Stars, Stripes and Diamonds

Stars, Stripes and Diamonds

American Culture and the Baseball Film

MARSHALL G. MOST *AND*
ROBERT RUDD

McFarland & Company, Inc., Publishers
Jefferson, North Carolina, and London

LIBRARY OF CONGRESS CATALOGUING-IN-PUBLICATION DATA

Most, Marshall G.
    Stars, stripes and diamonds : American culture and the
baseball film / Marshall G. Most and Robert Rudd.
       p.   cm.
    Includes bibliographical references and index.

    ISBN 0-7864-2518-0 (softcover : 50# alkaline paper)

    1. Baseball films—United States—History and criticism.
I. Rudd, Robert. II. Title.
PN1995.9.B28M67 2006
791.43'6579—dc22   2006009606

British Library cataloguing data are available

Cover photograph ©2006 Photodisc

Manufactured in the United States of America

McFarland & Company, Inc., Publishers
  Box 611, Jefferson, North Carolina 28640
   www.mcfarlandpub.com

For Jake and Crickett

Acknowledgments

The work you hold is the culmination of research that began late in 1990. Our original intention was modest — to produce a paper for the Third Cooperstown Symposium on Baseball and American Culture. The product of that initial effort was equally modest — a 23-page paper that drew upon a sample of only four films and focused on a single aspect of baseball's ideology as portrayed by Hollywood. We realized even before it was finished that a single paper would never begin to cover all the dimensions of baseball's cultural vision as expressed in American motion pictures about the National Pastime. With the kind assistance of a number of individuals, our research has been significantly broadened, the sample of films increased to more than 100, and a number of conference papers, journal articles and book chapters have been produced.

No one has been more helpful to us in our research than Steven Wood, of the University of Rhode Island and J. David Pincus, of the University of Arkansas, versatile scholars and baseball film researchers of some renown. We thank them not only for their assistance in the preparation of this manuscript, but also for their interest in, support of and thought-provoking discussions about our research, conversations that date back to the early 1990s. Our colleagues at Boise State University have always seemed a bit skeptical about research that sounded like it might be too much fun to be scholarly. They have, nevertheless, consistently supported the 15-year research agenda that made this volume possible. We appreciate our associates in the Department of Communication at Boise State, as well as our colleagues in the College of Social Sciences and Public Affairs, who supported our research with timely grants for research and travel. Such grants were often made by committees of fellow faculty members too numerous to mention. Deans include Dr. Michael Blankenship, Dr. Suzanne McCorkle, Dr. Jane Ollenburger and Dr. Robert Sims; and department chairs include Dr. Rick Moore, Dr. V. Marvin Cox and Dr. Robert Boren. We'd also like to thank our colleague Jane Freund for her help in putting together scene-by-scene summaries of many of the films we have viewed, and Erich Korte of Laughing Dog Press for his assistance with the photos.

We also extend our appreciation to Alvin Hall of East Stroudsburg University and all those at the National Baseball Hall of Fame and the State University of New York at Oneonta who have worked with Al to sustain the Cooperstown Symposium. The Symposium has afforded us and many other researchers a unique support system, providing a wonderful outlet for scholarly work on baseball and culture in an unparalleled venue.

Special thanks are extended to our wives, to whom this volume is dedicated, and to our other family members, for their loving support and interest (real and feigned) in our work.

And finally, our efforts over these many years were made easier by Jymson and Babba Luey, and their successors, Andre and Jack, companions who occupied our laps and inspired our writing (especially about *Rhubarb*) as we worked at our computers. Good kitties!

Table of Contents

Preface

As the writing of this book was completed, one of baseball's most well-known players—a man once considered a lock for election to the Baseball Hall of Fame—served a 10-day suspension for violating the game's ban on the use of steroids. The story was front-page news, receiving the level of attention that days before was reserved for such issues as the Iraq War, the economy, and famine in Africa. As sports commentators expressed their outrage, as Congress once again demanded the game be cleaned up once and for all, and as baseball fans across America lamented this latest tarnishing of the national pastime, one cannot help but wonder why this matters so much to us. Why do we care so deeply about this? In many ways, that is the central question addressed in this book.

In the film *Field of Dreams*, author Terence Mann, played by James Earl Jones, tells us that "this field, this game, is a part of our past. It reminds us of all that once was good, and that could be again." Quite simply, this is why the transgressions of one of the game's stars means so much. We have come to believe that America and the game of baseball are somehow intimately connected. At the most fundamental level, the identities of both baseball and America are deeply and inextricably intertwined. In the popular imagination baseball stands for all that is good about America. We have come to believe that the tarnishing of the game and what it stands for is also a degradation of America itself.

In the discussions which follow, we explore the nature of those connections between the game of baseball and American culture as they are represented in baseball films. All film, of course, serves to both reflect and shape cultural values and beliefs. At the same time that films represent and

1

reflect something within the cultural consciousness at the time they are produced, they also help to form that consciousness. But this is especially true of baseball films, we believe, which articulate a vision and a set of core values that have been a part of the American mainstream since well before the emergence (we hesitate to use the term "invention," given the contested history of the game) of the game itself in the late 19th century. Baseball films present not just an idealized view of the game and its heroes— and they are heroes in our culture — but also an idealized vision of America itself. And, in doing so, they contribute in a significant way to that cultural intertwining of the values and identities of baseball and America.

We begin in Chapter 1 with a review of the history and the central components of baseball's cultural vision — a vision which has been faithfully represented in baseball films since the earliest days of cinema. In Chapter 2, we provide a chronological review of baseball films since the late 1800s, offering brief narrative summaries of nearly 100 different films. In addition to providing an overview of the themes and central storylines of the past 100-plus years of baseball films, this chapter is intended to help the reader understand the historical context and evolution of baseball films through different eras, and in doing so to lay the groundwork for the analyses of the ideological dimensions of those films which follow.

Chapter 3 explores the theme of community in baseball films. The concept of community is central to baseball's cultural vision, and has thus been a primary theme of baseball films. In these films, viewers are offered images of idealized communities characterized by solidarity, equality, and diversity, in which individuals willingly put the good of the team/community first. In Chapters 4 and 5, we examine the ways the baseball hero— the idealized citizen of those baseball communities— are portrayed in baseball films. Chapter 4 focuses on the traditional, Puritanical moral code of the cinematic baseball hero, and Chapter 5 analyzes the motivations of the baseball hero. In sharp contrast to the seeming obsession of real-life baseball's superstars with lottery-sized contracts, baseball's cinematic heroes care little about the monetary rewards, playing the game simply for love of the game itself. This theme of devotion to the game is explored more fully in Chapter 6, in which we consider the treatment of the issue of gambling in baseball films, and Chapter 7, in which we examine representations of baseball owners in baseball cinema.

In Chapters 8 and 9 we examine the treatment in baseball films of two groups which have historically been denied membership in baseball's idealized communities—racial minorities and women. The final chapter discusses both the hegemonic and progressive dimensions of baseball's ideology as it is represented in baseball films. These films, we suggest, reflect a longing for a culture in which people such as Roy Hobbs and the cinematic Babe Ruth really do win; in which not only superstar athletes, but also the culture in which they perform and live, really do reflect the values of hard work, humility, and commitment to the greater good of the team/community. These cinematic portrayals of baseball and its heroes enable us to continue to hang on to a symbolic vision of what we would like our culture to become. It is a vision of the America that was meant to be.

1

America's Game

"God, I love baseball."
— Roy Hobbs, *The Natural*

The lessons have not been easy for Roy Hobbs. The day before the New York Knights face a one-game playoff for the pennant, the player who wanted to be, and might well have been, "the best there is" lies in a hospital bed; his career, once again, is possibly at an end. It is the result of a life in which his own dark side has often gotten the better of him. Prone to false pride, the seductions of beautiful women, and self-pity, Hobbs' life has taken on a familiar pattern. But this time, it will finally be different. His childhood sweetheart, Iris Gaines, who is also the mother of the child he does not know he has, has challenged him to listen to the lessons that life and baseball have to offer. "I believe we have two lives," she tells him. "The one we learn with, and the one we live with after that." With a simple utterance — "God, I love baseball" — Hobbs tells us he finally understands. The following night he hits the pennant-winning home run and then returns home to the farm with Iris and his son, and to the fulfillment he has so long sought. Roy Hobbs has learned the lessons of baseball, and of life.

It is called "the national pastime" and "America's game." For over a century the game of baseball, like no other game in America, has served as a defining feature of our cultural identity. For many, baseball serves as a metaphor for the American dream. It is said to embody the basic values that underlie the nation itself; to reflect the best that America has to offer. It is said to teach us the essential lessons of life; the lessons which Roy Hobbs and countless other cinematic baseball heroes have learned through more than a century of baseball films. Baseball is, without question, a part of our national ideology.

5

Robert Redford as Roy Hobbs in *The Natural* (Tri-Star Pictures, 1984).

The linkages between baseball and American culture are not coincidental. Both the promoters of the game itself, as well as those who have sought to mold the central values and identity of American culture, have consciously constructed these linkages in order to achieve their own ends. For baseball's owners, associating the game with the fundamental values of American culture served as an effective means of promoting the game to an increasingly affluent middle class in the early 20th century. For those seeking to construct a set of cultural values consistent with the needs of an urban, industrial society, the game of baseball has served to provide lessons and metaphors which can be applied to all aspects of life, throughout American culture. Together, the architects of baseball and of American culture have crafted a cultural vision in which the game of baseball and the culture of which it is a part are inextricably linked.

Although baseball's ideological frame did not fully crystallize until the 1920s, the groundwork of baseball's cultural vision was laid much earlier, in the late 19th and early 20th centuries, as America grappled with the dramatic changes brought on by the processes of urbanization and industrialization. While the shift to an industrial from an agrarian economy offered the promise of increasing prosperity, it also threatened traditional ways of life and deeply-held values as Americans moved from small, closely knit communities to earn their livings in large, impersonal and often threatening urban environments and highly structured industrial work places. As Fiske (1989), Ewen (1988), and other social historians have documented, the shift to an urban, industrialized America necessitated changes in fundamental American values, in order to create both a workforce and a consumer economy capable of supporting the nation's new industrial capacity. Long-held notions of individualism, as well as established Puritan admonitions against the elevation of materialist concerns and desires over spiritual ones were being challenged. And the escalating conflicts between the fundamental values these old and new ways of life represented posed real and significant threats to the stability of American culture. It was in response to these tensions that America's political and cultural leaders came to conceptualize and advocate sport as a site for molding the national character in ways that would preserve traditional republican and Puritan values in the shifting landscape of American culture. Where they had once been seen as a waste of time, distracting citizens from more productive and spiritually rewarding pursuits, sports and athletic activity came to be seen as potentially stabilizing forces in American society. Informal sporting clubs, for example, were created as a means of providing a sense of community, human contact, and a source of tradition and stability in response to the growing sense of chaos and instability resulting from urban and industrial growth (Gorn and Goldstein, 1993). Sport was to become the means through which to build the strong bodies and minds needed to service both a morally and economically strong industrial society.

Of particular concern to Progressive leaders of this era were the potential threats to the nation's moral constitution posed by the new economic order. Dryerson (1997) notes that while the middle-class Progressives of the late 19th century "worshiped the material plenitude and comfortable lifestyles that the machine process promised" (p. 126), they also feared that the "overly acquisitive and hypercompetitive sentiment" of both selfish industrial trusts and labor unions might infect the middle-class public as a whole, transforming them into "base economic creatures." There was, in their view, an evil dimension to the increasingly commercial world, which threatened to undermine traditional social values. As a means of ameliorating the undesirable social effects of a capitalist spirit run amok, they

7

turned to sport. For social theorists such as Price Collier, sport would teach essential moral principles "in days of commercial and social scrambling, when the Ten Commandments are mere rungs on the ladder of financial and social success" (Dryerson 1997, p. 130).

The concern of Collier and other proponents of the moral pedagogy of the sporting republic was that young men and women entering the new world of business and industry carry with them a sense of justice and fair play; that they possess the moral virtue necessary to resist the selfish, whatever-it-takes-to-win impulses of a commercial spirit focused only on the bottom line. Where the restricted nature of the modern workplace made it "insufficient for making the complete person" (Dryerson 1997, p. 124), sports would become the arena for building character and teaching ethics. Among the most prominent proselytizers of the moral virtue of the sporting republic was Theodore Roosevelt, who reiterated the classical notion that soundness in mind and body was the cornerstone of good character. The sporting society, in his view, would help to channel human energy for the public good, rather than simply for corporate profit and individual gain.

While obliteration of traditional religious and moral values by an overly materialist commercial spirit was a central concern of late 19th century critics of the industrial based capitalist wave sweeping through their culture at the time, it was not their only concern. For accompanying the synergistic phenomena of industrialization and laissez-faire capitalism was the increasing urbanization of American culture. In a culture with a long philosophical tradition of juxtaposing the physically healthy and morally virtuous agrarian lifestyle against the evils of city life, the shift from an agrarian to an urban culture in and of itself was seen to pose its own threats. Such vices as crime, illicit sex, drugs and alcohol were all associated with life in the city. Once again, the sporting republic, in which citizens engaged in regular physical activity and in which young people were taught the moral lessons sports had to offer through participation in organized teams sports such as baseball and football, was offered as the antidote.

There was to be no turning back the clock, however. Abandonment of the path American culture was now on, and a return to the rural, agrarian lifestyle, was not likely or even necessarily desirable. For while potentially poisonous, the fruits of the new industrial-urban economy were also alluring, promising a brighter future for all — provided that traditional moral values and civic virtues could be maintained. Sports were the mechanism for achieving that balance between the old world order and the new. Thus, at the same time that sports were perceived as a means of preserving traditional values in the face of urbanization and industrialization, and of maintaining moral virtue in a culture under siege by the forces of corporate greed and self-indulgent materialism, they were also presented as the method for socializing America's citizens into the new world order of the time; of inculcating in workers the new values and work ethic required by an industrialized economy. In their history of sports in America, for example, Gorn and Goldstein (1993) suggest that the organized sports which emerged in late 19th and early 20th century America both reflected and helped to shape the forces of modernization which were redefining the nature of American life. The values of most professional sports, as well as big-time amateur athletics, in the late 1800s—"competitiveness, aggressiveness, the will to win, discipline"—reflected the dominant male values of capitalist society (Gorn and Goldstein, 1993, p. 113). Baseball, they say, was foremost among those sports; a game shaped by and epitomizing the changing nature and emerging values of American culture and, at the same time, facilitating the acceptance of those changes within the culture at large. The values of industrial society — secularization, specialization of function, meritocracy, and quantification, for example — values which in many ways threatened the more traditional norms of American culture, were made to seem natural and enjoyable through sports such as baseball.

The need for such an ideological project in a time of rapid cultural change and potential volatility was not underestimated by those economic and political elites whose interests were served by the changing nature of American culture. As Fiske (1989) has written, "Industrialization and urbanization in the early nineteenth century produced, among other things, a widespread consciousness of the differences between classes and the growing fear that these differences constituted a real threat to the ability of the bourgeoisie to control the social order for their own interests" (p. 70). It was in order to maintain their control over the economic and social order, observes Fiske, that elites in both Britain and the United States turned their attentions to the leisure activities of the working class. In an attempt to impose the same sort of discipline on leisure that was imposed in the work place, and to eliminate the contradictions in values and behaviors between work and leisure, popular pleasures which were seen as lying outside of (and thus as a threat to) social control were defined by the middle class as antisocial, and as threats to the stability and moral health of the society. At the same time, leisure activities which were thought to reflect and promote the types of values consistent with the needs of the new, industrial workplace were actively promoted.

Ewen (1988) traces similar attempts by the corporate/industrial class to extend its control of the workplace to the leisure of workers in early 20th-century America. These attempts emerged out of "the need for society to achieve a compatibility between the worlds of work and daily life" (p. 188). Arguing that the private lives of workers must be consistent with needs of the workplace, industrial designers such as Le Corbusier even went so far as to advocate the use of architecture, in the home and workplace, as a means of making the private realms and lives of workers more consistent with the precise discipline required in the industrial workplace (Ewen, 1988).

The range of strategies documented by Fiske (1989) and Ewen (1988) reflect a concern of many political and economic elites of the time that workers adopt a set of meanings, values and behaviors in their private lives consistent with the needs of the industrial workplace, not simply to make them more reliable and productive workers, but also in order to minimize the potential of class conflict and disruption to the social order. Drunkenness, for example, was represented — as it still is today — not just as a threat to the worker's reliability and productivity, but also as a more general threat to the social order. As Fiske (1988) observed, much of the discourse of morality directed at controlling the meanings and activities of leisure of the late nineteenth century working class served to obscure the class and economic interests which actually underpinned these attempts to "reform" popular culture. So too would the moral discourse of baseball serve to redefine and universalize what were essentially the economic interests of society's economic elites as generalized moral imperatives.

On the surface, these two ideological functions—the simultaneous promotion of traditional, Puritan values and of the modern corporate/industrial norms which appeared to threaten them — seem contradictory. However, these seemingly conflicted purposes of sports reflect the conflicting tensions and pressures of the times. In light of those tensions, the dual functions of sports— the ability to promote dominant cultural values and social institutions and processes, while at the same time offering an escape from the strain and sense of estrangement generated by those same values and social processes— should not be viewed as contradictory, but as complementary. "By at once replicating some of the social forces altering America and denying them," Gorn and Goldstein (1993) write, "by offering both an elixir of modernity and its antidote, late-nineteenth-century sports symbolically reconciled contradictory reactions to contemporary life" (p. 114). The ability to incorporate both visions— the Puritan, agrarian past and the commercialized, urban future — within the ideological dimensions of sports accounts for the significant role of sports in helping American culture of the late 19th century confront and resolve the contradictory impulses it was simultaneously embracing as it made the transition into the new, industrialized order. It was out of these conflicts, and the accompanying movement to utilize sports as a means of addressing these tensions, that the ideology of baseball was born.

The Ideology of Baseball

While the game itself has been played in some form in America since Revolutionary War times (Ward and Burns, 1994), the *ideology* of baseball — the meanings we as a culture now associate with baseball and the privileged place we accord it in our own sense of national identity — did not fully crystallize until the early years of the 20th century. It was during this era that baseball became established as the "national pastime," as both the game's promoters and many sportswriters articulated the ideological vision of the game with which we are now so familiar. As suggested previously, the purpose of the ideology was not simply to promote the game itself, but also to use the game as a means of forging a set of values which would help resolve the tensions and conflicts of a changing American culture. Steven Riess (1980), in his history of the evolution of baseball's ideology, observes that since the early decades of the 20th century the game of baseball has been presented not simply as a form of entertainment, but as a contributor to both individual and national development. Baseball, in the eyes of its proponents at least, not only embodies the essential values of American culture, but serves to instill these values in players and fans alike, season after season. Baseball's mission is pedagogical. Its teachers are the game's heroes, who serve as role models for America's youth. Its lessons are of everyday life. The ideology of baseball is not just about baseball, but about America itself.

The ideology of baseball formulated in the early 1900s "looked back to a glorious past" (Riess 1999, p. 214). As Riess (1999) observes, baseball's proponents believed the game would cultivate in America's urban youth the same qualities that previous American youth had developed naturally on the frontier: characteristics such as honesty, patience, respect for authority, competitiveness and individualism. Baseball would bring the frontier into the city and teach the basic values of American society to new generations of America's youth. It was a vision which baseball owners, desiring to increase the game's appeal to middle-class audiences, were quick to embrace. They presented the game as a pastime which embodied traditional, middle-American values. They constructed an image of the game which spoke to the fears of middle-class America that the traditional moral values of American culture were in danger of being washed away in the tide of social and economic change.

The litany of moral virtues associated with the game was extensive. Baseball, it was said, would promote good health, honorable character, honesty, and a sense of fair play, as well as teamwork and respect for authority. Albert Spalding promised that the game would build manliness, character, and an ethic of success (Riess, 1999). And participation in baseball, as a player and as a spectator, would encourage sobriety — in a couple of ways. First, people attending baseball games, as players or spectators, were thought to be less likely to engage in less wholesome forms of leisure. Riess (1999) quotes a pre–Civil War article from the *Detroit Free Press* describing baseball as a "healthy exercise counteracting the growing tendency to visit saloons and other places of resort..." (p. 22). Secondly, baseball would teach the values of sobriety and moral purity to America's youth.

Especially important to the moral pedagogy of baseball were the heroes of the game, whom America's youth were encouraged to emulate. As Riess (1999) observes, despite the less than Puritanical realities of drinking, smoking and womanizing amongst many players, the sporting press of the time portrayed baseball players as virtuous, clean-living, Christian men who were the ideal role models for American youth. New York Giants' pitcher Christy Mathewson, known for his strong religious beliefs, was presented as epitomizing the values of clean living and fair play. The legendary Ty Cobb, it was said, taught by example the rewards and virtues of hard work. And even fictional characters like Frank Merriwell taught such values as loyalty, humility, and fair play, while warning against the evils of smoke and drink.

In addition to helping assure the moral virtue of America's citizens, baseball was also said to help assure the stability of the American workplace. As noted earlier, one of the functions of sports cited by advocates of the sporting republic was to serve as a relief valve for the frustrations of workers subjected to the new conditions of labor in an industrialized workplace. Baseball, according to its proponents, was particularly well suited to this task. H. Addington Bruce, observing that most city dwellers worked long hours in boring and repetitive jobs, suggested that attendance at baseball games would allow workers to release their aggression at the ballpark, rather than directing it at their families or employers (Riess, 1999). According to Bruce (1913), baseball would "perform this service the more readily because of the appeal it makes to the basic instincts, with resultant removal of the inhibitions that ordinarily cause tensions and restraint" (p. 107). Baseball's ideologists, according to Riess (1999), felt

> it was much healthier for society that the alienated and disappointed act out their hostilities at the baseball field than in the streets or at home. Their anger would be left at the ball game, and they would go home exhilarated and sober, prepared to work efficiently the following day [p. 216].

Baseball's contribution to a more efficient and productive workplace was thought to go beyond the provision of a site where alienated laborers could work off some of their tension and hostility, however. As Fiske (1989) has documented, there was a concerted effort during the late 19th century to delegitimize working-class forms of leisure which were thought a threat to social stability, and to replace them in the lives of American workers with more controlled forms of recreation. Indeed, during this era "leisure" itself was culturally redefined, as a time for workers to rest and "recreate" themselves, so they would be ready for work the next day. Baseball fit the bill perfectly. Through its emphasis on such values as a strong work ethic, humility, teamwork, devotion to the game, and abstinence from such activities as womanizing, drinking and smoking, the ideology of baseball defined a Puritanical moral code which reflected and served the economic interests of a newly industrialized society — a moral code of discipline and control which was part of the conditioning and mobilization of an industrial workforce. Riess (1991) reports that after the Civil War business executives actually began to view baseball as a source of improved morale and productivity in the workplace. Chicago business leaders in the 1870s, writes Riess, often granted their white-collar workers time off for practice and games "because it helped their staffs become more reliable, cooperative, and healthy, improved morale and loyalty to the firm..." (p. 67) as well as attracting positive press coverage.

Baseball, more than any other sport of the time, marked the transition from a rural to an urban culture; from an agrarian to a corporate, industrial economy; from individualism to teamwork. It was a game which, in the eyes of its ideologists, at least, duplicated the values and work experience of an industrial society. Through its "organization of a group to cooperate in the production process, in a predetermined order, and individual accountability combined with collective success or failure" (Gelber 1983, p. 10), baseball was thought to reflect the corporate ideal of the individual sacrificing his or her own interests for the good of the whole. Baseball itself became popular, argues Gelber (1983), precisely because it was consistent with and embodied those corporate values which were now dominant within an industrialized American culture.

As significant as baseball's contribution to the moral virtue of the individual was its purported role in creating a sense of community and an appreciation for democratic values in society at large. As the processes of rapid industrialization and urbanization uprooted people from their rural communities, and replaced the close-knit bonds of small town life with the social isolation and anonymity of existence in congested urban landscapes, baseball ideologists envisioned the game of baseball serving as the common bond to bring people together and to forge a new sense of community in America's new urban identity. In his analysis of the baseball novel, Timothy Morris (1997) writes that "the datum for most baseball novels is a fractious mess of different subjects" (p. 17), and that the central theme of the baseball novel is the assimilation of these various subjects into a team capable of pursuing a common goal. Assimilation has been a core theme of baseball's ideology from the beginning; not only the assimilation of diverse individuals within a particular team, but the assimilation of diverse social groups into the larger American community as well. Riess (1991) notes that mainstream, middle-class periodicals in the early 20th century "all accepted the cultural fiction that baseball was a useful sport that promoted social integration by instilling hometown pride, providing a setting where people from all walks of life could come together..." (p. 66). Baseball, it was said, would help promote community integration by instilling a sense of civic pride in fans who came to the ballpark to root for the local team. The democratic nature of the ballpark, it was believed, would translate into a greater sense of community in America's urban centers. And the values of fair play and sportsmanship, it was suggested, would promote good citizenship and an understanding of democratic institutions (Betts, 1974). It would teach the American way to the waves of immigrants landing on America's shores.

Fictional though the illusion may have been, it was nevertheless a crucial and compelling component of baseball's cultural vision. The game's owners and promoters, as well as sportswriters and journalists of the time, vigorously celebrated both the democratic and communal nature of the game. "Sportswriters were continually pointing out that ballplayers and fans were drawn from all levels of society, and that spectators mingled together on equal terms" (Riess, 1999, p. 28).

The cultural vision associated with baseball was clearly an idyllic one, which sought to provide both direction and reassurance in a time of rapid social change and uncertainty. The ideology of baseball, observes Riess, was designed to "provide the symbols, myths and legends society needed to bind its members together" (p. 5). It offered a newly industrialized, urbanized society a cultural vision in which traditional, small-town values were preserved; in which American youth would continue to learn the moral lessons that had long served as the foundation for a Christian nation. It offered the hope and assurance that the diverse cultures which characterized America's growing urban centers could be brought together as part of a common culture, with shared values and a shared national identity. It offered a vision of the America that was meant to be.

2

Baseball on Film: 1898–2005

"The one constant through all the years, Ray, has been base-ball. America has rolled by like an army of steamrollers; it has been erased like a blackboard, rebuilt, and erased again. But baseball has marked the time."

— Terence Mann,
Field of Dreams

For baseball ideologists, the role of baseball in American culture is to serve as an example which the rest of the culture might follow, and to instill in America's youth the values and sensibilities which will prepare them to become positive, productive members of that culture. The ideology of base-ball is not just about baseball, but also about America. Baseball films have played an important role in constructing that ideological vision. Indeed, as Bergan (1982) notes, Hollywood baseball films have been especially pure in reflecting an idealized image of the game, and in keeping the mythology of baseball intact. Although the news media, particularly since the 1970s, have often provided a critical focus on the game and those who play it, report-ing the unpleasant realities of drug abuse, escalating salaries and labor strife, and players and owners who seem to care only about themselves and the riches they can make from the game, baseball films have continued to pro-vide audiences with an idealized vision of the game; the way it is meant to be. It is a vision not just of baseball, however, but of America. It is this vision which we shall explore in the discussions to follow. We begin, though, with an historical overview of America's game in film — over 100 years of base-ball cinema. While few of the films produced prior to 1933 were readily available to us, we are fortunate that a number of authors have documented the films produced in the first third of the 20th century. We are indebted

James Earl Jones as Terence Mann in *Field of Dreams* (Universal Pictures, 1967).

in particular to baseball film historians Rob Edelman (1994), and especially Hal Erickson (2002) for their fine summaries of these early motion pictures, which we draw upon extensively in describing the first 20 years of Hollywood's baseball feature films.

1898: The Silent Years

Given the prominent, even privileged, status the game of baseball began to assume during the Progressive Era, it is no surprise the entrepreneurs of the fledgling film industry would make it the subject of some of the earliest American films. The first attempt to capture the game on celluloid was probably the Edison Company's 1898 kinetoscope short *The Ball Game*, which featured brief scenes of a Newark, New Jersey, baseball team. Edison's single-scene *Casey at the Bat* appeared the next year. Filmed at Edison's estate in West Orange, New Jersey, it depicts nothing more than a batter striking out and arguing with the umpire until the argument erupts into a bench-clearing brawl. Several similar kinetoscopes were produced in the next few years, but the sheer novelty of seeing moving pictures of baseball players would soon wear off.

Most of the commercial films made during the early 1900s were short features. Stories were kept simple, often resembling hurriedly-performed stage plays crammed onto one reel. Travelogues, comedy sketches, crude newsreels, and vaudeville turns were staples (Gomery, 1991). Films about baseball made during this era were little more than re-creations of baseball-related vaudeville routines or showcases for baseball's stars, with brief glimpses of game action (e.g., 1907's *Christy Mathewson and the New York National League Team*).

During the formative years 1905–1915, American films gradually grew longer, production and editing techniques more sophisticated, and subjects more complex. By 1917, Hollywood was giving the world feature-length narratives that would come to be called Classic Hollywood (Gomery, 1991). Baseball one-reelers were still well-represented during this period, notably by Universal's "Baseball Bill" series, featuring titles like *Baseball Madness* and *Strike One*, and Selig's "Mudville" series of comedy shorts. But movie audiences had come to expect feature-length films with well-known performers (the beginning of Hollywood's studio star system), and baseball films began to evolve into the full-fledged narratives familiar to contemporary audiences. Many of these studio star vehicles would take baseball as their subject, or treat it as a useful backdrop, plot device, or gimmick.

Little Sunset (1915) was just such a star vehicle for action film actor-director Hobart Bosworth. Generally regarded as the first feature-length baseball film, *Little Sunset*, like many early baseball pictures, can also be properly categorized as a melodrama, with baseball incidental to its plot. The storyline is typical of these early baseball melodramas: "Little Sunset" Jones is the young mascot of a minor league team, orphaned by his mother's death but befriended by the team's star player, Gus Bergstrom (Bosworth). When the boy becomes ill, a distraught Gus fails miserably in the field and at the plate. Frustrated, Gus leaves the team, but returns for a joyous reunion with Little Sunset, just in time to win the pennant for the team. The baseball backdrop is secondary to the plot, and the plot is designed to showcase Bosworth's screen talents.

Similarly, baseball serves as little more than setting in silent screen star Charles Ray's star vehicles *The Pinch Hitter* (1917) and *The Busher* (1919). However, Ray's films are notable for pioneering two staples— or clichés— of American baseball film. The first is the portrayal of the protagonist as hayseed-turned-hero. In *The Pinch Hitter*, Ray plays the rube ballplayer who leaves his rural home to play in the big city, only to become the brunt of urban ridicule until he wins the big game for his team. This presentation of the baseball protagonist would be reworked in numerous films, notably Associated Exhibitor's 1925 remake of *The Pinch Hitter*, Buster Keaton's 1927 comedy *College*, and Joe E. Brown's baseball trilogy of the 1930s.

Ray's other baseball film, *The Busher*, established a second staple used in many subsequent films, that of the minor-league talent whose success and promotion to the big leagues go to his head. The strutting braggart must then learn hard lessons in humility (in Ray's case, he is fleeced by a notorious woman and demoted back to the minors) before realizing success both on and off the field.

Baseball probably had less to do with the success of these films than did their stars. Just how important box-office appeal had become to the success of Hollywood films is witnessed in the miserable failure of the 1916 film *Casey at the Bat*. Rather than casting a popular screen star in the title role, the producers turned to DeWolf Hopper, a Broadway matinee idol whose presence in the film was designed "to add culture and class to a still unrespectable medium" (Erickson, 2002, p. 14). Hopper had popularized Ernst Lawrence Thayer's 1888 poem "Casey at the Bat," reciting it thousands of times on stage, but neither his name nor his reputation would substitute for a Hollywood film idol. Audiences found Hopper unconvincing — *Variety* reported that Hopper "failed utterly to look the part" and "acted it extremely badly" (quoted in Edelman, pg.51). Although Hopper's attempt to expand the *Casey* poem into a feature film was an unqualified flop, his popular stage performance of the piece was preserved on film with soundtrack six years later.

Audiences might not have accepted Broadway stars in motion pictures, but baseball stars were another matter. A pioneer in making the jump from the diamond to the silver screen was major league baseball star Michael Joseph "Turkey Mike" Donlin, who parlayed a successful playing career (a .333 life-time batting average, largely with the New York Giants) into modest film stardom. Donlin had dabbled in show business even while playing, teaming up with his actress wife Mabel Hite in vaudeville turns. In 1915, he starred in the feature *Right Off the Bat*, a film loosely based on his playing career. It is difficult to know just how much the story of Donlin's career was embellished for the film, but it is worth noting that some five years before the Chicago "Black Sox" gambling scandal broke, *Right Off the Bat* portrays gamblers attempting to bribe Donlin to throw a championship game. When bribery fails, the gamblers assault and kidnap Turkey Mike, but he escapes and arrives at the ballpark just in time to hit the home run that wins the game.

Right Off the Bat was not a critical success, but it did solid box-office business. Studios were thus convinced to cast other ballplayers in films roles. Donlin himself went on to play supporting roles in a half-dozen other pictures, sharing billing with Ty Cobb in *Somewhere in Georgia* (1916) and Babe Ruth in *Headin' Home* (1920).

Cobb was arguably the greatest player in the game when he starred in *Somewhere in Georgia*. The film — and Cobb's performance — received a lukewarm reception by critics, but found favor with audiences. Cobb plays a bank clerk who competes with a fellow employee for the affections of the bank president's daughter. Discovered by a Detroit scout while playing for the local team, Cobb is quickly signed and promoted to the big leagues. In his absence, the unscrupulous rival woos the girl and hires a gang of toughs to abduct Cobb. Cobb thwarts the scheme by thrashing his would-be captors, escaping their clutches just in time to win the big game and claim the hand of his true love.

A baseball name could also draw at the box office for a second feature, as Hall of Fame pitcher Christy Mathewson and his New York Giants manager John McGraw proved when they headlined the successful two-reel short *Breaking Into the Big League* in 1913. However, even the popular McGraw's presence as co-star could not rescue the inane five-reeler *One Touch of Nature* (1917), the tale of a fictional Giants second baseman who overcomes his prominent father's objections to his romantic involvement with a vaudeville performer by hitting a home run to win the World Series.

Both baseball and movie houses were, of course, racially segregated during this era, so there were no major league African American baseball players to cast in films, even those pictures produced exclusively for black audiences. There were, however, well-known black athletes, including heavyweight boxer Jack Johnson who plays himself in *As the World Rolls On* (1921). In the film, Johnson rescues a youth from a life of street crime by teaching him to box and play baseball. The young man goes on to play professionally for the Kansas City Monarchs of the Negro National League. The real Monarchs players are featured at the end of the film, perhaps the first African American ball players to appear in a Hollywood feature.

Headin' Home (1920) is noteworthy for reasons beyond Babe Ruth's film debut. One is the stark contrast of the story line with George Herman Ruth's real life and his entry into baseball. In the film, the Bambino plays George, a quiet, unassuming, clean living young man who lives with his aging mother and younger sister in the village of Haverlock. George is too shy to approach Mildred, the girl of his dreams, and his great passion (besides baseball and Mildred) is whittling bats from blocks of wood. He is judged a buffoon by Haverlock's locals, who are somehow unappreciative of his considerable baseball talents. George takes that talent to a bigger town, where he saves Mildred's brother from the clutches of a wanton woman, then returns to Haverlock to (in this order) rescue Mildred from the unwanted advances of a crooked big-city ball player, hit the game-winning home run for the local team in the big game, and sign a big-league contract with the New York Yankees. Only in his baseball prowess and his affiliation with the Yankees does George bear any resemblance to the real Ruth.

Another notable aspect of *Headin' Home* is that it is considered by some to be the last "pure baseball" release (i.e., a film about a baseball player playing baseball) made by Hollywood for nearly seven years. During this period, a number of film makers included a baseball element in their mix of subplots, gimmicks, settings, plot devices, and/or release titles. But as baseball-film historian Hal Erickson has noted, "baseball movies pure and simple were hard to come by" (2002, p. 15) from 1920 to 1927. Some of the films produced during this period come closer to fitting the baseball genre than others. The 1925 iteration of *The Pinch Hitter*, for example, is a barely-altered remake of the 1917 picture of the same title (although it can be argued that both versions were nothing more than melodramas dressed in a baseball uniform). Often considered a Western because it stars cowboy film hero Hoot Gibson and begins in a desert town, *Hit and Run* (1924) blurs the line between genres by marrying the baseball plot to the setting and stock characters of the Western. In *Hit and Run,* Gibson stars as Swat Anderson, the cowboy clean-up hitter for the Desert Twirlers. Discovered by a big-league scout (played by "Turkey Mike" Donlin), Swat is soon carrying his professional team, the Blue Sox, toward the league championship with his colossal home runs. Gamblers with their money on a rival team kidnap Swat, but he escapes in time to hit the home run that clinches the pennant for the Sox. Just as difficult to categorize (but much easier to criticize) is the 1926 baseball-Western *Out of the West*, in which cowboy/ballplayer Tom Hanley is kidnapped by rivals, but escapes in time to hit the game-winning home run in the big game. *Out of the West*'s only shred of originality comes in the finale, when Tom turns down a professional baseball contract to stay on the ranch and marry his sweetheart.

Producers also needed fresh angles and contexts for melodramas, a Hollywood staple during the first half of the century, so baseball is the incidental backdrop for films like *Trifling with Honor* (1923), *Life's Greatest Game* (1924), and *Catch as Catch Can* (1927). These melodrama-baseball films (and others, from *Little Sunset* in 1916 to *For Love of the Game* in 1999) might not even merit mention in a discussion of baseball cinema if not for their unwavering fidelity to the ideology of baseball, particularly their presentation of baseball's moral order, the dangers of gambling, the importance of marriage, and the celebration of the dedicated, honorable and stoic baseball hero. In *Trifling with Honor,* for example, Bat Shugreve is not only the star of the Pacific Coast League, he is also the escaped convict once known as the "Gas Pipe Kid." When crooked gamblers learn Bat's true identity, they confront him with his past and threaten to expose him unless he throws a game. Resisting their blackmail attempt, Bat goes to Judge Drury and make a clean breast of things. The judge has the blackmailers apprehended, then releases Bat in recognition of his recent status as a positive role model for America's youth. Bat returns to his team in time to pinch hit the home run that wins the big game.

Life's Greatest Game is more complicated but just as lachrymose. When Cubs pitcher Jack Donovan refuses to throw a game for a crooked gambler, the villain gets even by concocting a tale of marital infidelity that succeeds in breaking up Jack's family. Jack's wife and young son leave him, intending to leave the country by steamship, but literally miss the boat. By the time Jack discovers the gambler's chicanery, wife and child are (wrongly) believed to be lost at sea. Eighteen years later, Jack is managing the New York Giants into the World Series when the Giants sign a college pitcher for the stretch run. As scripted fate would have it, the rookie hurler is his son, Jack Junior. Seething because he still believes Jack Senior abandoned him and his mother, the younger Donovan intentionally loses a World Series game to spite his father. Upon learning the truth and discovering his father still loves him, Jack Junior pitches *and* slugs the Giants to victory in the Series' deciding game, and reunites his parents in the bargain.

Catch as Catch Can features a story line even more convoluted, thanks its subplot of political corruption. When baseball manager Reed Powers is accused of, then fired for, accepting a bribe to fix a game, only a handful of others know he is innocent. Reed takes the rap to protect the pitcher who did take the bribe and did throw the game: Phil Bascom, the brother of Reed's sweetheart, Lucille. Phil, a decent young man, was coerced into this act of corruption by crooked political operator Ward Hastings. When not bribing ballplayers, Hastings is busy trying to depose the city's mayor, who just happens to be the father of Lucille and Phil Bascom. Reed spends four of the film's five reels trying to expose Hastings' many schemes and clear his own name. This he does, of course, thus securing both the job of chief of police and the hand of the lovely Lucille from a grateful Mayor Bascom.

The hybrid of baseball and other genres was not confined to westerns and melodramas. During this period of quasi-baseball films, the national pastime would also make cameo appearances in comedies. In *The Battling Orioles* (1924), a Hal Roach farce (*sans* Harold Lloyd), the opening baseball sequence merely sets up the subsequent Roach slapstick feature. And *The New Klondike* (1926) is a comedy tale of the Florida land boom (which later turned out to be not so funny when the bubble burst) in which the principal characters only coincidentally happen to be employed in baseball, giving them a convenient excuse — spring training — to be in Florida in the first place.

1927: The Babe Saves Baseball — and Baseball Films

Ironically, when "genuine" baseball films returned in 1927, it was once again Babe Ruth who was largely responsible for their re-emergence. After the Babe's remarkable 1926 comeback culminated in an American League pennant for his New York Yankees, baseball's popularity soared and Hollywood rushed to cash in with four major studio releases devoted to the national pastime in 1927. Fittingly, the first of these was *Babe Comes Home*, starring Ruth as a ballplayer trying to give up chewing tobacco, not for health reasons, but because the stains it leaves on his uniform distress the woman (and laundress) he loves. She relents in her attempts to reform the Babe, even providing him a timely chaw during the big game. Babe responds by hitting a game-winning grand slam, then swears off tobacco in favor of love.

Ruthian influences are also evident in two of the other 1927 releases, *Slide, Kelly, Slide* and yet another version of *Casey at the Bat*. In both films, the title characters are prodigious home run hitters who display the sort of brash charm, colorful behavior, and good-humored swagger of the Babe.

The protagonist of *Slide, Kelly, Slide* is Jim Kelly, a rookie pitcher and power hitter whose cocky demeanor and penchant for practical jokes alienate his New York Yankee team mates, the Yankee manager, his love interest Mary, and even his pal little Mickey Martin, the Yankees' nine-year-old bat boy. Ostracized by the Yankees, who have lost all patience with his clowning, Kelly gets angry, then drunk the night before he is scheduled to pitch. To make matters worse, he aims a drunken tirade at his veteran catcher (Mary's father) and the Yankees' manager, then quits the team. The Yankees make it the World Series without Kelly, where they battle the St. Louis Cardinals to a 3–3 Series tie. But the Yankee pitching staff is completely spent, and Jim Kelly is their only hope. Little Mickey is sent to fetch Kelly to the ballpark, but on his way, the little tyke is hit by a car. In baseball cinema, modern medicine stands helpless in such situations, the only known remedy for children's injuries and diseases being a spectacular on-field performance by the small patient's hero. Hence, a humbled and remorseful Kelly takes the mound, pitches a masterful game, then wins the game with a thrilling inside-the-park home run. Kelly is forgiven by Mary, her father, the Yankees, their manager, the fans, and of course little Mickey, who is wheeled onto the field for the post-game celebration.

In contrast to Jim Kelly, Mike Casey — protagonist of *Casey at the Bat,* Paramount's 1927 baseball offering — is more bumbler than braggart, a slow-witted but well-meaning rube with a home run swing. Casey's prodigious appetite for beer and pretty girls completes the Ruth caricature. As the star of the Centerville town team, Casey's favorite bit of grandstanding consists of turning his back to the pitcher until there are two called strikes, then blasting the next pitch out of the ball park (and occasionally the Centerville city limits). Such power displays catch the attention of the New York Giants, who sign Casey and send him to the big club forthwith. As he leads the Giants toward the pennant, a crooked character named O'Dowd conspires with Casey's hometown rival, Elmer Putnam, to foil both Casey and the Giants' hopes. The pair first convince him that he is so sick he should not play in the pennant-deciding game. Casey finally sees through the scheme in time to arrive at the ballpark to pinch-hit in the bottom of the ninth, with two out. Turning his back on the first two strikes, Casey takes a mighty swing at the next pitch — and strikes out. But wait! O'Dowd has substituted a trick baseball for the regulation horsehide, one that is impossible to hit. O'Dowd and Putnam are exposed and led away by the police, and the final at-bat is replayed with results so predictable only the distance of Casey's home run is in question.

In complete comedic contrast to these Ruthian characters is Specs White, the hero of 1927's fourth baseball film *The Bush Leaguer*. Specs is a timid, bespectacled, absent-minded inventor whose inestimable pitching skills are of much less consequence to him than his latest invention — an advanced gas pump. Accepting a contract to pitch for the Los Angeles Angels only for the purpose of financing his invention, Specs discovers he suffers from "crowd fright" when pitching in the "big time." About the same time, he falls head over heels for Alice Hobbs, who just happens to own the Angels. Fortunately, Specs' love for Alice inspires him to overcome his phobia and pitch the Angels to victory. Alice is led to believe Specs has sold out to gamblers, a charge that appears to have some validity when he misses the start of the pennant-deciding game. But Specs' tardiness is due to his protracted yet successful negotiations to sell his invention for a bundle. He arrives at the ballpark in time to foil the crooked gamblers, hit the game-winning home run in the bottom of the ninth inning, and win the heart of Alice.

The financial success of 1927's baseball films led to fairly regular releases of baseball pictures for the next several years. Paramount's 1928 entry *Warming Up* would be the most forgettable of the lot if it could not lay claim to being the first baseball picture with sound. In the film, small-town pitcher Bert "Bee Line" Tulliver is as insecure as he is talented when he reports to the majors for a spring training tryout with the Green Sox. Things go badly for Bert as he is tormented and ultimately humiliated by a bullying teammate named McRae. Only the intercession of Mary Post, the daughter of the Green Sox owner and Bert's love interest, keeps the slumping Bert on the team. When McRae is traded to another team, Bert's confidence returns, his natural talent emerges, and he leads the Sox to the World Series. But his old rival McRae is playing for the opposing team, and Bert believes McRae has not only jinxed him, but is vying for the affections of Mary as well. Facing McRae early in the Series with the bases loaded, a jittery Bert walks his nemesis and is promptly benched. But Bert must pitch in the deciding game of the Series and, inspired by Mary, who pledges her everlasting devotion from the stands, Bert strikes out McRae and the Green Sox win the Series.

Warming Up failed in just about every way a film can — *Variety* described it as an "asinine concoction" (quoted in Erickson, 2002, p. 470) — but especially technically. In an attempt to cash in on the success of Warner Brothers' recent hit *The Jazz Singer*, the film was released with a hastily conceived phonographic system that attempted to match a musical score and sound effects on a disk with the pictures on the screen. The crude, unsynchronized noise it produced proved to be more a distraction than an enhancement.

1929: Baseball Speaks

The fact that *Warming Up* was a critical, technical, and financial loser did not discourage Paramount from trying again in 1929 with *Fast Company*, the first true "talkie" baseball film. A film adaptation of Ring Lardner and George M. Cohan's Broadway play *Elmer the Great, Fast Company* did little to change the formula of the baseball romantic comedy. Elmer "Hurry" Kane, the Yankees' power-hitting rookie, is a hayseed who falls for vaudeville actress Evelyn Corey. His love for her unrequited, Elmer begins to think about returning to his home town. Yankee skipper Bert Wade, fearing the loss of Elmer's considerable talents, forges a series of phony love letters to Elmer from Evelyn. The ruse succeeds, and Elmer powers the Yankees into the World Series. A gang of crooked gamblers try to coerce Elmer into throwing the Series, and when Elmer's average begins to slump, Wade believes they have succeeded. In fact, Elmer is off his game because he has learned the love letters supposedly sent by Evelyn are counterfeits. When Wade learns that his prize rookie is love-sick, not corrupt, he convinces Evelyn to come to the deciding game of the Series to cheer on Elmer. She agrees and to her surprise, decides she actually has a soft spot for the yokel slugger. Inspired by her affection, Elmer scores the game-winning run.

The musical *They Learned About Women* and the comedy *Hot Curves*, both released in 1930, could not sustain the box-office success of *Fast Company*, even though both featured the new technology of fully synchronized sound (to say nothing of suggestive titles). *They Learned About Women* even featured two popular vaudeville performers, Joseph T. Schenk and Gus Van, in the role of Blue Sox battery mates who moonlight as (not surprisingly) vaudeville partners. Between contrived musical numbers, a convoluted love triangle develops. The Wrong Guy — Blue Sox catcher Jerry Burke — is about to wed the Right Girl — Mary — but only because the Right Guy — Blue Sox pitcher and Mary's true love, Jack Glennon — has been tempted and then jilted by a scheming temptress. Such failures in romance can have only one consequence in baseball films and Right Guy Jack predictably goes into emotional and baseball funks. Not until Wrong Guy Jerry, noble friend and teammate that he is, realizes Jack and Mary were meant for each other and reunites the Rights will the Blue Sox have a chance to win the World Series.

Once reconciled with Mary, Jack shrugs off his slump in time to put down the opposing team's rally and win the World Series.

Hot Curves also featured a vaudevillian, comic Benny Rubin, who plays Benny Goldberg. Benny is signed by the Pittsburgh Cougars ostensibly as a catcher, but in reality because Cougar management believes he will attract more Jewish fans to the games. Nonetheless, Benny proves his worth to the team, as does Benny's pal, rookie pitcher Jim Nolan. As the season progresses, Jim's pitching steadily improves and he strikes up a courtship with Elaine McGrew, daughter of the Cougars' manager. Enter romance-wrecking jezebel Margie who proves so great a distraction for Jim that he is suspended for poor play before Benny can rescue him from the gold-digger. To add to the Cougar's woes, Benny is thought to have perished in a plane crash. But Jim is recalled to the team for the World Series and Benny turns up to catch him in the deciding game. With the Cougars down by a run in the final inning of game seven, Benny gets a single and Jim belts a home run to win the Series and reclaim the affections of Elaine.

Despite mixed results realized from the baseball releases of the late 1920s and early 1930s, Hollywood continued to produce baseball films through the 1930s. Perhaps the best of them were comedian Joe E. Brown's trilogy, *Fireman, Save My Child* (1932), *Elmer the Great* (1933), and *Alibi Ike* (1935). Each casts Brown as a naive, small-town ballplayer who is used, insulted and/or duped in the big leagues, disappears for a few games, makes an unlikely return, leads his team to victory in the late-innings of the big game, and wins the heart of his love interest. It was a predictable formula but with Brown as the lead, Warner Brothers had an accomplished ball player and popular screen star to give credibility and box office appeal to the three money-making films.

The other baseball films of the decade were generally less memorable, be they comedic shorts like *One Run Elmer* (1935), a two-reel talkie starring Buster Keaton in a series of slapstick gags with a baseball backdrop, or features like the lamentable *Swell Head* (1935), a melodrama about a ball player blinded after being beaned and his struggle to recover his sight and his true love. Almost all dialogue with only a smattering of baseball, it is a point of some dispute as to whether *Swell Head* is even a baseball film. The same judgment might be made of *Girls Can Play* (1937), a murder mystery in which the star pitcher of a women's softball team ferrets out the killer of her team's catcher. "Murder mysteries abounded in the early days of talking pictures" according to Erickson (2002, p. 145), and film makers cast about for novel ways to frame these programmers. *Girls Can Play* uses baseball (or more correctly, softball) as little more than a unique setting into which the mystery formula is dropped.

Perhaps the only film that can truly claim to straddle the baseball and mystery genres is *Death on the Diamond* (1934), in which St. Louis Cardinal pitcher Larry Kelly turns sleuth to find out who is poisoning, shooting, strangling, and bombing his teammates in an attempt to derail the Cardinals' pennant drive. Kelly himself is framed, set up to appear to be a conspirator with corrupt gamblers. In a climax true to the formula for both genres, Kelly redeems his reputation, apprehends the killer (with a well-aimed pitch), then slugs an inside-the-park home run to win the season's final game and clinch the National League pennant.

Whether *Death on the Diamond* is properly categorized as a baseball film, while *Girls Can Play* is not, is a point worth arguing only as it affects the calculation of another lull in the production of baseball films. For at least five, and as many as eight years (depending on how one defines a baseball film), Hollywood lost interest in making baseball pictures.

Ironically, it was the Brooklyn Dodgers, a team previously notorious for ineptitude, who rekindled film makers' interest in baseball movies. After nearly twenty years of franchise futility, the Dodgers captured the hearts and imaginations of fans across America by winning the National League pennant in 1941, and that in turn captured the attention of Hollywood. So strong was fan affinity that the Dodgers would be depicted in several more feature films in the following two decades, but Twentieth Century Fox was the first studio to try to cash in on the Dodgers' newly acquired popularity with the release of *It Happened in Flatbush* in 1942. Mirroring the Dodgers' rags-to-riches story, the underachieving and unnamed Brooklyn team in this feature is whipped into shape by their feisty new manager Frank Maguire. Along the way, Maguire faces challenges that include torpid players, new ownership interested mostly in profits, a romance with Kathryn Baker who just happens to be a member of that new ownership group, and a petition circulated among disgruntled players requesting his ouster. Undaunted, Frank relentlessly pushes the team to the pennant.

1942–1962: Biopics, Kids, and Fantasy — The Golden Age of Baseball Film

In 1942, RKO Pictures released *The Pride of the Yankees*, the film biography of New York Yankee great Lou Gehrig. *The Pride of the Yankees* recounts the spectacular baseball career and untimely death of Gehrig, a victim of amyotrophic lateral sclerosis. Released in the first year of America's entry into World War II, the film's opening narration pointedly reminds viewers that Gehrig's "valor and fortitude" in the face of death would be necessary virtues for many young Americans in the years ahead. *The Pride of the Yankees* was calculated to appeal to a broad spectrum of film goers, combining elements of comedy, drama, and even a musical number. The film's focus on the relationship between Gehrig and his wife Eleanor have led many to categorize it as a romance, but its depiction of the life and career of one of the game's finest players places it squarely in the baseball genre.

The Pride of the Yankees is something of a landmark in baseball film for a number of reasons. In contrast to its mainly second-rate predecessors in the baseball genre, *The Pride of the Yankees* was a high quality production with top box-office performers, acclaimed by critics and moviegoers and nominated for eleven Academy Awards, including Best Picture. Moreover, it revised the way Hollywood portrayed the baseball player. Although *The Pride of the Yankees* includes echoes of a past in which baseball was not entirely respectable and baseball players were typically portrayed as either semi-comic egotists, or naive, post-pubescent rubes, Lou Gehrig as portrayed in this film is no bumpkin, nor does he possess an insecurity, immaturity, or some character flaw that baseball must mend. The Gehrig played by Gary Cooper in *The Pride of the Yankees* is mature, decent, intelligent, humble, urbane, hard-working, and worthy of the public's adoration. The film is perhaps the first to elevate its baseball-playing protagonist to fully heroic proportions on and off the field.

The Pride of the Yankees not only altered the way the cinematic baseball hero is portrayed, it ushered in a succession of biographical films of baseball heroes in the next decade and a half, depicting the lives and playing careers of Hall of Famers like Jackie Robinson, Dizzy Dean, and Grover Cleveland Alexander, as well as players who overcame enormous odds, like Robinson, Monty Stratton, and Jimmy Piersoll.

Ironically, Hollywood's next baseball offering after *The Pride of the Yankees* was the unfortunate baseball B-comedy *Ladies' Day* (1943). Wacky Waters is the ace of the Sox pitching staff and victory is assured when he takes the mound unless he is distracted by a "dame" (which we are led to believe in the early scenes he frequently is). His latest distraction is a Latin movie star named Pepita Zorita. With the Sox in the midst of a pennant race, Wacky's preoccupation with Pepita threatens to cost the other players and their insatiably materialistic wives the money they will realize from a World Series victory. When Wacky and Pepita are married, the other wives hatch a variety of "comic" schemes to keep the newly-weds apart during the championship game, including assault, kidnapping and false diagnosis of a serious disease. Pepita's absence does not improve Wacky's pitching, and seems in fact to have the opposite effect. When she finally overcomes the machinations of the other wives to arrive at the ballpark, it is Pepita's very presence that inspires Wacky to pitch the Sox to victory.

The next in the succession of baseball biopics was *The Babe Ruth Story* (1948). In this worshipful film biography completely at odds with the reality of Babe Ruth's life, the Bambino is an oafish, innocent, and always well-intentioned fellow who rises from a happy childhood at St. Mary's Industrial School for Boys, to professional baseball, to virtual sainthood. Even the disappointments of his later life are tempered by his happy marriage to Claire Ruth. His feuds with management and teammates (notably Lou Gehrig), his carousing and promiscuity, and his failed first marriage are never depicted. The Babe Ruth of this film heals crippled children, rescues little dogs, beats up gamblers, saves baseball, and as he lays dying, volunteers to help others by trying an experimental drug. In any discussion of the worst baseball film of all time, *The Babe Ruth Story* will figure prominently.

A more pleasant baseball fantasy, *It Happens Every Spring*, was released the following year. Vernon Simpson is a baseball fan, research chemist, and instructor at Norworth University who is having little luck finding the formula for a substance that, when applied to tree bark, will repel insects. Such a discovery would secure both munificent funding from chemical and timber interests and his future with fiancé Debbie Greenleaf, daughter of the university's president. While working in his lab one day, a baseball from a nearby sandlot game sails into his lab and smashes the lab equipment containing his latest experiment. Retrieving the baseball from the resulting mess, Vernon discovers the ball now repels wood. He salvages what he can of the formula from the debris of his experiment and concocts a plan to raise the money he needs to continue his research and ensure a future for Debbie and himself. He abruptly takes a leave of absence from Norworth, and pesters skeptical officials of the St. Louis baseball team into giving him a tryout. Thanks to a ball doctored with his formula, the powerful St. Louis lineup is literally unable to get any wood on his pitches and Vernon is immediately signed to a contract. Soon he and his secret wood-deflecting potion are dominating the league's batters. Seeking to hide his true identity for fear university officials will not approve of his actions, Vernon plays under the name "King Kelly," goes to comic lengths to avoid photographers, and sends Debbie letters so ambiguous in regard to his whereabouts and circumstances that she becomes convinced he must be engaged in criminal activity. Vernon pitches St. Louis into the World Series against New York, but just before the deciding game of the Series, Vernon spills the remaining formula and must rely solely on his own dubious pitching skills. With New York threatening to rally for the win in the final inning, Vernon barehands a hard line drive for the final out, in the process breaking his throwing hand and ending his "pitching career." He returns home with the money he had hoped to earn, but also with the certainty that Debbie and Norworth officials will now want nothing to do with him. On the contrary, the entire campus has learned Vernon is the great King Kelly and he arrives home to a heroes' welcome. In winning the big game and the girl of his dreams, earning lots of money and the affection of the hometown fans, Vernon realizes the typical rewards conferred upon cinematic baseball heroes, as well as a prize it is safe to say is unique in baseball cinema — Vernon is named head of Norworth University's new research lab.

A notable aspect of *It Happens Every Spring* is the way in which film makers attempt to mitigate the plainly illegal doctoring of the baseball to win games. As baseball historian Hal Erickson writes:

> ... Yes, the hero of *It Happens Every Spring* is cheating. No, *It Happens Every Spring* does not advocate cheating; nor does it state flat out that the team could not have won *without* cheating. The script very carefully underlines several plot points that take the curse off the loaded-ball gimmick [2002, pp 237].

Viewers have far less moral ambiguity to contend with in another 1949 release, *The Kid From Cleveland*, a cautionary morality play about juvenile delinquency that seems tragically innocent today. Mike Jackson, a broadcaster for the Indians, befriends young Johnny Barrows and helps him become a batboy for the Tribe. Johnny is a runaway, the product of a bad home environment. The redeeming milieu of baseball, we are led to believe, rescues the boy from a life of crime. In the end, Mike is romancing Johnny's analyst, Johnny is straightening out his life and family relationships, and the Indians are winning the 1948 World Series.

The Stratton Story is the inspiring 1949 baseball biography of Monty

Stratton, an All-Star pitcher for the Chicago White Sox who wounds himself in a hunting accident following the 1938 season. Stratton loses his leg as a result of the accident, and despite the unflagging and patient support of his wife Ethel, he broods over his misfortune for months. As he helps his infant son learn to walk, Monty decides it is time for him to learn to use his prosthesis to do the same. Father and son are soon taking walks together, and more, Monty is throwing again, pitching to Ethel in the yard of the family farm. As he adjusts to life with his artificial limb, Monty's spirits are restored. The Strattons decide to attend a Texas League All-Star game between the Western and Southern All-Stars at the invitation of the Southern All-Stars' manager. Unbeknownst to anyone except the manager is the fact that Monty means to pitch in the game, to prove to himself and others that despite the loss of his leg, he is "just the same as anybody else." Things do not go well for Monty in the early innings, but his shakiness proves to be mostly rust and nerves. As the game progresses, he is increasingly effective, and even hits and runs bases tolerably well. Frustrated opponents bunt to try to reach base, but the tactic fails when Monty proves he can field as well as he pitches. Behind Monty's gritty effort, the Southern All-Stars win the game, but more importantly, Monty Stratton has triumphed over a cruel tragedy.

Take Me Out To The Ballgame was the fourth baseball film of 1949, but the first musical comedy set to baseball since the release of *They Learned About Women* in 1930. The musical numbers and drollery dress up a plot that is pretty ordinary baseball cinema. Eddie O'Brien and Dennis Ryan play for the Wolves and the spend the off-season performing as a vaudeville team. Arriving at spring training in Florida prior to the 1906 season, they discover that the Wolves have a new owner, K.C. Higgins, who happens to be a woman (and one who knows baseball, at that). In their first encounter during a Wolves batting practice session, Eddie is insubordinate and K.C. shows him up. Worse, her strict rules for the team threaten to cramp his moonlighting as a song and dance man. But as Eddie attempts to soften up his new boss, he ends up falling for her, and she for him. Enter the inevitable gambler: Joe Lorgan is the owner of a vaudeville club who has bet heavily against the Wolves' success. He attempts to protect his wagers by hiring Eddie as the top act for his club, a move calculated to wear him out rehearsing all night. Eddie slumps and so do the Wolves, their division lead dwindling rapidly as the season draws to a close. When K.C. learns that Eddie is breaking training, she assumes he is chasing after chorus girls and fires him, and Lorgan, his scheme working better than he hoped, does the same. Eddie's fans will have none of it, however, and their chants force K.C. to reinstate Eddie just before the critical game of the pennant drive. K.C. forgives Eddie when she learns of Lorgan's plot and in a farce of mistaken intentions, Dennis gets on base and Eddie hits a home run to win the big game.

Just three years after breaking major league baseball's color barrier, Jackie Robinson himself starred in *The Jackie Robinson Story* (1950). Unlike some of the earlier baseball biopics, the film is largely faithful to the events of Robinson's life and baseball career, although it often softens the nature and intensity of the abuse Robinson actually endured. The film chronicles Robinson's stellar achievements as a multi-sport collegiate star at Pasadena City College and UCLA, and his frustration in searching for meaningful work in "Jim Crow" America following graduation. After serving in the military, Robinson becomes a star second baseman for the Kansas City Monarchs' Negro League team. He is scouted and recruited by Brooklyn Dodgers general manager Branch Rickey, who selects Robinson to break the color barrier based on the player's background, character, ability and most of all, the courage to play through the discrimination and hostility he is sure to face. Rickey warns young Jackie that the task of integrating baseball will be an unpleasant and harrowing one, and indeed Robinson faces open and ugly racism from fans, opponents, and even teammates, first on the Dodgers' Montreal farm club, then in the major leagues. Jackie perseveres, demonstrating both his talent and mettle, proving the skeptics wrong, helping the Dodgers win the National League pennant, and ushering in a new age of race relations in America.

The other 1950 baseball release, *Kill the Umpire* also serves up a lesson in understanding, albeit one of rather less social significance. Bill Johnson is a former baseball player, a rabid fan and a baiter of umpires. He attends spring training games near his Florida home, but appears to enjoy loudly disparaging umpires more than the game itself. He misses work to take in a ballgame once too often, however, and is fired. With his long-suffering wife threatening to leave him and his angry father-in-law, a former umpire, pressuring him, he reluctantly enrolls in a school for umpires. Although initially (and intentionally) the worst student in the school, Bill begins to take his role as umpire seriously and upon graduation is assigned to the Texas Interstate League, a circuit notorious for its fans' abuse of game officials. Now Bill is on the receiving end of the harassment, but he steadfastly maintains his composure and integrity, even when threatened by perfidious gamblers and angry crowds.

Another lesson in the redemptive powers of baseball, *Angels in the Outfield* (1951) is the fantasy tale of crusty, bellicose Guffy McGovern who manages a Pittsburgh Pirate team wallowing in the National League cellar. McGovern prowls the dugout bellowing obscenities, perhaps understandably, as he manages an embarrassingly inept Pirate team. One evening, while alone in Forbes Field, McGovern receives a visit from the Angel Gabriel, who takes the manager to task for his belligerent and profane ways, and makes it clear a kinder, gentler approach will yield the miracle his Pirates need to win. And so it does—McGovern changes his attitude and his habits, and the Pirates go on a ten-game winning streak. When he reverts back to his old manner, the team slumps. Helping Guffy find the better man inside him are his love interest, novice sportswriter Jennifer Paige and a little orphan girl, Bridget White, whose prayers summoned Gabriel in the first place. Things are going well for the reformed McGovern until late in the season when he is stunned by a line drive. In his dazed condition he mentions to the press the unique arrangement with angels. Baseball officials order a hearing to determine Guffy's mental competency, but the Commissioner ignores the testimony of a psychiatrist in favor of that of three clergymen. On to the big game, where Guffy performs his greatest act of kindness. He has learned from Gabriel that fading veteran pitcher Saul Hellman is destined to die in the off-season. With the pennant on the line, Guffy gives Hellman one more shot at glory, and Hellman responds with a gutsy performance to win the game. Predictably, the reformed Guffy marries Jennifer and they adopt little Bridget.

Those who prefer their supernatural influences on the game to be a bit less celestial might find 1951's other baseball comedy, *Rhubarb*, more to their liking. Rhubarb is the feline companion of millionaire Thaddeus J. Banner, owner of the Brooklyn Loons. When the eccentric Banner dies, he bequeaths the team and $30 million to Rhubarb, and designates his press agent Eric Yeager as the cat's guardian. Imbroglios abound. It seems Rhubarb is not the only heir—Banner's conniving daughter Myra vainly attempts to depose Rhubarb throughout the film. Eric's life is complicated when his fiancé (and daughter of the Loons' manager) Polly Sickles discovers she is allergic to Rhubarb. And the Loons are none too happy about having a cat for an owner. Yeager convinces the team Rhubarb will bring them luck, and much to his surprise, that is exactly what happens. Rhubarb becomes a fixture in the Brooklyn dugout, the players petting their feline good-luck charm before they go to bat, and in no time the once-hapless Loons bust out of the cellar and into the pennant race. None of this success is lost on the spurned Myra. She hatches a plot with crooked gambler Pencil Louie, a bookie with heavy bets against the Loons, to kidnap Rhubarb during the World Series. Eric manages to find the kidnapper's hideout and Rhubarb escapes to turn up at the ballpark in time to inspire a Brooklyn victory. Polly discovers she is not allergic to Rhubarb, but to the lining of his cage, clearing the way for her marriage to Eric, and a big happy family with Rhubarb and his many offspring.

Two more baseball biographies were released in 1952, and while both claimed to be "true stories," neither is a particularly accurate account of their protagonists' lives. *The Pride of St. Louis* is the story of Hall of Fame pitcher Jerome "Dizzy" Dean, a congenial, cocksure young pitcher who climbs the baseball ladder from an Ozarks minor league team to the St. Louis Cardinals' "Gas House Gang" of the 1930s. Along the way he meets and marries the love of his life, Pat Nash. Dizzy averages 24 wins a season during a five-year span and, along with his brother Paul "Daffy" Dean, pitches the Cardinals to a World Series championship. The brothers become wildly popular, clowning with fans, charming the sportswriters, and generally acting like kids in a major league candy store. But this is a baseball biopic, so it is all too good to last. Dizzy is injured while pitching in the All-Star game, and he never recovers his form. He is traded to the Cubs, then sent to the minors. He broods, begins to drink and gamble, and he hits bottom when Pat, tired of waiting for him to grow up, leaves him. His salvation is, of course, baseball — Diz gets back in the game as the Cardinals' radio announcer. His distinctive, folksy radio presence rekindles his popularity with fans, but his mangling of syntax and grammar brings down the wrath of what appears to be every teacher of English within the sound of his voice. A chastened Dizzy offers to quit the broadcast booth in the interests of the youth of Missouri and Southern Illinois. In what he thinks is his farewell broadcast, he counsels his young listeners to get the education he never had, and to "give it everything you've got." The teachers are so moved, they drop their complaint. Pat is so moved, she returns to his side. The sponsors are so moved, they keep Dizzy in the booth, where he becomes one of the game's most beloved announcers.

The Winning Team, released a scant six weeks after *The Pride of St. Louis,* is an even more inaccurate (to say nothing of mawkish) baseball biography that ostensibly chronicles the life and career of Hall of Fame pitcher Grover Cleveland Alexander (played by Ronald Reagan). As a young man, "Alex," has no plans for baseball beyond the few dollars he might earn playing in the bush leagues to put toward a farm, where he will settle down with his sweetheart Aimee. But as Alex moves up to higher levels of play (and pay), his thoughts turn to the possibility of a big-league career. Those dreams seem to be shattered after he is hit on the head by a line drive and begins to suffer from spells of double vision. Apparently unaware of his injury, the Philadelphia Phillies pick up Alex's contract. As he contemplates a return to the game, Alex's double vision suddenly clears and his pinpoint control returns. Aimee, never much in favor of being married to a baseball player, sees what the game means to Alex and becomes his biggest supporter as he returns to baseball and rises to fame in the majors. Alex is traded to the Chicago Cubs just about the time he is drafted and sent to Europe to fight in World War I. Stunned by an explosion in combat, his spells of double vision and vertigo return. Shortly after his return to civilian life and the Cubs, he collapses during a game. Despondent when a doctor tells him the relapse will mean the end of his pitching career, Alex goes out and gets very publicly drunk. Now word in the league is that his problem is booze, a rumor made more credible by the stoic Alex's refusal to tell anyone, including Aimee, what is really wrong with him. Turning to drink in earnest, he is soon out of the big leagues. Aimee leaves him. He becomes a vagabond, playing exhibition and pick-up games for a few dollars, and is eventually reduced to a carnival sideshow act. In the meantime, Aimee discovers the truth about his real affliction, and along with Alex's old friend, St. Louis Cardinals' manager Rogers Hornsby, rescues him from his degrading circumstances. Hornsby offers him a contract, Aimee supplies the inspiration, and Alex is soon making a comeback, one that culminates in a masterful pitching performance that wins the World Series for the Cardinals.

The Big Leaguer, released in 1953, is the only baseball film that takes place entirely in training camp. Veteran baseball man Hans Lobert is a scout for the New York Giants. Each year, he sifts through the Giants' new prospects at the team's tryout camp in Melbourne, Florida. Only a very few of these rookies will be good enough to stick with the Giants' organization, and fewer still will ever make it to the big leagues. A collection of young men — reminiscent of the typical group of diverse characters thrown together as comrades in war movies— vie to make an impression that will keep them in professional baseball. The camp is important to the players, but Hans' job might also be on the line should he fail to accurately assess the talent assembled for the two-week camp. The brightest prospect seems to be Adam Polachuk, a young man from Pennsylvania coal country who is supposed to be in college fulfilling his father's wish that he become a lawyer. Instead, he is taking his shot at the big leagues. Lobert's niece and assistant Christy takes a shine to Adam, providing the obligatory romance angle. Adam's father uncovers Adam's deception and shows up in Melbourne, but after watching his son play, he gives his blessing to the young man's baseball aspirations. His faith in Adam, as well as Hans' evaluation of him as a legitimate big-league prospect, are validated when Adam smacks a game-winning home run in the culminating event of the camp, an intersquad game against the Dodgers' rookies.

When *The Kid from Left Field* debuted in 1953, it ushered in another distinct and enduring trend in baseball films — the presence of children as central characters. Of course, children are seen in many other baseball films prior to 1953, but they are confined to relatively minor roles, usually cast as objects of pity and/or willing subjects for inspiration by the film's baseball hero. However, *The Kid from Left Field* and later films including *Roogie's Bump* in the '50s, *Safe at Home* in the '60s, *The Bad News Bears* in the '70s, *Rookie of the Year* in the '90s and *Hardball* in the '00s place children on the field and at the center of the narrative. The title character of *The Kid from Left Field* is Christy Cooper, nine-year-old son of Larry Cooper, a widower who was once a major league star for the Bisons. Despite a wealth of knowledge and gifted insight about the game, Larry has been reduced to a mere peanut vendor in the Bisons' ballpark. When he shows more interest in the action on the field than in peddling peanuts, Larry is fired by his despotic boss. Young Christy approaches the team owner, Mr. Whacker, in an attempt to have his father reinstated. He succeeds in saving Larry's job and in the process so impresses Whacker that the owner makes Christy a Bisons batboy. In the dugout, Christy begins passing on advice to the players, tips on hitting and strategy he has heard from his father. Although initially skeptical about the kid's coaching, it does not take long for the Bison players to realize this is good stuff. Following Christy's suggestions, the team begins to turn its woeful season around, no thanks to their incompetent and malicious manager Billy Lorant. When the resentful Lorant learns Christy is managing the team behind his back, he dismisses the lad. Predictably, the team goes into a slump. Eventually, Whacker learns it was

Christy who was responsible for the Bisons' earlier success and, always looking for a clever marketing angle, the owner fires Lorant and names Christy the new manager of the Bisons. Larry keeps providing Christy the information he needs to successfully manage the ballclub, but the elder Cooper will take no credit and swears Christy to secrecy about their father-son collaboration. But when Christy is hospitalized with pneumonia, he must reveal it was his father who was the coaching genius behind the Bisons' success. Christy is lauded for his honesty and Larry is named the new manager of the Bisons.

Roogie's Bump (1954) combines the fantasy element of *Angels in the Outfield* with the emphasis on youth of *The Kid from Left Field* to create a really dreadful movie, a serious contender for designation as worst baseball film ever. Young Roogie Rigsby hasn't much going for him as the story opens. Uprooted from his Ohio home after the recent death of this father, he finds himself living in Brooklyn with no friends. The neighborhood kids will not let him into the local sandlot games and bully him because he is short. Roogie's luck changes when he is visited by the ghost of the great Brooklyn pitcher Red O'Malley. O'Malley's spirit gives the youngster a bump on his right arm, a bump which confers upon Roogie phenomenal pitching ability. "Phenomenal" may be an understatement — Roogie is now able, with the assistance of crude animation, to throw a baseball through a brick wall and bring down great industrial smokestacks with what one would assume is his four-seam fastball. Roogie manages to get himself a tryout with the Dodgers. The Brooklyn manager, Coach Boxey, wants to sign the boy and let him play when he grows up, but Dodger publicity agent P.A. Rikert overrules the coach and has the boy put on the Dodgers' pitching staff immediately. Roogie's freakish talents make him both an instant hit with fans and an instant target of all sorts of commercial interests seeking to capitalize on his fame. Boxey, infuriated by this corporate exploitation of the boy, takes Roogie off the roster — at least until the outcry of the fans and pressure from baseball officials force him to reverse his decision. Roogie is reinstated just in time for a relief appearance in the late innings of a crucial game. Alas, the ghost of Red O'Malley, having regrets about placing the boy in such a situation, reappears and revokes Roogie's powers. Still, Roogie has great value to the Dodgers as their good-luck charm, and he remains with the team as they go on to win the pennant.

In *The Great American Pastime* (1956), suburbanite lawyer, father, and baseball fan Bruce Hallerton decides coaching his son's Little League team would be just the thing to promote father-son bonding. Bruce soon realizes that: 1) His own son has been assigned to a different team than the one he's coaching; 2) He has been handed the worst team in the league; 3) The players' parents expect him to win every game while giving their sons preferential playing time. Despite pressuring from the parents to win even if it means bending the rules, Bruce holds firm to the ideals of play fair, teaches his young charges to play the game well, and leads them to victory in the season finale against the league's top team. Released twenty years before *The Bad News Bears*, *The Great American Pastime* does not have the sardonic edge (nor the profane and insolent children) of *The Bad News Bears*, but it does consider what happens when adults organize kids' games and turn sand lot sport into miniature major leagues.

The 15-year run of baseball biopics would in end in 1957 with the release of *Fear Strikes Out*, loosely based on the story of Boston Red Sox outfielder Jimmy Piersall's battle against mental illness. From the opening of the film, where we see Jimmy as a child playing catch with his father John, the younger Piersall is constantly pushed (and frequently berated) to play better by John, who is vicariously living his dream of baseball stardom through Jimmy. Despite stellar high school and minor league careers, Jim's best never seems good enough for his father. While in the minors, Jimmy meets and marries Mary Teevan, a nurse who offers support, but no solution to his problem. The constant pressure applied by his father to achieve ever more begins to take its toll on Jim's psyche. By the time he makes the Red Sox' major league team, he is moody, paranoid and hostile. Jimmy finally snaps, suffering a mental collapse in the middle of a game, screaming and climbing the backstop until he is subdued by teammates. He is admitted to a mental hospital, where he works for months with a therapist to come to grips with his condition. The dawning awareness that his father's unrelenting demands lie at the root of his problem leads to a brutally direct confrontation between Jim and John. Freed from the heavy burden of his father's expectations, reunited with Mary and reconciled with John, Jimmy returns to the Red Sox to play for himself and his love of the game.

Damn Yankees (1958), a film adaptation of the hit Broadway play, has the distinction of being the last baseball musical produced by Hollywood. The Washington Senators are the worst team in baseball, but they haven't a bigger fan than Joe Boyd. There is not much the aging, pudgy Boyd can do to help his beloved Senators except curse their rivals, the perennially successful New York Yankees. But one day the devil, calling himself Mr. Applegate, appears and offers to transform Joe into the slugger the Senators so desperately need. Joe agrees to sell his soul, with one stipulation: he can void the deal and return to his former life by walking away from the Senators at any time, right up until the penultimate day of the baseball season. And so Joe Boyd becomes Joe Hardy, a 22-year-old power-hitter. What Joe does not know is that Applegate's machinations include snatching the pennant away from the Senators and handing it to the Yankees on the final day of season, even as he snatches away Joe's soul. Joe Hardy proves to be just what the underachieving Senators need, and his remarkable prowess drives the Senators to the top of the standings. Success on the field is fine, but Joe misses his wife, Meg, and rents a room in her home just to be closer to her. Applegate fears Joe's devotion to Meg might spoil his plans, so he summons "real sexy babe" Lola to seduce Joe. Joe proves to be a man of profound fidelity, and Applegate's schemes are thwarted when Joe and Lola become friends and join forces to outwit the devil. The Senators win the pennant, Joe returns to his loving wife and former life, and Applegate is left seething but powerless in the face of Joe's overwhelming virtue.

1962: Baseball Stops Going to the Movies

Despite the box office success of *Damn Yankees*, it would be four years until another baseball film would be released, and it would take the excitement generated by Roger Maris and Mickey Mantle's 1961 home run race to inspire the production of *Safe at Home* (1962). A morality play about the evils of fibbing, *Safe at Home* is the story of ten-year-old Little Leaguer Hutch Lawton, who is having trouble fitting in with the other kids. Attempting to impress his peers (and to defend his oft-absent father), he tells the other boys that his dad has friends on the New York Yankees team, including Mantle and Maris. Hutch is pressed to invite the two Yankee sluggers to the Little League banquet and he sneaks off to the Yankee's Fort Lauderdale training facility to find the two players and ask them to extract him from the lie by appearing at the dinner. He does manage to attain an audience with Mantle and Maris themselves, but instead of helping the boy perpetuate his deceit, they give him a stern (to say nothing of stiff and badly delivered) talking to about the importance of honesty and send him back home. Expecting to be further disgraced, but ready to face the consequences of his dishonesty upon his return, Hutch is redeemed when Mantle and Maris invite Hutch's team down to Florida to spend a day with the Yankees.

It would be easy to blame the miserable *Safe at Home* for the eleven-year drought of baseball films that would follow. Not until 1973 would Hollywood produce another baseball film. One can posit numerous other explanations for this hiatus, from the social upheavals of the 60s and 70s, to overly cautious attitudes bordering on the paranoid about producing certain types of movies, to struggles within Hollywood's power structure, to simple coincidence. Whatever the case, the drought would end with only a trickle of films in the 1970s and would not again reach a steady flow of baseball releases until the 1980s.

Bang the Drum Slowly (1973) is one of only two baseball films produced in the 1970s that is about adults, rather than little-leaguers, playing baseball. (*The Bingo Long Traveling All-Stars and Motor Kings* is the other.) It is also one of the first baseball films to portray (albeit rather circumspectly) issues like racial tensions in the clubhouse and labor disputes as elements of professional baseball. But the film is primarily about the relationship of two players on the New York Mammoths, pitcher Henry Wiggen and third-string catcher Bruce Pearson. Wiggen is a bona fide star while Pearson, his slow-witted roommate, is a marginal ballplayer who is not expected to make the team. The two share a secret learned in the off-season: Bruce Pearson is dying of Hodgkin's disease. At the time, Henry is in the process of bargaining a new contract with the Mammoths and when negotiations reach an impasse, he offers a compromise: He will accept less money if he is contractually tied to Pearson. Or, as Wiggen puts it, "Whatever happens to one must happen to the other. Traded. Sold. Whatever." The chance to sign Henry Wiggen for less than his true value is an offer too good for the miserly Mammoth club officials to pass up, so the deal is done and Pearson makes the team. Not that making the New York Mammoths is an entirely good thing. The team's clubhouse is wracked by dissension, petty jealousies, and constant ragging, and the discord carries over into the Mammoths' performance on the field. But when word spreads through the team that Pearson is dying, the players' attitudes change, along with the team's fortunes. They quietly rally around Pearson and begin to support each other as well. Finally given an opportunity to play, Bruce becomes a good hitter and Henry helps him become a better catcher. The Mammoths clinch the pennant, but it is obvious at that point that Bruce is too ill too continue playing. He leaves the team before the playoffs begin but the Mammoths go on to win the World Series. A few months later, Henry Wiggen is the only member of the Mammoths organization — player or management — to attend Bruce Pearson's funeral.

The Bingo Long Traveling All-Stars and Motor Kings (1976) is probably better-known for its softball treatment of the racial discrimination faced by black ballplayers in the first half of the 20th century than its critique of the treatment of ballplayers by ownership. Like The Jackie Robinson Story a quarter of a century earlier, Bingo Long offers a largely sanitized account of the scale and harshness of the bigotry confronting black ballplayers and African Americans in general prior to the civil rights movement. Bingo Long is a star pitcher for the Ebony Aces of the Negro leagues in the late 1930s. The Aces are owned by Sallison Porter, a mean-spirited, exploitive owner. When Porter releases an injured Aces player, then docks the pay of the other players to pay the hospital bill, Bingo decides he has had enough. He and Elite Giants catcher Leon Carter contact some of the best players in the Negro leagues and together they organize a barn-storming baseball team. The team proves so popular with fans, and steals so much talent from the Negro leagues, that Porter and the other owners conclude they had better put the Traveling All-Stars out of business before the All-Stars do the same to them. They organize a boycott of the Traveling All-Stars' games, but Bingo and Leon keep the team in business by playing exhibition games against White semi-pro and town teams, clowning their way through the games like baseball versions of the Harlem Globetrotters. Porter's hired thugs beat up one of the Traveling All-Stars and stab another, but the players will not be intimidated. Porter finally offers Bingo a deal: The Negro League All-Stars will play Bingo's Traveling All-Stars in a winner-take-all game. If Bingo's team wins, they will become a member of the league, but if they lose, the Traveling All-Stars will disband and the players will return to their original teams. Of course, Sallison Porter is too corrupt to play the game on the up-and-up, so he schemes to undermine Bingo's chances. None of those machinations look likely to succeed, except the kidnapping of the Traveling All-Stars' clean-up hitter Leon Carter. But Leon escapes his captors and shows up just in time to hit the home run that wins the game. The Traveling All-Stars have won a place in the league, but the signing of one of Bingo's talented young players by the Brooklyn Dodgers after the big game foreshadows the end of the Negro leagues themselves.

The Bad News Bears (1976) was the first and easily the best of the four films about little leagues that dominated baseball cinema in the 1970s. It is a parable about middle-class parent's over-organizing kids' sports, their obsession with winning, and their willingness to hire out the chore of developing their own children because they are too busy to do the job themselves.

One of those parents, Los Angeles City Councilman Bob Whitewood, threatens legal action to force the ultra-competitive and very white suburban North County League to include the Bears, a team as diverse as they are inept. Whitewood hires former minor league pitcher Morris Buttermaker, paying him under the table to coach the Bears. Buttermaker, now a swimming pool cleaner by trade, is content to let the kids play while he sits in the dugout and swills beer. That changes after the league's best team, the Yankees, and their arrogant, overbearing coach Roy Turner embarrass the Bears in a 16–0 drubbing. North League officials and Turner tell Buttermaker everyone would be better off if the Bears just dropped out of the league. The Bears themselves make it clear to Buttermaker they do not appreciate his laissez-faire approach to coaching and threaten to walk. All of this seems to awaken Buttermaker's competitive instincts. He talks the Bears out of quitting, collectively and individually, whips them into shape, and recruits a couple of key players. One is Amanda Whurlitzer, daughter of his ex-girlfriend and an accomplished pitcher. The other is Kelly Leak, a young hoodlum and the best player in the league. Buttermaker's dramatically improved team begins to win, and by the end of the season they find themselves in the championship game against the Yankees. As the prospect of a championship grows nearer, Buttermaker's competitive fires begin to burn too hot. He orders Kelly Leak to run teammates off fly balls to ensure they are caught, tells another player to allow inside pitches to hit him so he can reach first base, and contemplates risking injury to Amanda Whurlitzer's overworked pitching arm. When the Bears do not seem to share his obsession with victory and the vindication he believes it will bring them, Buttermaker launches into a profanity-laced tirade about winning and revenge. As he looks into the faces of his players who sit in the dugout in stunned silence, it becomes apparent to him that he is coaching like Roy Turner. That fact becomes even more evident to him as he watches Turner berate and then strike his own son, who is pitching for the Yankees, for failing to follow instructions. Reminded of the true purpose of kids' sports, Buttermaker inserts his reserves — the team's worst players — into the lineup to finish the championship game. Incredibly, the scrubs keep the game close and put on a valiant rally in the bottom of the final inning. But in a close play at the plate, Kelly Leak is tagged out trying to stretch a triple into a homer, and the Bears fall short by one run. After the game, the teams meet at home plate where the Yankees are presented a four-foot high championship trophy and the Bears receive a seven-inch runner-up token. When one of the Yankee players offers a condescending congratulation to the Bears, the second place trophy is thrown into the dirt at his feet and the Yankees are told to "Wait till next year." This sparks a wild, beer-squirting celebration by the Bears and their parents.

The sequels that followed *The Bad News Bears* in the subsequent two summers are, at best, pale reflections of the original. *The Bad News Bears in Breaking Training* (1977) features most of the original team, *sans* coach Buttermaker and pitcher Amanda Whurlitzer, making a trip to Houston to play a game in the Astrodome against a team from Texas for the right to play a game in Japan. No explanation is offered as to why the Bears were selected for this singular honor, but it provides a handy device for various Bad News Bears status offenses and other misdemeanors, scatology, and prolific cussing to take place on a road trip. Produced for a teen audience, one of the film's themes is that responsible adults are mostly imbeciles, so the players run off their new, authoritarian coach, dupe their parents into thinking they will be properly chaperoned on their trip to Texas, then drive themselves to Houston, leaving a good many hoodwinked grownups in their wake. Once in Houston, a run-in with the law produces a demand by authorities that they produce an adult supervisor. As luck would have it, Kelly Leak's father Mike lives in Houston. Although father and son are estranged since Mike divorced Kelly's mother, the elder Leak agrees to his son's request and pretends he is the Bears' coach to get the kids off the hook. It soon becomes obvious even to the Bears that they need a real coach, and Mike again agrees to step into the role, drilling the Bears into readiness for the big game which they win in dramatic fashion. Mike and Kelly are reconciled and the Bears are off to Japan.

The saga mercifully ends with *The Bad News Bears Go To Japan* (1978). Although the Bears have earned the right to play in Japan, the Junior League decides to cancel the game because the Japanese champions are too competitive. The Bears make a public appeal for support, and their plea is answered by Marvin Lazar, a luckless publicity agent of dubious character. Lazar manages to get the Bears to Japan, where he engages in a series of schemes to promote a game between the Japanese champions and the Bears. The game is finally on, but gamblers bent on fixing the outcome compel Lazar to add three illegal and obviously overage players to the Bears' roster. The Bears are not happy about their new teammates and the Japanese players, who earlier befriended the Bears, discern the plot. Realizing the game is a sham, both teams walk off the field. Later that day, the Japanese team and the real Bears meet in a sandlot for game of baseball untainted by media hype and adult corruption of the game. The kids get to play, and Lazar gets a valuable lesson in the true meaning of sport.

Here Come the Tigers (1978) is the final and by far the most wretched of the four little league films of the 1970s. In this utterly predictable B-picture, good-hearted Eddie Burke, a rookie police officer, takes on a motley group of lascivious, foul-mouthed adolescent screw-ups and turns them into league champions.

Although the 1980s saw a resurgence in the production of baseball pictures, with some of them classified among the best baseball films of all time, the decade did not get off to a very promising start when *Blue Skies Again* was released in 1983. A low-budget film that perhaps justifies the long hiatus in the production of baseball pictures that proceeded it, *Blue Skies Again* is the tale of Paula Fradkin, who aspires to be the first woman to play not merely professional baseball, but major league baseball. With the assistance of baseball players' agent Liz West, Paula secures a tryout with the Denver Devils during spring training. Despite an impressive hitting exhibition for Devils manager Dirk Miller, it does not appear that Paula will get a fair tryout. The Devils players resent her, but the primary obstacle standing in her way is the wealthy, vain, obnoxious and borderline misogynist owner of the Devils, Sandy Mendenhall. When Miller, West and others urge Mendenhall to give Paula a shot at making the team, he agrees. But Mendenhall stacks the deck, ordering his players to heckle and insult her, a chore they take up with a venomous and vulgar enthusiasm. Paula naturally loses her concentration during this barrage of ridicule from her ostensible teammates and performs poorly. Mendenhall smugly assumes the case is closed, but Paula's supporters, including Miller, arrange to have Paula pinch-hit in a spring training game against the Memphis Blues. Once again, Paula is up against a hostile team, but this time they are opponents, not her own teammates. Facing the Blues' toughest (and judging from his nickname — "Brushback" — their nastiest) pitcher, Paula smacks a line drive to left and hustles it into a double. Brushback gives her a smile of grudging respect. The fans go wild. And Sandy Mehdenhall, when swarmed by the media after the game, changes his stripes and takes credit for finding the first female big leaguer.

1984: The Natural — Baseball's Cinematic Revival

With its big budget, a cast of genuine Hollywood stars including Robert Redford in the lead, and a celebrated director in Barry Levinson,

The Natural (1984) marked the revival of baseball films as major Hollywood productions. In this loose film adaptation of Bernard Malmud's novel,
young Roy Hobbs, a "can't miss" minor league prospect, leaves his rural
home for a tryout with the Chicago Cubs. He also leaves behind his fiancé
Iris, but promises that he will send for her when he has made it big. Shortly
before Roy reports to the Cubs, he is shot and badly wounded by a deranged
woman, who then kills herself. Roy knocks around, always on the fringes
of the game until he finally returns to professional baseball 16 years later as
an outfielder for the New York Knights. His spectacular play transforms the
bumbling Knights into contenders, a turn of events that threatens to upset
the plans of the Judge, the team's corrupt half-owner, who stands to win
sole control of the ball club from his partner, team manager Pop Fisher, if
the Knights fail to win the National League pennant. The Judge had already
conspired with gambler Gus Sands, and his moll/temptress Memo Paris, to
wreck the Knight's chances by buying off right fielder Bump Bailey. But
when Bailey is killed in a freak accident and Roy emerges as Bailey's replacement and the Knight's savior, they turn their attention to corrupting
Hobbes. Paris seduces Roy and distracted by her charms and the nightlife
of New York, he falls into a terrible slump. Roy's past is destined to catch
up with him and it does when the Knights travel to Chicago. His long-lost
love Iris contacts Roy after learning he will be playing in Chicago and the
erstwhile lovers are reunited. An inspired Roy Hobbs breaks out of his
offensive malaise with a barrage of home runs. Once again, the Knights are
on a roll, one that carries them into first place with only three games remaining in the season. Desperate to derail the Knights' charge to the pennant,
Gus Sands arranges to have Memo poison Hobbs. Roy falls into a coma and
awakens three days later to learn the Knights have lost three straight in his
absence and will now have to play a one-game playoff for the National
League championship. Against the advice of doctors and despite a final
attempt by the Judge to bribe and blackmail him, Hobbs plays in the game
and, inspired by Iris and the news that she bore him a son, now a teenager,
Hobbs wins the game with a towering, pyrotechnic home run. As the film
ends, we see Roy and his son playing catch in the same fields where Roy
and his father once played.

Perhaps encouraged by the example of a project as ambitious as *The
Natural*, the producers of *The Slugger's Wife* (1985) used much the same
formula: a sizeable budget, a notable director in Hal Ashby, a capable cast
of stars, and a screenplay by reliable hit-maker Neil Simon (the film's full

release title was in fact *Neil Simon's The Slugger's Wife*). Despite all that firepower, *The Slugger's Wife* was a flop. When Atlanta Braves star Darryl Palmer marries singer Debby Huston, it appears to be a good personal and career move. Inspired by Debby's presence, Darryl has never played better. But when she leaves to perform on the road, Darryl falls into a slump and becomes convinced Debby must be at every game if he is to hit well. His insistence that she always attend his games becomes so suffocatingly oppressive that she finally leaves him to pursue her career. Eventually he realizes that it is wrong for him to expect her to give up her career for his, and that he can play well when she is absent. The film ends with a hint of the couple's reconciliation.

The rocky-romance-plus-baseball formula surfaced again in *Bull Durham* (1988), a film often cited as the most realistic cinematic depiction of minor league baseball. The film's protagonist is minor league journeyman Crash Davis, a AAA-league catcher sent down to the A-league Durham Bulls to tutor raw but talented rookie pitcher Ebby Calvin "Nuke" LaLoosh. Annie Savoy is a local baseball aficionada who "hooks up with" a Bulls player each season to impart lessons on baseball, romance, literature, and mysticism. This season's candidates for Annie's attentions are Nuke and Crash. Crash refuses to "try out" for this role as Annie's lover but Nuke eagerly accepts it. Over the course of the season, Crash and Annie transform Nuke into a legitimate major league pitching prospect, but Annie comes to realize she has chosen the wrong man. Near the end of the season, Nuke is called up to the majors, and the Bulls organization, no longer needing a mentor for Nuke, releases Crash, who finds solace in the arms of Annie. Crash leaves Durham to finish the season in Asheville but returns to Durham and Annie, and the film ends with the promise of a managerial career for Crash and true love for both.

Eight Men Out (1988), a film version of the Eliot Asinof book by the same title, recounts the infamous "Black Sox" scandal in which several members of the Chicago White Sox baseball club conspired with gamblers to intentionally lose the 1919 World Series to Cincinnati Reds. The film portrays the White Sox as a talented team racked by internal dissent but harboring a common loathing of conniving, miserly team owner Charles Comiskey. Eight of the players are either participants in or aware of the scheme to throw the Series, including one of the game's greatest players, "Shoeless Joe" Jackson, and Buck Weaver, who learns of the plot but refuses to either participate in the fix or report it to baseball officials. During the

Series, the money promised to the players by the gamblers is not forthcoming and some of the players begin to have second thoughts about their complicity. They play to win, stave off elimination, and begin to look as if they might even win the Series. But the gambling syndicate headed by the notorious Arnold Rothstein has serious money riding on the outcome and they dispatch a thug who threatens to kill pitcher Lefty Williams' wife if he wins the next game. Williams throws the game and Cincinnati wins the Series, but suspicions and rumors of the conspiracy abound. Baseball writer Hugh Fullerton, with help from Ring Lardner, investigates and publishes a series of articles that force both baseball and government officials to act. With some nifty legal maneuvering by prosecutors and baseball's lawyers, confessions are obtained from several of the eight conspirators. When those confessions mysteriously "disappear" during the players' controversial criminal trial on fraud charges, all eight players are acquitted. But even as the players celebrate their acquittal with members of the jury, the new Commissioner of Baseball, Kennesaw Mountain Landis, decrees that all eight will be banned from organized baseball for life.

All this information about the Black Sox scandal would come in handy for film goers who viewed *Field of Dreams* the following year. *Field of Dreams* has the distinction of being only the second baseball film nominated for the Academy Award for Best Picture (*Pride of the Yankees*, nominated in 1942, was the first). "If you build it, he will come," an ethereal voice instructs college-radical-turned-farmer Ray Kinsella. Kinsella obediently constructs it, "it" being a baseball diamond in his Iowa corn field. And he builds it despite the ridicule of his neighbors and the financial difficulties that threaten foreclosure on his farm. His behavior is particularly strange given that Kinsella rejected baseball during his rebellious youth as part of his campaign to alienate his now-deceased father, a former baseball player. When the diamond is finished, the spirits of ballplayers from the past (most notably "Shoeless" Joe Jackson and the other players banned from baseball in the 1919 Black Sox scandal) appear — but only to Kinsella and his family — and play each evening on the field. The mysterious voice then instructs Kinsella to fetch Terence Mann back to the ballfield. Mann, a Sixties writer, is now an embittered recluse living in Boston. Understandably skeptical when first approached by Kinsella, Mann also receives mysterious communications and agrees to go see Kinsella's field himself. Once there, Mann's idealism and optimism are restored, and he explains the mystic phenomena of the cornfield (sort of). Kinsella finally understands the meaning of the phrase "if you build it, he will come" when his estranged father appears on the field as the young ball player Ray never knew, and Ray has the chance to put to rest their feud. Reconciled with his father, the younger Kinsella is also about to be financially solvent as well, as hundreds of fans stream toward his farm for the chance to pay to see the remarkable goings-on in his corn field.

A more conventional baseball film, *Major League,* was also released in 1989. The Cleveland Indians' new owner is Rachel Phelps, a haughty, conniving former showgirl who inherited the team from her late husband. Her ambition is to move the franchise to Florida (a notion not as far-fetched in 1989 as it seems now), but to get out of the club's stadium lease, season attendance must fall below 800,000. Phelps makes a number of highly questionable personnel decisions, divesting (she believes) the team of its best talent and replacing them with untested rookies and aging journeyman ballplayers. In the process, she brings together a roster of baseball's strangest characters to ensure a losing season and miserable attendance. What Phelps has not taken into account is the team's latent talent and competitive fire, a fire that is stoked white hot when the players detect Phelps' scheme. The Indians unite behind veteran catcher Jake Taylor and manager Lou Brown, begin to win games, and more importantly, to draw fans. In a thrilling finale, Cleveland wins the American League East title on the final day of the season and thwarts Phelps' machinations.

Malevolent ownership is also a prominent feature of 1991's *Talent for the Game.* The film's protagonist is California Angels scout Virgil Sweet, a former player who now scours the countryside looking for big-league talent. His latest scouting mission is conducted under a dark cloud, as Virgil has recently learned the new owner of the Angels, wealthy yuppie Gil Lawrence, plans to scrap the traditional scouting system and replace it with a computerized system of statistical player evaluation. To make matters worse, Virgil is stranded in a tiny village in rural Idaho when his car breaks down. It doesn't take long for the silver lining to show up in the form of local baseball prodigy Sammy Bodeen, a pitcher of remarkable promise. After assuring Sammy's parents the boy will be well looked after, Virgil and his new prospect are off to Anaheim and a formal tryout for the Angels brass. Sammy performs erratically during this audition until Virgil dons the tools of ignorance and catches for him. With Virgil behind the plate, Sammy begins to deal overpowering pitches, awing the front office personnel. Virgil is promoted to an executive position, but a different sort of promotion is planned for Sammy. Gil Lawrence decides to cash in on the youngster's talent immediately, advertising him as the team's savior in a publicity blitz. Lawrence then decrees Sammy will make his professional debut in the major leagues, despite warnings from Virgil and others that it could prove disastrous to the youth's psyche and career. Sure enough, the pressure gets to Sammy and he disappears before his inaugural game. Talked into returning by Virgil, Sammy reluctantly takes the mound and pitches horribly in his first inning. An incensed Lawrence orders the young pitcher relieved, which prompts Virgil to upbraid the owner and quit his new high-paying position. Virgil's resignation prompts a walk-out by the other Angels employees present, and Lawrence is left to fume alone in his luxury box. Virgil rushes to the clubhouse between innings, disguises himself as the Angels catcher, and takes the field to catch for Sammy. His confidence bolstered by Virgil's presence, the young pitcher shows his real ability, overwhelming the opposing team and winning the game.

Pastime (1991) may be one of the lesser-known baseball films of the 1990's, but is regarded by many critics as one of the best. Set in 1957, *Pastime* is about aging minor-leaguer Roy Dean Bream's final season. Bream clings to the lowest rung of the professional baseball ladder as a marginal relief pitcher for the Tri-City Steamers entry in the California D-league. Doggedly pursuing his failed dream of baseball stardom has consumed virtually all his 41 years. He is without family, friends, or prospects, with nothing to show for a lifetime in the game except a yellowed newspaper clipping of his only major league appearance. Steamers manager Clyde Bigby recognizes this, and despite his impassioned defense of Roy Dean to ownership, it is clear Bigby keeps the old timer on the roster as a simple act of kindness. The one thing that keeps Bream going is a shot at baseball immortality — if he pitches in six more games, he will tie the professional baseball record for pitching appearances. Roy Dean is so quick with a helpful tip for his considerably-younger teammates and so hopelessly optimistic despite his dismal circumstances that the other Steamers players consider him a buffoon. He is joined in the role of team outcast by the only black player on the Steamers, a teenage rookie pitcher of great promise named Tyrone DeBray. Their common antagonist is pitcher Randy Keever, a self-important bigot who loathes Roy Dean for costing him wins and Tyrone because he represents a threat to Keever's supremacy on the pitching staff. Befriending Tyrone, Roy Dean imparts lessons learned in his many years in the game. Unfortunately, even all that knowledge cannot make up for the physical skills that have abandoned Roy Dean, and after a particularly poor pitching performance, Steamers management decides they must release him. Roy Dean receives this news at a party from a gloating Keever, and trying to hide his embarrassment, he runs from the party to the ballpark. Once there, he turns on the stadium lights, grabs a bag full of baseballs and takes the mound one last time. While pitching this imaginary career finale, Roy Dean suffers a massive coronary. His body is discovered by Tyrone, who has been sent out to search for him. Neither the story nor Roy Dean Bream's dream end there, however, for Tyrone, inspired by his mentor, will eventually reach the major leagues.

Three notably dissimilar baseball films made their way into theaters in 1992, including a Babe Ruth biopic, the first baseball biography to come along in thirty-five years. If the 1948 film *The Babe Ruth Story* is a hopelessly sappy and worshipful portrayal of the Bambino, 1992's *The Babe* is its mirror image — a characterization that is grotesque, unflattering, at times even sinister. In *The Babe*, George Herman Ruth is portrayed as an abused, forlorn orphan whose enormous baseball talent cannot compensate for his utter lack of social awareness. He is crude, boorish, naive, desperately lonely and seems alternately dim-witted and deranged. He is regarded by first the Boston Red Sox, then the New York Yankees, as an "overgrown child." Ruth's hedonistic appetites match his baseball prowess, leading to a disastrous first marriage, and a career and personal life in shambles. His marriage to second wife Claire helps him salvage his career and find personal fulfillment. When Yankees management makes it clear he will never fulfill his dream of managing the team, he signs with the Boston Braves. After learning his is being used as little more than a side-show attraction by Braves' management, he hits three massive home runs in a single game and quits, leaving the game on his own terms.

A much happier portrayal of a bit of baseball history turns up in *A League of Their Own* (1992). In this fictionalized account of the All-American Girls Professional Baseball League's inaugural season, young women from across North America are recruited to play baseball in a women's league conceived by major league owners as a way to preserve baseball despite the manpower shortage precipitated by the Second World War. Sisters Dottie Hinson, a catcher, and Kit Keller, a pitcher, are recruited out of an Oregon softball league to play for the Rockford Peaches. The Peaches are ostensibly managed by former major league star Jimmie Dugan. But Dugan is a drunk who is bitterly resentful that his last chance to stay in baseball is what he considers the humiliating task of managing a women's team. At one point, he confronts his boss and thunders "I haven't got ballplayers, I've got girls! Girls are what you sleep with after the game, not what you coach during the game!" Dugan's attitude is shared by skeptical fans in the sparse crowds that attend the League's early games. But over the course of the season, Dugan comes to appreciate the skill and dedication of his players. As he takes an increasing interest in managing, his drinking diminishes and, with his help, the Peaches become one of the best teams in the league. The fans' doubts about women's baseball are also reversed, due largely to the efforts of Ira Lowenstein, the league's director and publicist, and the outstanding play of the women, especially Dottie Hinson, who emerges as the league's marquee player — the "Queen of Diamonds," as Lowenstein dubs her. The players, a diverse group of women from all walks of life, form a close-knit "family" and prove to a skeptical public that "girls" can play baseball.

Baseball's international appeal finally received recognition from Hollywood with the release of *Mr. Baseball* in 1992. The title character is Jack Elliott, an aging New York Yankee slugger who is the worst stereotype of the modern professional athlete — arrogant, boorish, promiscuous, self-absorbed. When Elliott's contract is sold to the Chunichi Dragons, a Japanese team, he is resentful and defies Japanese cultural mores and baseball conventions even as his game slumps as badly as his behavior. Confrontations with teammates and Dragons manager Uchiyama lead to fines and suspension. Largely through the efforts of his love interest (and the manager's daughter) Hikoro Uchiyama, Elliott begins to appreciate the Japanese approach to the game and the wisdom of his manager. Jack doggedly works himself back into shape, apologizes to his teammates in Japanese and gains their acceptance, then sets about leading them to the top of the standings. In the end, Elliott wins the pennant, the girl, and a coaching job with the Detroit Tigers.

Films centered on children and baseball had been absent from the big screen for 15 years when Hollywood rediscovered the formula and released four such pictures in a two-year span. Both baseball films released in 1993 are about kids playing the game, the first a fantasy with a plot highly reminiscent of 1954's *Roogie's Bump*. When marginal little leaguer and Chicago Cubs fan Henry Rowengartner falls and breaks his arm in *Rookie of the Year*, it appears that his baseball career is over for the summer. Shortly after the cast is removed from his throwing arm, Henry attend a Cubs game where he catches an opposing team's home run ball in the outfield bleachers. As Wrigley custom dictates, Henry throws the ball back onto the field. To the astonishment of all, Henry's throw is a frozen rope all the way to the Cubs catcher standing at home plate. The youngster's arm has apparently healed in such a way that he is now capable of throwing a baseball with overwhelming velocity. In this film, at least, the Cubs front office is not peopled by dummies and Henry is quickly signed to a contract. In no time, he is the most dominant relief pitcher in the major leagues and an instant celebrity. Henry's mom, a single mother, ties to protect her son and keep his life relatively normal but her devious boyfriend sets himself up as Henry's agent, and along with the team owner's duplicitous nephew, schemes to sell Henry's contract to the New York Yankees. When kindly Cubs owner Bob Carson gets wind of the plot, he quashes the deal and demotes his nephew to hot dog vendor. It would not, however, have mattered to Henry because, as he tells Carson, he will not be back next season. Tired of the notoriety, he just wants to be a 12-year-old kid again. But before that precocious retirement, Henry is called on to pitch the ninth inning of the pennant-deciding final game. Just as the dramatic inning is about to get underway, Henry falls on his pitching arm and it returns to its normal condition. His overpowering fastball gone, Henry must resort to unorthodox methods, including a hidden ball trick and a slowpitch softball delivery to win the game and the pennant for the Cubs.

What is in some ways the negative analog to the *Bad News Bears*, the 1993 film *The Sandlot* "recalls" the purity and innocence of the game when kids played baseball just for the fun of it. Recent arrival Scotty Smalls seeks acceptance from the kids in his new neighborhood, but they are almost constantly engaged in a sandlot baseball game and Scotty has never learned to play the game. He is befriended and tutored by the sandlot's best player, Benny Rodriguez and soon becomes one of the gang, sharing their love of baseball as well as the summer's adventures. When the group finds itself in need of a baseball one day, Scotty borrows his step father's prized Babe Ruth–autographed baseball, which Benny hits out of the sandlot and into the yard of "the Beast," a vicious-looking dog protecting the property of the feared, reclusive Mr. Mertle. Always a team, the kids band together to help retrieve the treasured ball and save Scotty the terrible retribution of his step father. Always the leader, Benny takes it upon himself to take on the Beast and confront Mr. Mertle. It turns out that neither Mr. Mertle nor the Beast are very dreadful but the Beast has made a meal of the ball. After they befriend Mr. Mertle, the boys discover him to be a former Negro League baseball player, a contemporary of Ruth and Gehrig, as well as a kind and lonely man eager to talk baseball with the youngsters. Mr. Mertle replaces the Babe Ruth baseball with one signed by the entire 1927 Yankee team, an act of kindness that saves Scotty and seals the bonds of friendship with all the boys.

The year 1994 was a rare one for baseball film, as no fewer than five baseball features were released. And as in 1993, two films about kids playing baseball would make it to the big screen. *Angels in the Outfield* (1994) is a remake of the 1951 film of the same name. Among the many story changes is the replacement of the Pittsburgh Pirates team featured in the original with a team with a far more appropriate mascot — the California Angels. (The remake is a Walt Disney Pictures film, but the Disney corporation did not buy the Angels franchise until 1996, at which time the corporation renamed the team the Anaheim Angels). In this updated version, the child who summons the divine influences is 11-year-old Roger Bomman. Roger is dumped into foster care by his reprobate of a father, who tells the child that there is as much chance of the family reuniting as the California Angels have of winning the league. The last-place Angels team is mired in a fifteen-game losing streak, but Roger, who takes his father's mean-spirited analogy a bit too literally, begins praying for the team in hope of securing a normal family life. Al the Angel dutifully appears to Roger, telling the boy he and his heavenly host will help the California team win, but only Roger will be able to see them assisting the ballplayers. In return, Roger must continue to believe in the angels even in the face of the skepticism he will surely encounter. Initially, there is no greater skeptic than George Knox, the belligerent, short-tempered manager of the Angels. But George can find no explanation other than a miracle when the Angels team begins to win with spectacular play. A kinder and gentler George emerges, befriending Roger and his best friend J.P., and even publicly defending the notion of heavenly intervention. A pennant for the California team seems assured, but some sort of heavenly restriction more difficult to fathom than Major League Baseball's Rule V draft dictates that angels cannot assist players in a championship game. However, the California team has a bond of faith strong enough to overcome any adversity, and they win the big game. The miraculous season leaves George Knox a changed man, one who will adopt Roger and answer the boy's prayers for a permanent home and a loving family.

If the previous three films fail to remind us that baseball is a kid's game, *Little Big League* (1994) will certainly make the point. When Minnesota Twins owner Thomas Heywood dies, he leaves the team to his twelve-year-old grandson Billy Heywood. Billy fires the Twins' overbearing, abusive manager and names himself manager of the underachieving and self-absorbed Twins, a team that seems more concerned about long-term contracts and investments than baseball. At first skeptical and uncooperative, the Twins are won over by Billy's encyclopedic knowledge of baseball and his enthusiastic admonitions to play the game for fun, just as they did when they were his age. Playing like kids, the Twins begin to win. But as his team becomes more successful, Billy begins to behave like an adult — to be precise, like the obnoxious adult manager he recently fired. Chafing under the bossy regime of their child manager, the Twins team grows bitter and their play begins to suffer. Before all is lost, Billy realizes what has happened to him. He apologizes to the team, and once again playing the game for fun, the Twins return to their winning ways. Although their season ends with a heartbreaking loss in the pennant-deciding game, their love for the game is restored and they receive a thunderous ovation from the home crowd despite the loss.

Major League II (1994), the first of two sequels to 1989's *Major League*, sends a similar message about the proper motivations for playing baseball. The Cleveland Indians return from their thrilling pennant run of the prior season with big contracts and bigger heads. Prima donna third baseman Roger Dorn has purchased the team from evil owner Rachel Phelps and expectations for the team are high. But the Indians are distracted by their new-found fame, wealth, and status, and the team begins to struggle badly, falling to the bottom of the standings. With bickering in the clubhouse and the stands nearly empty, Dorn begins to lose money and is forced to sell the team back to Phelps. At the same time, manager Lou Brown, frustrated by his players attitudes, has a heart attack in the clubhouse. Once again united by adversity and a common nemesis, the team pulls together behind catcher Jake Taylor. As the Indians return to their unorthodox but genuine ways, they rediscover the true values of baseball and win the American League pennant.

While there are no children in *The Scout* (1994), an emotionally immature character, the child-like ballplayer Steve Nebraska, extends the mid–1990s theme of children and baseball. The title character is Al Percolo, a major league baseball scout with a penchant for finding players with physical talent and psychological problems. After his latest disastrous signing — a young pitching prospect with a great arm but debilitating stage fright — his employer has had enough and banishes Percolo to scouting's worst circuit — rural Mexico. There Percolo stumbles across Steve Nebraska, a young American who is clearly the best baseball player in human history. Percolo can hardly believe his luck and quits his scouting job to act as Steve's agent, shopping his new prospect to major league teams. Naturally, the New York Yankees outbid everyone else for Steve's services with a record-breaking contract, but it becomes increasingly obvious that Steve is yet another talented psychotic discovered by Percolo. Abused as a child, Steve struggles to maintain his mental equilibrium. When he is scheduled to make his debut as the starting pitcher in Game One of the World Series, Steve suffers a mental meltdown and flees to the roof of Yankee Stadium. Percolo, by now something of a father figure to the young man, reassures Steve, helps him confront his fears and talks him down. Steve takes the mound and pitches a perfect game, a triumph for both the player and the scout.

A film that is not a tidy fit in the baseball genre, *Cobb* (1994) is a biopic set in the final months of baseball great Ty Cobb's life. Cobb hires writer Al Stump to author the long-retired player's authorized biography. Flashback scenes reconstruct Cobb's life, but little in the film relates directly to baseball and only one scene shows Cobb playing (and, characteristically, attempting to injure an opponent while sliding into base). It soon becomes apparent to Stump that Cobb is a vicious, racist, unbalanced, lonely, and paranoid old man who both anguishes over and glories in his reputation as baseball's most despised hero. Stump creates two versions of the Cobb biography, the sympathetic portrait that is eventually printed, and the unpublished version that makes it clear "the greatest baseball player who ever lived was also the greatest bastard," as Cobb's character in the film puts it.

A similarly dark film, *The Fan* was released in 1996. A deranged baseball fanatic named Gil is obsessed with San Francisco Giants' all-star outfielder Bobby Rayburn. Gil neglects job and family to attend Giants games, where he is loud and vulgar in expressing his support for Bobby. When Bobby goes into a slump, Gil imagines emerging Giants star Juan Primo is to blame. Gil murders Primo, then begins stalking Bobby, seeking some sign of appreciation for eliminating Bobby's "rival." When Bobby tells Gil he is not happy that Primo is dead, that his teammate's death has given him a fresh perspective on life and that baseball is no longer his all-consuming passion, Gil is pushed completely over the edge. He kidnaps Bobby's son and holds him hostage, demanding that Bobby hit a home run in the Giants' next game. Gil then disguises himself as the plate umpire in the game to ensure its outcome, but he is recognized by Bobby, confronted by the Giants team, and gunned down by security on the pitching mound as Bobby's son is found and rescued by police.

The second release of 1996, *Ed*, is no more credible but strikes a much different tone. Country boy pitcher Jack Copper loves to play baseball and he makes the roster of the Santa Rosa Rockets. But once in professional baseball, he begins to try too hard, spending endless hours studying pitching and practicing throwing until the game becomes a chore and he falls into a slump. To make matters worse, he is assigned as a roommate Rockets mascot Ed, a chimpanzee who turns out to be a decent third baseman, and who becomes Cooper's friend. As Ed's renown spreads, the Rockets' scheming owner sees a chance to make a profit by selling the talented chimp to another team, which treats poor Ed like — well, like an animal. All this shakes Jack from his funk. Realizing there are more important things in life than perfecting his pitching, Jack rescues Ed and in the process finds renewed enjoyment in baseball as a game instead of a job. His mental attitude properly adjusted, Jack wins the big game and signs with the Dodgers.

While baseball films have been released on a fairly regular basis since 1996, the pace has slowed to fewer than one per year. When the third film in the *Major League* trilogy, *Major League: Back to the Minors* was released in 1998, it had been almost two years since a baseball feature appeared in American theaters. *Back to the Minors* recycles a smattering of characters from the first two films, including former Indians third baseman Roger Dorn, now the owner of the world champion Minnesota Twins. Dorn is in desperate need of a capable manager for the Twins' woeful AAA minor league team, the South Carolina Buzz. He turns to Gus Cantrell, a journeyman minor league pitcher and a solid baseball man. The team Cantrell inherits is the typical ragtag collection of baseball misfits, including several former Indians from the previous *Major League* installments. Cantrell turns the fortunes of the Buzz 180 degrees, but in the process makes an enemy the of manager of the Twins' major league club, the smug, self-important Leonard Huff. As a reward for their outstanding play, the Buzz are give the opportunity to travel to Minnesota to play the Twins in an exhibition game, a contest which turns into something of a personal duel between Cantrell and Huff. The game is tied in the ninth with the Buzz threatening to take the lead, but the conniving Huff has the indoor stadium's lights shut off and the game ends in a tie. Later in the season, after the Buzz have won their AAA league title, Cantrell challenges Huff and the Twins to another game. To make the contest more interesting, Cantrell promises his salary for the year to Huff should the Twins prevail, but if the Buzz win, Huff must yield the helm of the major league team to Cantrell. Of course, the Buzz win in dramatic fashion, but the honorable Gus Cantrell turns down the chance to coach the Twins, choosing to remain with his team of loveable minor league misfits.

As the 1999 melodrama *For Love of the Game* opens, aging Detroit Tigers pitcher Billy Chapel is having a particularly bad day at the end of a particularly bad season. Billy has just learned the Tigers have been sold and the new owners intend to trade him in the off-season. Just as troubling to Billy is the news that his long-time love interest Jane Aubrey is leaving late that evening for a new job in London. And the day will not end until Billy has pitched his final game for the mediocre Tigers, a game in which he must face the playoff-bound Yankees in the season finale in Yankee Stadium. As Billy takes the mound against the Yankees, he reflects on his life, his playing career, and especially his sometimes-rocky relationship with Jane, recollections the audience shares in continual flashbacks between innings. Such distraction apparently serves Billy well, as he retires the Yankees in order, inning after inning. Meanwhile, Jane's flight is delayed and she passes the time in an airport lounge watching the ballgame. By the time all his reminiscing and ruminating are done, Billy has pitched a perfect game against the Bronx Bombers. Jane, unable to tear herself away from the drama of Billy's no-hitter, misses her flight. Seizing the opportunity to leave baseball a winner, Billy sends a message to Detroit management that he is retiring "for love of the game," then bolts for the airport just in time to tell Jane he is retiring and that he wants her to stay. We're left with the very strong impression that Billy will convince her to stay, and that his passion for the game will be replaced by his passion for Jane.

2001: Baseball in the New Millennium

With the debut of *Summer Catch* in 2001, baseball cinema had its first back to back chick-flicks. The film is set in the Cape Cod League, the best amateur baseball circuit in the country. Each summer top prospects, mostly college players, come to play with the hope they will enhance their status with the major league scouts who frequent the league's ballparks. One of those prospects is local kid Ryan Dunne, who gets a chance to pitch for the Chatham Aces. A Boston College dropout who was kicked off his junior college team for fighting with a teammate, Ryan now cuts grass for his father's lawn care business. Early in the season, he shows talent but still struggles on the mound due at least in part to complications in his personal life. His romantic interest, Tenley Parrish, is the daughter of prominent, wealthy Chatham resident Rand Parrish, who disapproves of his daughter's involvement with the young ballplayer who mows his extensive lawn. Late in the season, Ryan is called on to pitch the opening game of the playoffs after the Aces' best pitcher is kicked off the team. At the same time, he learns Tenley plans to leave for a job in San Francisco. Ryan is pitching the game of his life, a no-hitter into the eighth inning, when Tenley appears at the ballpark to see him on her way out of town. As he takes the mound for the ninth, he looks to the stands and sees she is gone. Two outs from a no-hit shut-out, he takes himself out of the game and rushes to the airport. He finds Tenley, pledges his love, and is immediately approached by a scout for the Philadelphia Phillies, offering him a contract and a signing bonus. As the credits role, we see Ryan in his first major league appearance with the Phillies.

Two very different baseball films found their way into theaters in 2002. *The Rookie* is a biopic based on the true story Jim Morris' long journey to the major leagues. Jim has nurtured a life-long love of baseball. As a child he plays little league baseball in Connecticut despite the indifference of his father, a career navy man with neither time for nor interest in his son's passion for the game. The resulting rift between father and son becomes a chasm when the elder Morris moves his family to West Texas, a region largely devoid of baseball. Jim is heartbroken, but sustains his dream of a baseball career. After his pitching days are ended in the minor leagues by a shoulder injury, he becomes a high school science teacher and baseball coach. Pitching batting practice to his high school players, Jim discovers he still has a lot of life left in his thirty-something pitching arm. His players insist that he should try out for the pros, and while he finds the suggestion laughable, Jim does make a bargain with his underachieving team: If they start winning games, he will try out for the Tampa Bay Devil Rays organization. Of course, they win. Of course, he goes to the tryouts and stuns the Devil Ray scouts with his 98 mph fastball. Sent to Tampa's minor league system, he struggles with the separation from his family and the uncertainty of pursuing what may be a dead end. Frustrated and on the verge of returning home, Jim gets the call to the big leagues, at 35 the oldest rookie in baseball. His success is due in no small part to the unwavering support and patience of his family. It is a family made whole when his appearance in the majors proves to be the long-overdue wake-up call to his father, with whom he finally, if awkwardly, reconciles.

Something of a contrast to the feel-good story of Jim Morris, the other baseball film of 2002, *Hardball* is the tale of Conor O'Neill, an aimless young man whose life seems to consist of little more than scalping tickets, gambling and drinking. When he calls on a friend, financial analyst Jimmy Fleming, to ask for money to pay a gambling debt, Jimmy refuses to loan him the money. Instead he offers Conor a job coaching the Kekambas, a little league team from the notorious Cabrini Green housing project in Chicago. Only because he is desperate for cash does Conor reluctantly take on the chore, and after the first practice it appears his reluctance is well-founded. As in almost every motion picture about little league baseball, the Kekambas do not appear to be much of a team initially, absorbing an embarrassing loss in the season's first game to the sort of well-drilled (not to mention better-attired) rival team typically found in such films. Unlike the kids in other baseball films, the Kekambas must also deal with the off-field realities of abject poverty and gang violence, factors Conor must also come to grips with. With hard work and Conor's guidance, the Kekambas are transformed into a winning team, earning a trip to the championship game. Conor begins to appreciate his importance to the players and their influence in helping him become a better man. The bond between players and coach is cemented when the team's smallest player, "G-Baby" Evans, is killed by a gang-banger's errant bullet. Overcoming this tragedy, Conor and the Kekambas triumph in the championship game.

Mr. 3000 (2004) slightly alters the oldest plot line in baseball cinema — the struggle of the baseball hero to learn humility, selflessness and virtue before he can realize true success. But in the end, the result is a film true to baseball film's enduring tradition. Nine years after his retirement, former Milwaukee Brewer great Stan Ross is waiting to get into baseball's Hall of Fame. Although a statistical shoe-in by virtue of his 3,000 career hits, Stan's election has been delayed, perhaps indefinitely, by the fact that he is intensely disliked by former teammates and the media who know him to be an arrogant, obnoxious, selfish bore who quit the Brewers as soon as he had his 3,000th hit. But when a record-keeping error is discovered, Stan is left with only 2,997 hits and a much longer-shot at entering the Hall of Fame. Along with Milwaukee's profit-oriented general manager, who sees a chance for the Brewers to sell a few more tickets, Stan concocts a scheme to return to the Brewers at age 46 to get back to 3,000 hits. What follows is the typical cinematic transformation of talented-but-self-absorbed-player into true baseball hero. Stan works hard to get back into shape, rediscovers the love for the game he'd known as a boy, comes to see the error of his way in quitting the game, and tries to pass along these lessons learned to his younger teammates. His old flame Maureen, now an ESPN reporter, returns to cover his comeback, and he begins to regret losing her years ago. By the final game of the season, Stan is still one hit short of 3,000 with only one at-bat remaining. Understanding at last what it means to be a team player, Stan lays down the sacrifice bunt that scores the winning run but leaves him with 2,999 hits. It's a sacrifice that earns him a thundering ovation from the fans, the love of his once-hostile teammates, the respect of the press, and eventually his election to the Hall of Fame, along with the promise of a permanent relationship with Maureen.

Just as the Brooklyn Dodgers' unlikely 1941 pennant run inspired films like *It Happened in Flatbush,* so the Boston Red Sox' improbable 2004 World Series championship serves as the subtext for the romantic comedy *Fever Pitch* (2005). Ardent (and often obsessed) Red Sox season-ticket holder Ben meets and courts his love interest, a rising young professional woman named Lindsey, during the off-season. Hence, Lindsey has no sense of just how intense is Ben's devotion to his beloved Red Sox. She finds out as soon as the season is underway and the resulting strain on their once-perfect relationship threatens to end it by September. Ben experiences an epiphany on the proper perspective of the game at just about the same time Lindsey realizes how much the game means to Ben, and how it might bring them together. With Ben on the verge of selling his season ticket rights to prove his love for her, Lindsey sprints across the field at Fenway Park and stops him from signing the contract. As the film ends, the happy couple is celebrating Boston's first world championship in 86 years.

From 1898 to the present — more than a century — baseball, and its vision of American culture, have been reflected on the silver screen. We now turn to the nature of that vision — the values it celebrates, the ideological assumptions upon which it rests. We begin with the theme which is most central to baseball's cultural vision, and to baseball films; the theme of community.

3

The Community of Baseball

"We're a team on the baseball field, and in the potato field."
— Leon Carter, *The Bingo Long Traveling
All-Stars and Motor Kings*

It has been a rough road trip for Bingo Long's barnstorming all-stars. Star right-fielder Charlie Snow, caught alone under the stands during a night game, is severely slashed with a razor by thugs working for Ebony Aces owner Sallison Porter, who is determined to put the All-Stars out of business. Near death, Snow is rushed to the hospital. It takes all the team's money to pay his medical bills. Broke and unable to pay their hotel bill, the team finds their car has been confiscated by the sheriff, to be sold at auction. Without their means of transportation from one small town to the next, the barnstormers will, indeed, be out of business. But the players don't give up. And the team doesn't come apart. They take a job digging potatoes, in order to try and buy their car back. It is hot, dirty work. Looking around him at his teammates, sweltering in the dust and the sun, Leon Carter's face breaks into a big grin. "We're a team on the baseball field, and in the potato field," he proclaims. This is what being a team is all about.

And, ultimately, this is what baseball films are all about, as well. More than anything else, baseball films through the years have offered viewers visions of the ideal community. This overriding emphasis on community in baseball cinema is not surprising, for the concept of community is central to baseball's cultural vision. Baseball, according to its ideologists, is about the very process of building community.

Since the end of the 19th century, when the rapid pace of industrialization and urbanization began to reshape the American cultural landscape,

Billy Dee Williams (left) as Bingo Long and James Earl Jones (center) as Leon Carter in *The Bingo Long Traveling All-Stars and Motor Kings* (Universal Pictures, 1967).

and to erode the identity of a rural, agrarian society, sports have been accorded a special role in creating and fostering a sense of community in American life. From the informal sporting clubs of the late 1800s, which "provided human contact, a sense of community, and a source of tradition and stability amid the chaos of urban-industrial growth" (Gorn and Goldstein, 1993), to the modern, professional "ritualized sports spectacles" (Jhally, 1984), one of the most important cultural functions of sports has been the creation of a sense of community, for participants and spectators alike.

As the national pastime, baseball in particular has been accorded a preeminent role in fulfilling this cultural mission. Ever since the ascension of baseball to the status of national pastime in the 1920s, the idealized view of the game disseminated by its proponents has emphasized the game's ability to build a strong sense of community in an increasingly fragmented urban environment (Betts, 1974; Jhally, 1984; Riess, 1980). Baseball's advocates have argued that not only does the game build a strong sense of unity and community among those who play it, through such values as teamwork and devotion to the game, but that it also serves to create a sense of community in the cities where it is played, by bringing together fans of all ages and all ethnic and social backgrounds to root for the home team.

As the historical analysis of Riess (1980) and others suggests, the authors of baseball's cultural vision — primarily sports writers and journalists writing in the early 1900's — were deeply concerned about the impact of urbanization and industrialization on American society. The meanings they constructed for "the national pastime" were intended to bind society together (Riess, 1980). It was within this cultural context that baseball's advocates advanced an almost utopian vision of community as a hopeful alternative to the increasing fragmentation and isolation of American social life.

Such a vision, of course, is not unique to baseball. The writings of a diverse range of cultural theorists have posited "community" as a more ideal and more natural form of social relationship, in contrast to the more formal and impersonal relations which dominate modern, industrialized society. In his analysis of social organization, for example, Ferdinand Tonnies (1963) draws the distinction between Gemeinschaft and Gesellschaft — community and society. The Gemeinschaft is characterized by a strong sense of unity and shared identification with the larger community among its individual members. Community members are linked through interpersonal bonds, and social relationships reflect compassion, friendship and nurturance. In such a community, community members serve as a source of support and assistance for one another, and individuals are comforted by the knowledge that those around them genuinely care about them and what happens to them. The Gesellschaft, by contrast, is characterized by superficial, impersonal, and essentially contractual forms of relationship. There is little sense of shared community or interpersonal bonds between its members, and individuals pursue their own self-interests with little genuine concern for other members of the community or the community itself.

Raymond Williams (1963) elaborates on the characteristics of an ideal, Gemeinschaft form of community, emphasizing the conditions of equality of being, tolerance of diversity, and solidarity. In such a community, all members of the community are valued equally, regardless of differences in skills, knowledge, etc. In addition, argues Williams, the community must be fully open, tolerating and even encouraging diversity and differences. Finally, community members must place the common good above individual self-interest, defining the common interest as true self-interest and finding "individual verification primarily in the community" (p. 332). It is

64

only through a commitment to equality of being, tolerance of diversity, and solidarity, says Williams, that communities can continue to grow and survive.

The characteristics of the ideal community outlined by cultural theorists such as Ferdinand Tonnies and Raymond Williams are not unfamiliar to citizens of 20th-century America. For it is precisely such images which are regularly invoked in nostalgic representations— although not necessarily accurate ones— of America's rural past. Movies, television sitcoms, commercial and political advertising all regularly manufacture fog-filtered glimpses of small-town, rural America, portraying it as a pastoral ideal; a peaceful, cohesive community governed by shared, deeply-held traditional values. And this is the vision of community which permeates baseball films. One after another, baseball films portray nurturing, tolerant communities in which people are motivated by such traditional values as compassion, justice, hard work, and devotion to the game, and in which individuals are able to achieve fulfillment within, and through, the larger community.

> "I would like to apologize to you all. From now on, I would
> like to make an effort to be a real member of the team. And,
> between us, I'd like to build a bridge of friendship."
> — Jack Elliot, *Mr. Baseball*, 1992

As noted earlier, a central component of Raymond Williams' (1963) true community is solidarity, a voluntary and freely accepted commitment by all community members to place the common good above their own individual self interest. Solidarity is the lesson Jack Elliot had to learn.

In *Mr. Baseball* (1992), fading New York Yankees superstar Jack Elliot is traded to the Chunichi Dragons, the only team to express any interest at all in his dwindling talents, where he discovers in the Japanese leagues a style of baseball, and a way of life, that demands a greater subordination of individual to team. It is not a lesson easily learned. The abrasive, self-centered former Yankee quickly alienates his teammates and manager. A scene early in the film, in which Elliot is filming a television commercial captures the essential conflict. During a confrontation with the commercial's director, Hiroko, who also happens to be the daughter of the Dragons' manager, as well as Elliot's love interest in the film, he laments the "Japanese way. Shut up and take it." Her reply is the lesson he must learn to gain acceptance in this unfamiliar community: "Jack's way: me, me, me," she chides him. "Sometimes, acceptance and cooperation are strengths, also." Over time, and often with considerable frustration, he gradually learns these lessons and, after apologizing to his teammates, achieves the acceptance of the community. It is only then that he begins to fulfill his potential as both a player and a person. It is only then that manager Uchiyama finally tells him, "Now, you are ready to hit." Eventually Elliott is able to make his own contribution to the community, by helping his team and manager understand the psychological nuances of the game. In the end, this fully unified team triumphs over their heavily favored archrival the Tokyo Giants.

This theme of team/community first is reiterated more than a decade later in the 2005 release, *Mr. 3000*. In this film, Milwaukee Brewers superstar Stan Ross is despised by his fellow teammates and just about anyone else who has any contact with him for his arrogant, self-centered attitude and behavior. The lack of commitment to anyone but himself is most clearly demonstrated when he announces his immediate retirement from the game near the end of the season, when the Brewers are in the middle of a pennant race, after getting what he believes at the time to be his 3,000th hit, and ticket to the Hall of Fame. It is only when he returns to the Brewers 9 years later — after baseball's records keepers discover that Mr. 3000 is really only Mr. 2997 — to try to get those final 3 hits, that Ross learns the lessons of community. Now seeing himself in younger stars of the game, and not liking what he sees, Ross comes to understand and value the importance of putting the team first. He apologizes to his manager for abandoning the team at the end of the season 9 years previously, telling him "It was wrong the way I quit on the team back then. I was young, Skip. I was young." Ross also teaches the lessons of team rather than self to the Brewers' new young superstar, T-Rex. And, most symbolically, in his final at bat in the final game of the season, he foregoes his last opportunity to become Mr. 3000 by laying down a sacrifice bunt, and driving in the winning run, giving the Brewers a 3rd place division finish.

The ultimate expression of solidarity, of course, is the willingness not just to lay down a sacrifice bunt for the team, but to be willing to sacrifice one's own life for the team. Thus, it is not surprising that in the 1934 baseball mystery *Death on the Diamond*, St. Louis Cardinal's ace pitcher Larry Kelly insists on taking the mound to pitch the final, pennant deciding game of the season, despite the fact he risks assassination by the same unknown evil forces who have already murdered two of his teammates. Kelly does so not simply to helps his team win, but also for the community of baseball itself, and for the millions of fans whose national pastime is threatened by evil. In explaining the baseball way to his fiancée, who has begged him not to pitch, Kelly tells her she probably *wouldn't* love him if he weren't the type of person willing to take such a risk. Such a profound commitment is also the central dramatic tension in *The Natural* (1984), in which Roy Hobbs, after repudiating his selfish goal to be "the best there ever was," risks death to play in the championship game, not simply to help his New York Knights win the championship, but, more importantly, to save the team for manager Pop Fischer. And while the potential consequences are perhaps not quite as dire as those faced by Larry Kelly and Roy Hobbs, *The Sandlot's* (1993) Benny Martinez risks being devoured by "the beast," a frighteningly large and vicious sounding dog which inhabits the unknown neighbor's yard, in order to retrieve the Babe Ruth–autographed baseball which Scotty Smalls had "borrowed" from his step-father, without his knowledge or permission.

Typically, though, solidarity is not a life and death matter in baseball films. It is most often a matter of doing what is best for the team and one's teammates—laying down a sacrifice bunt, for example, instead of seeking personal glory by trying to hit the game-winning home run. In some films, however, putting the team first means giving up something which, as we are told in *For Love of the Game* (2000), may mean even more than life. It may mean giving up the game itself. In *The Pride of the Yankees* (1942), an ailing Lou Gehrig courageously pulls himself out of the line-up, ending his record setting string of consecutive games, because he realizes his play is hurting the team. An aging Pete Haines quits the Bisons for the same reason (*The Kid from Left Field*, 1953). And sitting in the dugout between innings, near the end of the first and only perfect game of his career, 40-year-old 19-year veteran pitcher Billy Chapel writes a note on a baseball and has it sent up to the owners' box. Earlier that day, Chapel learned from long-time owner Gary Wheeler that the team had been sold, and the new owners wanted to trade Chapel, a Tiger his entire career, to the Giants. On the baseball, Chapel has written, "Tell them I'm through. For love of the game" (*For Love of the Game*, 2000).

While Lou Gehrig, Pete Haines, and Billy Chapel all end their careers for the good of their teams and the game itself, in a few films we also see baseball heroes bringing an early end to their careers—or at least threatening to do so—over matters of life and principle which are even more important than the game itself. In *Field of Dreams* (1989), for example, a briefly youthful Archie

Graham leaves Ray Kinsella's magical baseball field, and the opportunity to live his dream of playing major-league baseball into eternity, in order to save the life of Kinsella's daughter. And, in one of the strongest portrayals of baseball's idealized form of community, *A League of Their Own* (1992), prize recruit Dottie Henson and her sister, Kit Keller, are willing to sacrifice their careers before they have even begun, in order to help a fellow player. When a scout for the league refuses to sign talented hitter Marla Hooch because she is not pretty enough to play in the league, the two sisters are outraged and refuse to board the train bound for the league tryouts without Marla, forcing the scout to relent. Whether it be for the good of the team, the game, or the community at large, the message of baseball films since the 1930s is unmistakable. The true baseball hero is willing to give him or herself up for others.

> *"You're one of us. You're a Rockford Peach."*
> — Helen Haley, *A League of Their Own*, 1992

Individual commitment to the team is a central tenet in the ideology of baseball films. Its virtues have been clearly and consistently expounded through the decades. Loyalty is not one-way street in these films, however. For his or her loyalty to the community and commitment to the common good, the individual baseball citizen is in turn rewarded with the strength and support of that larger community. With few exceptions, baseball films have offered viewers nurturing, caring communities whose members, in a variety of ways, provide strength, assistance and friendship to one another. When New York Mammoth catcher Bruce Pearson's teammates learn he is dying, for example, they pull together to support him, and do everything they can to make his final days happy ones (*Bang the Drum Slowly*, 1973). Roy Hobbs's (*The Natural*, 1984) teammates visit him in the hospital not because they are concerned about the loss of their star player, but because they have come to care about Roy Hobbs as a friend and member of their family. In *Bull Durham* (1988) we see a discussion on the mound about, among other things, what kind of wedding gift to get a fellow teammate. The player is later married on the field, with all of his teammates forming an arch of baseball bats, similar to the wedding scene in *A League of Their Own* (1992), for the happy couple's wedding procession. And in *Mr. Baseball* (1992), once Jack Elliot learns humility and makes the commitment to place the team's needs above his own, the other members of the team demonstrate their support and affection for him by joining him in running extra wind-sprints as he tries to get back in shape.

One of the most powerful portrayals of a caring, nurturing community comes in *A League of Their Own* (1992), the fictionalized drama about women's baseball in the 1940's and 50's. The coming together of individuals from all walks of life — beauty queens, dairy workers, students, housewives, and dance hall bouncers — to form a community characterized by genuine caring and support for one another is a central theme of this film. In one early scene, for example, which takes place just after the first tryouts for the All-American Girls' Professional Baseball League have been completed, the team rosters of those women chosen for the league have been posted on a bulletin board at the edge of the field. Those who did not make the league have left, dejected. Those who were lucky enough to make the grade are grouped with their new teammates, sitting on the field, waiting to learn about the new league — and their futures. One woman, however, stands alone at the bulletin board, in tears. "Are you on the list or not?" the male manager who conducted the tryouts impatiently demands. If she's not on the list, she'll have to leave. She doesn't respond. Out of the group sitting on the field, Helen Haley, future first-baseman of the Rockford Peaches, approaches the traumatized woman. "Honey," she gently asks, "can you read?" The answer is no. Haley asks the woman her name, and then scans the list. "There it is," she joyfully announces. "Shirley Baker. You're one of us. You're a Rockford Peach." In later scenes, we see May Mordobitto teaching Baker how to read. The gentleness and compassion of these scenes are a marked contrast to the abusive treatment of the illiterate Shoeless Joe Jackson in *Eight Men Out* (1988). In numerous scenes throughout the rest of *League of Their Own* (1992) we see the players as they live together, take charm school classes together, sneak out for a night on the town together, and share their common grief at the news that the husband of one of their friends has died in the war. The bonds they form are so strong they will last half a century, as we see in the film's concluding reunion scenes.

However, the individual baseball citizen finds much more than friendship, caring and support in the baseball community. He or she also finds individual success — not simply on the field, but in life, as well. For at the same time that baseball films define the ideal community as one in which individuals place the common good above their own self interest, they also go to some lengths to demonstrate that individual fulfillment also can and does occur within the parameters of community. In fact, the *only* path to personal fulfillment and achievement, these films suggest, is through a commitment to the team/community.

This linkage of individual fulfillment and happiness with a commit-ment to the larger community in baseball films reflects the inherent ten-sion between the values of individualism and community — both within the game of baseball, and in American society itself. At the same time, it offers a reconciliation of that tension. Within baseball itself, the linkage between commitment to community and individual fulfillment reflects the need, if a team is to be successful, to temper individualism with an appre-ciation of teamwork. In many ways, baseball is the most individual of all team sports, with nine individual performances blending to create the whole (Riess, 1980), and therefore the task of convincing individual athletes to place the good of the team above their own self-interest is a challenging one. Thus, in baseball — and baseball films — the promise of individual fulfillment is located within a commitment to the larger community. In these films, we consistently see individuals who, having first made the com-mitment to the good of the community as a whole, are able to realize their individual dreams.

The potential for conflict between the interests of the individual and the interests of the larger team, community, nation, or corporation is not unique to baseball, however. It is woven throughout American culture. And the lesson of baseball films is not just for ballplayers, but for all of us. The path to individual greatness and happiness is through a commitment to community first. And it is the only path. In no film is the individual fulfillment offered by a commitment to community more spiritual and more profound than in *Field of Dreams* (1989). In this film, characters who will-ingly make the decision to sacrifice for others achieve both individual suc-cess and spiritual fulfillment within the context of their community. The idyllic community represented in *Field of Dreams*, writes Aden (1994), is one in which the values of individualism and community are harmoniously synthesized; individuals are afforded the freedom to pursue their own paths, in ways that provide inner peace and spiritual satisfaction, along with mate-rial success, and which simultaneously benefit the larger community. By maintaining their faith in each other and in the game, members of the Kin-sella baseball community achieve both success and fulfillment. Kinsella is reunited and reconciles with his dead father, disillusioned writer Terence Mann has his faith restored, and the ghostly players are granted a place to continue fulfilling the dream of an endless season. And, the thousands of people streaming toward the Kinsella farm are granted a Garden of Eden where they can find inner peace (Aden, 1994). "For," as Terence Mann explains to Ray Kinsella, "it is money they have. It is peace they lack" (*Field of Dreams*, 1989).

In *Major League* (1989), as a result of their commitment to community, the Cleveland Indians players win more than just a division title. Catcher Jake Taylor recovers the one true love of his life. Third baseman Roger Dorn rediscovers the fulfillment of playing the game for the joy of playing, rather than as a way to make money. And pitcher Ricky Vaughn makes the unlikely transition from convict to baseball hero. In *Back To The Minors* (1998), the second of two sequels to the original *Major League*, it is only when "Downtown" Anderson learns, as manager Gus Cantrell tells him, "We're a team, here. We do what's best for the team," that he is able to successfully make the jump to the major leagues. Similarly, by holding fast to baseball's moral order and putting the team first, *The Natural's* (1984) Roy Hobbs fulfills his own dreams— saving the team for Pop, reuniting his family, living up to his father's expectations and achieving true greatness. And in the unshakably strong community found in *A League of Their Own* (1992), individual fulfillment is nearly universal, with the various players finding what each has been seeking: May Mordobitto achieves respectability, Marla Hooch love, Doris Murphy satisfaction with own her identity as a ballplayer, and Kit Keller independence. Even former major league star and coach Jimmy Dugan stops drinking and reclaims his dignity. At the end of the film, in a reunion scene at the Baseball Hall of Fame, we are not surprised to learn that the players have all led happy, fulfilling lives since their playing days fifty years before. And in *Mr. 3000*, once Stan Ross learns the lessons of community he wins the heart of his ESPN reporter love interest, the respect of his team, election to the Hall of Fame, and inner peace.

As a core virtue in baseball's cultural vision, the value of community is taught from the very beginning of one's baseball career. From T-Ball on up, parents and coaches instill in young players that the baseball way is to put one's team and one's teammates first. Not surprisingly, then, the importance of community is a central theme in baseball films featuring children. One of the best portrayals of baseball's vision of community among kids is *The Sandlot* (1993). In this film, team leader Benny Rodriguez adopts the newcomer Scotty Smalls, an initially awkward kid who can't even throw a baseball, into the team community, teaching him not only to play baseball, but how to make friends, as well. The team of youths in *The Sandlot* (1993) are a tightly-knit community, centered around their involvement in baseball. Not only do the team members spend hours playing baseball together, they eat together, go swimming together, experiment with chewing tobacco together, have team sleepouts, and, as noted earlier, when one of them loses his stepfather's prized baseball, autographed by Babe Ruth, they all confront their fear together — "risking their lives" to retrieve the ball from the neighbor's yard. In the end, the young players in *The Sandlot* find through baseball what all young people search for — self-confidence, friendship, and a sense of belonging in a caring, supportive community. In a much grimmer portrayal of this same essential theme in Hardball (2001) it is through baseball that the young players on the Kimbakas, an inner-city little-league team, are able to find a brief respite from the poverty and violence that surrounds them. And through the support and comraderie of the team, they begin to discover and express their individual capabilities within their baseball community; to find opportunities for individual growth and happiness denied them by American society at large.

Unambiguously, communities characterized by nurturance are the overwhelming norm in baseball films. The notable exceptions to this pattern are *Eight Men Out* (1988), the story of the Chicago "Black Sox" scandal of 1919, *The Babe* (1991), the film biography of the career of Babe Ruth, and *Cobb* (1996), the story of the painful, lonely life of one of baseball's greatest legends, Ty Cobb. Rather than challenging the idealized vision of nurturing communities portrayed in most of their counterparts, however, these films serve simply to reinforce that vision by confronting viewers with the consequences of the absence of such a community. In these films, it is the lack of a true, shared community which serves as the source of tragedy for the central characters. The central theme of *The Babe* (1992), for example, is the tragic Babe Ruth seeking, often grotesquely, to create the caring, nurturing community he never had as a child. And in *Cobb* (1996), viewers are confronted with the bitter and isolated existence of an aged ex-hero, despised by his family, ex-teammates, and just about anyone else who has ever had occasion to meet him.

The most striking example of the consequences of a dysfunctional community, however, is John Sayles' *Eight Men Out* (1988). Sayles' film story of how the Chicago White Sox conspired with gamblers to throw the 1919 World Series begins with a scene in which the White Sox infield turns a double play, then trot off the field bickering at each other. The divisions and infighting extend from owner Charles Comiskey down to even insignificant players like Fred McMullin. Despite the constant sniping and genuine dislike for one another, the 1919 White Sox are portrayed as far and away the best team in baseball, and are expected shoe-ins to win the World Series. In the end, however, the decision to place their self-interests above those of the team not only cost the White Sox the world series, but also cost the eight "Black Sox" the ultimate price baseball can exact — banishment from the game. Without a genuine sense of community and solidarity, the 1919 White Sox were unable to survive as a team — on or off the field.

In real life, of course, affection for one's teammates off the field and success on the field do not necessarily go hand in hand. The Oakland Athletics of the early 1970s are but one example of a team which was notorious for its infighting and the personal conflicts among players, but which still managed to play together as a team on the field, winning three straight world championships. In baseball films, however, teamwork and interpersonal comraderie are inextricably linked. When cinematic players do not get along, they cannot play well together, nor succeed as a team. Perhaps with the exception of *Eight Men Out* (1988) this cinematic reality is expressed nowhere more eloquently than in *Bang the Drum Slowly* (1973). Repeatedly in the early scenes of the film, the point is made that the New York Mammoths are the strongest team in the league, and should be running away with the pennant, but they have not been able to pull together as a team. Instead, they have started ragging on one another. In a voice-over, star pitcher Henry Wiggin comments he's afraid that one day he'll wake up to find out he's not even speaking to himself. In a fit of frustration, manager Dutch Schnell lectures his team on the consequences of such constant dissension, explaining that the reason the "hand" of the New York Mammoths has not been able to reach up and pluck the nagging, buzzing fly of the Baltimore Orioles out of the air and crush it, is that the fingers on the hand are not working together, but are instead fighting with one another. It is only when the Mammoths put aside their individual differences and concerns, and unite as a family in their efforts to make dying catcher Bruce Pearson's last days as a Mammoth happy ones, that they begin playing together as a team. Similarly, it is only when the Cleveland Indians (*Major League*, 1989) put aside their petty differences and unite — not just as teammates, but as friends as well — in their common struggle against evil owner Rachel Phelps that they are able to begin playing together and winning as a team. The link between teamwork and success is also driven home in *Back to the Minors* (1999). Despite a team full of high-priced superstars, the Minnesota Twins are one of the worst teams in the league. In a statement of the philosophy which will enable his Triple-A Buzz to eventually defeat the Twins in an exhibition game, Buzz manager Gus Cantrell tells the arrogant Twins manager, Leonard Huff, "Maybe you've got too much talent, not enough team."

Given that the promise of community has been central to baseball's cultural vision since the early years of the 20th century, it is not surprising that images of the ideal community have characterized baseball films in all eras. However, where films of earlier eras seem to take the notion of community as a given, more recent films focus much more explicitly on the hope and process of achieving community through the game of baseball. In film after film since the mid 1970s, we have seen the transformation of teams into caring, nurturing, human communities emerge as a principle story line. In these films, the formation of community is not a brief, tangential element within a larger story, but is frequently the central storyline of the film.

The Bingo Long Traveling All-Stars and Motor Kings (1976) and *A League of Their Own* (1992), for example, are, more than anything else, stories about collections of different players becoming close-knit families. In *The Sandlot* (1993), Scotty Smalls' attainment of a close group of friends is the primary plot-line. In *Major League* (1989), the main theme is that of a group of various individuals from radically differing backgrounds coming together as a community in their solidarity against evil owner Rachel Phelps. In *Mr. Baseball* (1992) and *Mr. 3000* (2005), the principal plot-lines are the transition of Jack Elliot and Stan Ross from selfish, and failing, individuals into successful, happier and more spiritually fulfilled members of their teams. In films such as *Bang the Drum Slowly* (1973), *Little Big League* (1994), and *Major League II* (1994) we see teams of separate individuals, focused on their own interests and well-being and often sniping at one another, transformed into close-knit, supportive, and successful, communities. In the Bad News Bears trilogy (*Bad News Bears*, 1976; *Bad News Bears in Breaking Training*, 1977; *The Bad News Bears Go to Japan*, 1978), we see a group of misfits come together to develop the support and sense of community most of them otherwise lack in their lives. And in *Hardball* (2001), we see kids trapped in a contemporary urban hell develop a close, caring community amidst the bleak desolation, fear, and deadly violence that are part of their daily life on Chicago's South Side.

Such portrayals of caring, nurturing baseball communities are especially striking in light of the competitive and individualistic nature of sports in contemporary society. For the past three decades, in sharp contrast to the real world experiences of baseball players and fans, baseball films have presented viewers not with communities in which the values of individualism and competitiveness dominate, but rather with communities characterized by a shared sense of interdependence, affection and mutual support. They offer viewers images of close, caring communities; the kinds of communities all too many in our culture are unable to experience in their own lives.

"People will come, Ray. And they'll watch the
game. And it'll be as if they'd dipped themselves in
magic waters. People will come, Ray."
— Terence Mann, *Field of Dreams*, 1989

In addition to their more pronounced emphasis upon the formation of community amongst the players of cinematic baseball teams, more recent baseball films have also emphasized baseball's potential as a means of bringing together communities of fans as well, both within and beyond the confines of the ballpark. In baseball films, the achievement of the ideal of community is not limited to the teams themselves, but is extended to the larger culture in which these teams play. And the communities that are created through baseball are communities that are accessible to all. This cinematic portrayal of baseball's ability to build communities beyond the ballpark's outfield fences is consistent with a fundamental postulate of baseball ideology first advanced during the Progressive Era, which holds baseball to be a vehicle for social integration as fans from all segments of society come together to support the home team (Jhally, 1984; Riess, 1980). Thus, with the exception of crazed super-fan Gil in *The Fan* (1996), fans are not regarded as autograph-seeking nuisances in these films, but as members of the community, and exemplify how we all might become part of that community, sharing the team's goals and celebrating the team's achievements. Of course, baseball films in all eras have featured crowds of cheering fans, rooting for the home team and their favorite heroes. But in a number of films since the 1980s, these scenes are constructed quite explicitly within the context of the achievement of community. In *Major League* (1989) for example, as the Cleveland Indians come together as a community amongst themselves, and thus begin to achieve success on the field, we not only see scenes of the stadium crowds growing larger, but we also see scenes of people all across Cleveland getting involved in the excitement of the team's success, and uniting as a community in the process. In the final scenes during the championship game against the New York Yankees, film audiences not only see thousands of fans joining together in the stadium, screaming the theme song ("Wild Thing") of their hero, pitcher Rick Vaughn, but also scenes of people in a Cleveland bar, joining together to cheer the Indians. The involvement of the larger community is signified by the appeal of the Indians' broadcaster, who invites people, wherever they are, to join in the cheering. The achievement of community is further accentuated in a scene in a bar, in which people are cheering and hugging following the Indians' victory. At one point, a stereotypical looking "redneck," in white T-shirt and baseball cap and a stereotypical looking "punker," with spiked hair and leather jacket, hug one another. They stop, look at each other, and hug again. The Cleveland Indians have brought the city together. Not to be outdone, however, California Angels fans even dress like angels for the final game, and stand to wave their wings in unison, in support of struggling pitcher Mel Clark (*Angels in the Outfield*, 1994). The list goes on, as the Durham Bulls *(Bull Durham,* 1988), Chicago Cubs (*Rookie of the Year*, 1993), and Chunichi Dragons (*Mr. Baseball,* 1992) all create excited, joyous communities of fans who share the teams' success. Even Ray Kinsella's cornfield promises to set attendance records when, at the end of *Field of Dreams* (1989), we see a solid line of headlights headed for his farm, where they will find the peace and sense of community that they lack. This process is repeated in films such as *The Natural* (1984), *A League of Their Own* (1992), *Rookie of the Year* (1993), and *Little Big League* (1994), in which, as each team begins to develop a sense of community within itself, and achieve the success that, according to baseball's ideology, accompanies the blending of individual personalities and interests into the shared identity and goals of a larger community, scenes of empty stands of isolated, and often negative, sniping fans, are gradually replaced by scenes of stadiums packed with cheering, happy fans, united in support of their team. Again, baseball films of all eras have featured large crowds, of course, cheering for their teams. What distinguishes these types of scenes in more recent films is the more explicit thematic emphasis on the process of winning teams bringing larger communities together. And, significantly, this process occurs within the larger context of these cinematic teams themselves making the transition from collectives of individuals to true communities. In a number of films since the 1980s, these two processes—the achievement of community within teams and the achievement of community beyond the ballpark—are inextricably linked.

This appealing sense of community is extended even further, however, beyond the teams and fictionalized fans portrayed in these films, to the audiences of these films, as well. A significant appeal of these films, we believe, and a large reason for their popularity, is that the movie audience is also invited into this larger circle of community fandom, and invited to participate, however briefly, in the warmth and security of a close, caring community. In his discussion of the consequences of modernity on individual identity in 1973, Peter L. Berger argued that modern man suffers from "a deepening condition of homelessness" (p. 82); an increasing sense of alienation from the social structure and an undermining of personal identity. Berger's analysis was confirmed in 1982 by Daniel Yankelovich. In his survey that year of American attitudes, Yankelovich reported a dramatic increase during the preceding ten years in the percentage of Americans seeking to "compensate for the impersonal and threatening aspects of modern life by seeking mutual identification with others..." (1982, p. 248). During that 10 year period, he found, the percentage of Americans "deeply involved in the search for community," had increased to 47% (p. 248).

Given this renewed search for community in the 1980s, it is not surprising that we also witnessed a renewed popularity of the baseball film at that time, beginning with *The Natural* in 1984 and extending into the new millennium. For, as we have emphasized repeatedly, the concept of community is central to baseball's cultural vision. In these films, audiences are able to immerse themselves in a sense of human community that is too often missing from their daily lives. They are able to celebrate communities whose members nurture and support one another; communities whose members place the good of the community above their own self-interest; and, since the 1950s, communities of diversity and equality. These cinematic portrayals are a marked contrast to the lived experiences of the audiences which have flocked to theaters to view them. For the reality of many Americans during the latter decades of the 20th century was an increasing sense of isolation and loss of community. Baseball films have served as a familiar and comfortable form through which to express the contemporary longing for community. We should not simply view these films as nostalgic longings for an idealized, and perhaps fictional past, however. While some of these films clearly do portray an idyllic and innocent small-town of America's past — *Sandlot* (1993) being the best example — others, such as *Major League* (1989) and *Mr. Baseball* (1992), locate the ideal community squarely within modern, industrialized, urban centers. The popularity of these films does not reflect simply a longing for an earlier time, but also the desire for, and possibility of, community within the conditions of modern American life.

4

Booze, Broads, and Baseball

*"Booze and broads. Booze and broads. You can't live like that
and play baseball. No man alive can."*
— Miller Huggins

"I can."
— Babe Ruth, *The Babe*

There is both anger and frustration in Yankees manager Miller Huggins' voice. The Great Bambino, the greatest player the game has ever seen, has arrived late for another Spring Training. Soaked with booze, overweight, and with the swagger of a man who knows full well he is the greatest player the game has ever seen, Babe Ruth has yet to learn the lessons that will eventually transform him into a true baseball hero. For now, values such as hard work, humility and sobriety are not among the Babe's repertoire. And his path to Cooperstown will not be easy.

In Chapter 3, we examined the principal vision of baseball films, that of an ideal community characterized by caring, nurturance, support, equality, and solidarity; a community in which players/citizens willingly place the good of the team/community above their own interests, and in doing so achieve their own individual fulfillment and happiness. In this chapter, we explore the characteristics of the ideal individual within that exemplary community, the cinematic baseball hero. For, in the end, it is through the collective commitment and efforts of its individual citizens that the baseball film's idyllic community is achieved. Consistent with that idyllic vision of community, therefore, baseball films present prototypical icons who exemplify the virtues advocated by baseball's ideologists since

John Goodman (left) as Babe Ruth in *The Babe* (Universal Pictures, 1992).

the early 1900s. These films offer us images of the hero that was meant to be; a hero who lives the values of hard work, humility, and purity of body and soul.

Given baseball's perceived role of teaching youngsters the "traits that would be important in the business of life" (Riess, 1980, p. 22), it is not surprising that a commitment to the values and benefits of hard work has been central to baseball's ideology, nor that cinematic portrayals of the baseball hero have often served as a celebration and reaffirmation of the American work ethic. In both subtle and not so subtle ways, audiences are reminded that the true baseball hero/citizen achieves his greatness only through hard work and dedication. *The Pride of the Yankees* (1942), a film which has served as the template for baseball films ever since its first release, provides one of the more blatant celebrations of the heroic work ethic. Lou Gehrig's commitment to hard work is documented by a montage of newspaper headlines chronicling his minor league season in Hartford: "Gehrig Tireless Worker Says Manager," "Human Dynamo Never Takes It Easy," "Strives for Perfection By Endless Effort." Later in the film, Gehrig attributes the early symptoms of the illness that will kill him to a need for greater effort. "You can't try too hard," he tells a coach. "I need a lot of work."

The importance of hard work is a lesson young Roy Hobbs (*The Nat-*

ural, 1984) learns early in his life. *The Natural* opens with a scene of the idyllic pastoral vision, a boy and his dad playing catch. We see the boy running through waste-high waves of golden grain to catch a soaring fly, shattering a board on the side of the barn with a fastball — dead center in the circle his father has drawn for him to aim at — and tossing the ball back and forth with Dad in front of the tractor. Gently, approvingly, with just enough of a hint of underlying threat to insure his message will haunt Roy throughout the rest of his life, the father tells the son, "You've got a gift Roy, but it's not enough. You've got to develop yourself. Rely too much on your own gift and you'll fail." It is a message not lost on Roy, who, years later, will leave his sickbed on the eve of his final game to take batting practice.

The importance of a never-failing commitment to hard work is also firmly established in *Bull Durham* (1988); although considerably more subtly. After walking out on love interest Annie Savoy early in the film, Crash Davis, the minor-league journeyman who knows he is near the end of his career, pauses in his melancholy wanderings to pull a cardboard tube from a dumpster and practice his batting swing in the reflection of a hardware store window — a quiet testimony to the true hero's obsession to always work at being the best. The message in these films is clear. One's individual talents, no matter how great they may be, are not sufficient to insure success.

A similar lesson emerges in both cinematic portrayals of the person many consider to be the greatest talent the game has ever known, Babe Ruth. In *The Babe Ruth Story* (1948), the audience learns that it is hard work and a rededication to the game that revive the Babe's fading career at age 32. When he is reminded by his mentor, Brother Matthias, that "the crippled children you visit so often ... never give up," Ruth stages a dramatic comeback. And, after his final game as a player, the Babe takes a Boston rookie aside and passes along the wisdom of hard work, instructing him, "Give (baseball) everything you've got and baseball will be good to you." Almost fifty years later, even the less flattering re-make of the Sultan of Swat's career (*The Babe*, 1992) features scenes of an overweight and struggling Ruth returning to his Massachusetts farm during the off-season, where he works out, chops wood, and tempers his hedonistic lifestyle, enabling him to revitalize his career.

Resurrection through hard, honest toil is also a principle theme of *Mr. Baseball* (1992). When fading superstar Jack Elliot quits attempting to get by on his past accomplishments and talents, begins taking the advice of his manager, and dedicates himself to getting back in shape, he recovers his past form and starts to hit again. As in many baseball films, evidence of his newfound work ethic is dramatized through scenes of the born-again athlete working out, running up and down stadium stairs, and running wind sprints until he is on the point of collapse. It is not until Elliot regains both the discipline and the physical conditioning that comes through hard work that he is able to begin hitting again. Similarly, only when "Downtown" Anderson is humbled by being sent back to the South Carolina Buzz after a disastrous, short-lived trip to the majors, and commits himself to the hard work and daily grind — the "sweat, sweat, and more sweat" — of really learning to hit, is he able to revive his career (*Major League: Back to the Minors*, 1998).

In addition to developing and sustaining one's natural abilities, a commitment to hard work is also presented as a means of achieving the respect of one's teammates. Lou Gehrig, of course, was revered by his teammates as well as fans as "the iron horse" of baseball (*The Pride of the Yankees*, 1942). In *Mr. Baseball* (1992), when Jack Elliot finally does commit himself to hard work, he regains the respect of his fellow Chunichi Dragons, who join him in running wind sprints as a means of showing their support and providing encouragement to him. As bat-boy for the Bisons, young Christy Cooper quickly gains the affection and admiration of the team with his hard work and enthusiasm, winning the ultimate compliment from a ball-player: "You're all right. You've got a lot of hustle" (*The Kid from Left Field*, 1953). Later, as manager of the Bisons, Christy stays up late into the night, spending long hours developing strategies, to the point that he finally becomes ill and physically collapses. In *Major League* (1989), prima donna third-baseman Roger Dorn is able to win back the respect of his teammates, as well as regain his form, only by taking ground ball after ground ball in extended workout sessions.

In baseball's morality plays, the rewards of hard work are often made more dramatic through the portrayal of the humble beginnings of the dedicated, hard-working baseball hero. Babe Ruth is shown as a boy laboring in the family saloon on the rough Baltimore waterfront. Mistreated by his father and in trouble with the law, Babe leaps at the chance to return to a Baltimore orphanage, where he will be allowed to play baseball (*The Babe Ruth Story*, 1948). *The Pride of the Yankees* (1942) opens with a scene in which young Lou Gehrig, the poor son of struggling immigrants, plays sandlot ball in a declining New York neighborhood. When he breaks a merchant's window with a long home run, the Gehrigs cannot pay the $18.50 to fix it. It is through hard work, together with their natural, God-given talents, that these cinematic heroes are able to rise above their impoverished beginnings. Similarly, Monty Stratton is depicted walking several miles to and from games. And, when he finally gets home in early evening, after pitching nine innings and walking the several miles home, he finishes the chores on the farm where he lives with his widowed mother (*The Stratton Story*, 1949). In *The Winning Team* (1952) Grover Cleveland Alexander is shown working as a telephone lineman, trying to scrape together enough money to buy a farm and get married, and pitching in local games whenever he can. Perhaps not as dramatically as in these earlier films, the notion that hard work can serve to elevate individuals from their limited beginnings is also validated in *Major League* (1989). Motivated by the machinations of evil owner Rachel Phelps, the various misfits, losers and ex-cons who now comprise the Cleveland Indians are shown in a series of scenes buckling down and working hard to become a real team, and exact their revenge on Phelps, by winning the American League East. In the end, through their solidarity, commitment, and hard work, this team of misfits and losers does just that.

While baseball films generally adhere to Lou Gehrig's philosophy that "you can't try too hard," there are some notable exceptions. In *Fear Strikes Out* (1957), for example, driven by an ambitious father, Jimmy Piersall works relentlessly throughout his entire childhood to become a major leaguer. The constant pressure eventually leads to a mental breakdown. And, as we shall explore more fully in Chapter 5, a number of films of the 1980s and 1990s tempered the emphasis on a strong work ethic with an equally strong emphasis on the idea that baseball is supposed to be fun, and that players should have a good time playing the game. Nevertheless, the lesson of baseball films is clear. It is the lesson taught throughout the culture of industrial America; America and baseball are fields of opportunity. If one works hard enough, she or he can rise from the slums of Baltimore to the life of an America hero.

> *"Aw, cut it out."*
> — Babe Ruth, *The Babe, Ruth Story*, 1948

If, as Crash Davis tells Nuke LaLoosh (*Bull Durham*, 1988), baseball players are supposed to play the game with fear and arrogance, to remain cocky even when they're getting beat, baseball heroes are also expected to be paragons of humility. The cockiness and arrogance referred to by the aging Durham Bulls catcher is contained and disciplined; the confidence tempered by a humble recognition of one's place in the larger scheme of things. And, by the standards of the real world of modern baseball, at least, even the confidence, cockiness and arrogance of cinematic baseball heroes are nothing short of genteel. You will never see a baseball film hero holding a freshly-stolen second base above his head shouting "I am the greatest." Nor is there is any gloating over beaten opponents; no high-fiving, forearm-bashing, finger-pointing, homerun strolls, or home plate dances. Such is not the way of heroes. The true baseball hero, these films tell us, possesses a quiet, dignified humility.

The Pride of the Yankees' (1942) Lou Gehrig is the proto-type of humility, as well as every other heroic characteristic, as the film's prologue makes clear, describing Gehrig as "a lesson in simplicity and modesty to the youth of America." Later in the film, Lou's pal, sportswriter Sam Blake, lectures a colleague (and cynics in the audience) about the value of Lou's character: "Let me tell you about heroes. I've covered a lot of 'em and I'm saying Gehrig is the best of 'em. No front page scandals, no daffy excitements, no horn piping ... but a guy who does his job and nothing else." Lou Gehrig epitomizes the myth of the common man.

In similar fashion, *The Natural* (1984) proclaims the humility of fictional protagonist Roy Hobbs. The narrator of a newsreel reports, "although embarrassed by praise and shy of the press, Hobbs is always there for an autograph." And, not only does the modest Hobbs never display untoward delight in his own personal accomplishments, he noticeably bristles at the conceit of others and invariably triumphs over the arrogant antagonist. Likewise, *Bull Durham*'s (1988) Crash Davis is also offended by what he considers excessive or inappropriate arrogance displayed by other players. And, like Lou Gehrig and Roy Hobbs, Davis shies away from publicity about his own personal accomplishments. He refuses publicity for hitting a minor-league record 247 home runs, calling it "a dubious honor."

This sense of quiet humility characterizes nearly all of baseball's cinematic legends. Despite being the greatest player in the game, Washington Senator Joe Hardy (*Damn Yankees*, 1958) remains extremely polite and reserved; his newfound status as the Senators' savior never goes to his head. (Perhaps selling one's soul to the devil encourages an extra degree of humility and sense of place in the larger scheme of things.) Similarly, Grover Cleveland Alexander (*The Winning Team*, 1952) displays a gentle, often joking, typically Reaganesque humility throughout the film. In one scene, he faces a struggling Rogers Hornsby. Hitless all game, Hornsby is probably going to be sent down to the minors if he goes 0 for 4. Alexander, whose Philadelphia Phillies are well ahead, floats a fat one to Hornsby, allowing him to get a hit. His own achievements are not the only things that matter to Alexander; a striking contrast to the image presented by many modern real-life players, who often appear concerned about nothing else.

Humility comes less easily for Babe Ruth, however, who spends the better part of *The Babe Ruth Story* (1948) and *The Babe* (1992) learning the virtues and rewards of humility. In the 1948 version, for example, the initially arrogant and undisciplined Great Bambino is a constant aggravation to manager Miller Huggins, who even suspends Ruth for two weeks during the 1925 season. It is only as Ruth acquires, through bouts with alcohol, age and baseball's institutions, a more humbled evaluation of himself and a subsequent concern for the feelings and well-being of others, that his public persona shifts from one of admired player to that of beloved American icon. Indeed, it is the learning of humility that salvages the Babe's professional and personal life, and elevates him to true heroic status. Thus, at the end of the 1927 season, and the film, a now matured Ruth has resurrected his career by hitting a record-setting 60 home runs. And when a dying Miller Huggins says to Ruth — who is at this point still unaware of his manager's condition — "Babe, I never dared tell you this before. But you're the gosh-darndest, greatest ballplayer that ever entered the game," the now humble and heroic Ruth responds with the natural modesty of a true baseball hero. "Aw, cut it out," he gushes. This is a Babe Ruth we can now all truly admire.

A similar process of enlightenment occurs in *Little Big League* (1994), when young Billy Heywood, owner/manager of the Minnesota Twins, begins taking himself much too seriously, eventually becoming the same sort of mean, arrogant, egocentric manager that he had earlier fired. Soon no one — his team, friends, not even his mother — wants to be around him. It is only when he recognizes what he has become, and is able to regain his humility, and the easy-going commitment that baseball should be fun, that he is able to regain the love and admiration of those around him. It is only then that the slumping Twins resume their winning ways. Humbled by the murder of rival Juan Primo, which "puts it all in perspective," San Francisco Giants' slugger Bobby Rayburn regains his hitting form, as he comes to realize true fulfillment comes from the quiet joys of family, not through the arrogant power trips of a baseball prima-donna (*The Fan*, 1996). As mentioned earlier, before he can commit himself to becoming a true major-league hitter, *Major Leagues: Back to the Minors'* (1998) "Downtown" Anderson must first become humbled by failure. Once he accepts that he still has much to learn, apologizes to manager Gus Cantrell for his arrogance, and dedicates himself to learning what Cantrell has to teach, Anderson is able to fulfill the promise and potential of his natural ability.

In *Back to the Minors* (1998) and *Mr. 3000* (2005), Leon Curtis and Stan Ross are presented as caricatures of the contemporary egoistical, trash-talking sports superstar. In *Back to the Minors*, Curtis, the Minnesota Twins slugger who has proclaimed himself a religion, is finally put in his place, backing down in a confrontation at the mound with a minor league pitcher. In *Mr. 3000*, Stan Ross eventually does learn the lesson of humility, thus achieving things he never had before — the respect and admiration of his teammates, true love, and election to the Hall of Fame.

Learning the lessons of humility is one of the most common themes in baseball films, as we witness the growth of the talented player into the full bloom of a true baseball hero. It is the process of coming to learn that talent is not enough, and that it is such virtues as humility which enable the individual with great, natural talent, to fully develop his or her abilities, and to achieve true heroic stature. Because of the centrality of humility in baseball's moral code, in nearly all baseball films, the hero either possesses a strong sense of humility, or acquires it in the process of becoming a "true" baseball hero. In only a few films are we presented with central characters who seem genuinely arrogant or conceited, and who apparently maintain those characteristics throughout the film. In these cases, that self-centeredness is typically tempered by other characteristics or circumstances. In both *Elmer the Great* (1933) and *The Pride of St. Louis* (1952), for example, the central characters— Cubs' pitcher Elmer Kane and Cardinals' pitcher Dizzy Dean — are not at all shy about assuring everyone around them that they are the best. Elmer Kane, for example, who has just arrived from Gentryville, Illinois, where he delivered groceries and played for a semi-pro team, stalks off the playing field during spring training, shouting "I ain't gonna play with no rookies," when he learns the only players in camp to this point are the rookies, like himself. Dizzy Dean assures the St. Louis Cardinals that they are making a big mistake when they decide to start him out in the minors, rather than bringing him straight to the major leagues after signing him (*The Pride of St. Louis*, 1952). This confident braggadocio is a characteristic both players maintain throughout the film.

In both cases, however, their cockiness and apparent conceit is presented as part of their country charm and naivete. Both are of "rural" backgrounds, in the purest sense of the word. And both are presented as endearing, likable characters. While Kane's conceit initially offends some of his teammates, they come to see that his behavior is more a result of a lack of refinement, and apparently forgive him for his initial abrasiveness. Dean's lack of humility does not seem to offend anyone in *The Pride of St. Louis* (1952). Quite the contrary, Dean's country-style self assuredness quickly endears him to his future wife, Patricia.

Typically, however, a cinematic baseball hero's apparent lack of humility is explained away as a protective cover for other, more forgivable personal weaknesses. In *The Big Leaguer* (1953), pitcher Bobby Bronson initially appears extremely arrogant and self-centered. He is the kind of kid the director of the Giants' tryout camp, Hans Lobert, knows needs to be taught a lesson. In the end, however, Bronson's arrogance is recognized as a cover for his own insecurity. We learn what kind of person he really is during a crucial intra-squad game, in which Bronson is getting hit pretty hard. Adam Paluchek, the one real major league prospect in camp, realizes this, and has decided to let Bronson strike him out. After Paluchek takes two pitches right down the middle, Bronson senses what is going on, and knocks Paluchek down with a high, tight fastball. This apparently brings Paluchek to his senses. As Paluchek gets up, he quietly says, "Thank you, Bobby," and hits the next pitch out of the park. Bronson would not allow Paluchek to sacrifice his chances for him, even if it meant he, Bobby, would probably be cut himself. Indeed, he is cut. But, as he walks out the door, even Hans Lobert comments to one of his coaches, "You know Mac, I might have just booted one." In *Fear Strikes Out* (1957), Jimmy Piersall's apparent arrogance, evidenced by his constant taunting and riding of his Red Sox teammates for not working hard enough or not playing as well as he thinks they should, turns out to be the early manifestations of a mental breakdown, brought on by his own father's treating him the same way throughout his childhood.

The most notable example of a lack of humility, however, is represented in the film biography of one of baseball's cockiest and least humble superstars, Ty Cobb (*Cobb*, 1996). There is little endearing about the Ty Cobb depicted in this film, who is portrayed as a dirty, vicious player, as a racist and misogynist, and as generally deranged in all respects. No one in this film likes Ty Cobb. Even when the dying Cobb tries to visit his sister near the end of the film, she pulls her curtains and will not allow him in the house. Cobb is presented as the antithesis of everything a true baseball hero should be. Indeed, the central purpose of the film is to document that the real Ty Cobb was nothing like the heroic image of him that has prevailed in much of the popular media. But, even here, Cobb's poisonous personality is explained as a result of childhood traumas; seeing his mother's lover kill his father, and then lying to protect his mother in court. If, for whatever reason, a baseball hero turns out to be something less than the humble, virtuous ideal, there must be a good reason.

Such depictions of a less than humble central character are rare, however. Overwhelmingly, the central characters of baseball films reflect the quiet, genuine humility characteristic of the true baseball hero. True arrogance is typically reserved for minor characters who serve as foils for the hero's righteousness, such as the bit-player Barnett who, extremely confident he will make it to the show, is meanly derisive of players who get cut. His manager calls him a "pain in the ass" (*Ed*, 1996). In *Major League II* (1994), the villainous slugger Jack Parkman's vicious arrogance makes him immediately disliked by fellow players, as well as by film audiences. Pitcher Eric Van Leemer's self-centered arrogance is held up as the antithesis of the baseball way in *Summer Catch* (2000), and eventually gets him into enough trouble that he is kicked off the team.

Baseball's cultural vision attempts to strike a balance between the values of individualism and community. Consistent with this ideological project, the humility exhibited by the cinematic baseball hero serves to temper the "excesses" of individualism which may accompany star status, and to reassert the primacy of the larger community. Despite their own personal accomplishments true baseball heroes recognize that, ultimately, the good of their team, the game, and the fans matters more than their individual achievements. Consistent with baseball's emphasis on community, it is a humility which reminds them — as it serves to remind other citizens/workers throughout American culture — that the good of the organization/team comes first, and that what is good for the team is, in the end, what is best for the individual hero, as well. Humility, along with hard work, baseball films repeatedly tell us, is the stuff real baseball heroes are made of. Not to mention an heroic level of moral discipline.

> *"I was a fool. A grand-slam, double-barreled fool. Breaking training, hitting the bottle, you don't stay up there very long. And by the time I learned my lesson, I was out.*
> — Barney Wiles, *The Stratton Story*, 1949

The ideology of baseball places considerable emphasis upon the game's role as a purveyor of strong moral values to American youth. As Riess (1980) has noted in his review of the historical development of baseball's ideology, boys during the early 1900s were encouraged to model the behavior of their baseball heroes, who were presumably clean-living out of necessity, since a strong mind and body were critical for continued success. Despite the reality of drinking, venereal disease and other violations of the game's moral code, pulp novelists and the press portrayed baseball players as virtuous men, who abstained from such vices as smoking, drinking and carousing with wild women. Young boys were offered such heroes as the hard-working Ty Cobb, and the wholesome Christy Mathewson. According to Riess, the clean-living Mathewson, who "started playing ball at the YMCA and almost never pitched on the Sabbath" (p. 23) was particularly idealized. Following his death from tuberculosis in 1932, *Commonweal* wrote,

> Certainly no other pitcher ever loomed so majestically in young minds, quite overshadowing George Washington and his cherry tree or even that transcendent model of boyhood, Frank Merriwell ... Such men have a very real value above and beyond the achievements of brawn and sporting skill. They realize and typify in a fashion the ideal of sport —clean power in the hands of a clean and vigorous personality [cited in Riess, 1980, p. 24].

Given the centrality of clean-living and moral conduct within baseball's cultural vision, it is not surprising that baseball films reflect a moral code clearly Puritan in origin. The evil of such moral vices as drinking and womanizing are illuminated in no uncertain terms. And the linkage between moral virtue and heroic status is clearly established. As noted earlier, *The Pride of the Yankees'* (1942) Lou Gehrig serves as the exemplary cinematic baseball hero; the ideal to which others aspire. Lipsky (1981) characterizes Gary Cooper's portrayal of Lou Gehrig as that of an idol with no known vices or deficiencies; a good son, good student, good husband, and good provider.

Other cinematic heroes, however, have not been so blessed. For many of them, overcoming their moral transgressions has been a long and difficult process; part of the long path toward the status of hero. Babe Ruth, for example, liked to party. In the original, more timid version of his life story (*The Babe Ruth Story*, 1948), Ruth's excessive drinking is lightly broached. There is one crucial scene, however, in which a joyful Babe who, on his way into a children's hospital to deliver gifts after having had a bit too much

Christmas cheer, is reproached for his transgressions by moral savior and future wife Claire. She attempts to shame the Sultan of Swat into moral virtue by reminding him of his position as role model for America's youth. "How you act, they act," she tells him. Otherwise, Ruth's penchant for late-nights and lots of beer is more inferred than directly stated. And, his reputation for womanizing is never mentioned. Nevertheless, without dwelling on the issue, the impression is clearly established that Ruth had a tendency to enjoy his nightlife — and that he needed to change. But, it is not just the drinking that threatens Ruth's career and future heroic status. In this film, his lifestyle is presented as part of a larger pattern of irresponsibility and lack of discipline. It is only when Ruth reforms himself, by giving up this way of life, and rededicating himself to the game and the hard work it demands, that he is able to revive his sagging career and find true fulfillment through his marriage to Claire, who wanted little to do with baseball's greatest player ever, until he had matured.

The Babe (1992), nearly 50 years later, portrays Ruth's violations of baseball's moral code much more graphically. Unlike the "pulp novelists and obsequious press" cited by Riess (1980, p. 23), who, during the early decades of this century portrayed all ballplayers as paragons of moral virtue, at least some film makers of the 1990s were more willing to bare the less virtuous sides of baseball's heroes. Thus, the 1992 biography of Babe Ruth is much more open in its depictions of Ruth's drunkenness, gambling, and adultery. But, although more graphic in its depiction, the message in 1992 was still much the same as it was in 1948. It is only when Babe Ruth finally realizes the truth in manager Miller Huggins' advice, that no one can "live like that and play baseball," that he is able to revive his career and, more importantly, find the peace and fulfillment he has been seeking. And while the 1992 version of Ruth's life and career is much more direct in representing his moral transgressions, it is also much more direct in providing an explanation for those transgressions, attributing Ruth's behavior to a desperate grasping for family and community, the result of his own childhood abandonment.

Similar to Babe Ruth, fictional New York Knights superstar Roy Hobbs also finds his career threatened by his descent into the night life (*The Natural*, 1984). Having made a miraculous return to the game at age 35, Hobbs is literally knocking the cover off of baseballs, and leading the Knights to the pennant, until he becomes involved with the unsavory Memo Paris, and begins regularly breaking curfews as he frequents nightclubs with her.

Scenes of Hobbs and Paris spending their nights on the town drinking champagne, among other things, interspersed with scenes of a tired Roy Hobbs slumping, make clear that not only is Hobbs jeopardizing his own career, but that he is also taking the Knights down with him. And, this is not the first time Hobbs' career has been jeopardized by temptation. It was his attraction to the mysterious and seductive Harriet Bird, sixteen years earlier, that brought a sudden and tragic end to his baseball career then. As with Ruth, it is only when Hobbs abandons his nightlife, and refocuses his attention and energy on the game, that he is able to regain his earlier abilities. He, too, has learned that booze, broads and baseball don't mix.

While for Babe Ruth and Roy Hobbs the demon rum is a recreational temptation that eventually impairs their abilities and threaten their careers, for others, alcohol is a refuge, a place to hide and seek solace when their careers appear to be at a premature end. During an early scene in *The Pride of St. Louis* (1952), Dizzy Dean tells his future wife Pat that he doesn't smoke or drink — he quit moonshine when he was 7. Unfortunately, when a series of injuries finally result in an early end to the Diz's career, Dean seeks consolation through drinking and gambling. It isn't until his wife finally leaves him that Dean pulls himself back together, quitting his drinking and gambling, and beginning a second career as a baseball broadcaster.

Similarly, when his career is threatened by recurring double-vision and fainting spells, the result of being hit in the head by a ball in his first Triple-A game, Grover Cleveland Alexander (*The Winning Team*, 1952) also resorts to the bottle for comfort. His drinking, of course, only compounds the problem, as everyone attributes his dizziness and blackouts to alcoholism. Alexander's career comes to an end, and he ends up in a carnival sideshow. Thanks to the support of his wife Aimee, who had earlier left him because of his drinking, and friend Rogers Hornsby, Alexander is eventually able to make a comeback, leading the Cardinals to victory in the 1926 World Series.

Whether the baseball hero drinks for enjoyment, or for solace and escape, the effects are usually severe, threatening his career, his marriage, and his life. In films prior to the 1980s, there is usually no middle ground. Most cinematic heroes, such as Lou Gehrig (*The Pride of the Yankees*, 1942) do not drink at all. Those who do drink serve to impart the moral lesson by exhibiting the consequences of drinking. Inevitably, alcohol and failure, both professional and personal, are intertwined. For those who fail to take this lesson seriously, there is the haunting specter of Barney Wiles, an ex-major league catcher, now a disheveled drifter sneaking rides in boxcars (*The Stratton Story*, 1949). The morality lesson is unambiguous. Don't let this happen to you.

In the films of the 1980s and beyond, however, reflecting a greater social tolerance and acceptance of drinking, as well as the realities of the real world of baseball itself, portrayals of drinking have been somewhat looser, with occasional scenes of ballplayers drinking socially and in moderation, and without tragic consequences. In *A League of Their Own* (1992), for example, the Rockford Peaches sneak out to a speak-easy, to enjoy a beer and some dancing, with no disastrous results. *Bull Durham's* (1988) Crash Davis enjoys an occasional beer or glass of scotch, as do some of the Cleveland Indians (*Major League*, 1989; *Major League II*, 1994). However, even in contemporary films, ballplayers are rarely shown as drinking to the point of intoxication. And, when they do, the portrayal is critical. In *Cobb* (1994), the vicious and psychotic Ty Cobb drinks constantly; just one more symptom of his completely diseased personality. And in *The Slugger's Wife* (1985), when Braves slugger Darryl Palmer's wife leaves him, as a result of his unwillingness to allow her to pursue her own career as a pop singer, he immediately gets sloppily drunk. After spending some time commiserating with his dog — telling it not to fall for some good-looking cocker spaniel and to never get married, because all women care about is their careers— he goes to the stadium to practice his hitting. When his manager and a couple of teammates arrive to take him home, he comes completely undone, degenerating into a pathetic tantrum of sobbing, screaming and whining, eventually bashing the pitching machine with his bat.

Probably the mildest portrayal of drinking to the point of drunkenness occurs in *Ed* (1996), when the Santa Rosa Rockets get together in a bar to toast those who didn't make the cut. They are so hung over the next day that their manager, Chubb, cancels practice, telling them "You're all useless." While none of the Rockets experiences the same sort of descent into a long-term state of moral decay as Babe Ruth, Roy Hobbs, Dizzy Dean, or Grover Cleveland Alexander, the moral lesson is still the same. Booze and baseball don't mix.

While the moral admonition against alcohol has been somewhat tempered in more recent films, the portrayal of smoking, to the degree the issue has received any attention at all, has been consistently negative. For the most part, baseball films have delivered their anti-smoking message by portraying role models who lead by example. In contrast to the game's historic affinity for tobacco, we virtually never see a ballplayer smoking in these films. When the issue is broached, the references are consistently negative. As mentioned earlier, Dizzy Dean tells us he has never smoked (*The Pride of St. Louis*, 1952). In *Alibi Ike* (1935), the naive Ike Farrell warns a group of gamblers and thugs, whom he mistakenly thinks are members of a "young men's high ideals club" against the dangers of smoking. Similarly, in *The Babe Ruth Story* (1942), Babe Ruth sternly tells a group of young autograph seekers, "Now kids, I want you all to remember what I said about smoking. It'll stunt your growth." Then, pointing to manager Miller Huggins, standing next to him, "Look what it did to him." This earlier version of Ruth's life stands in stark contrast to the 1992 depiction of a morally decrepit Ruth shown frequently with a cigar in his mouth; yet one more symbol of his moral failings.

The strongest anti-smoking statement comes in *Angels in the Outfield* (1994), in which we regularly see aging pitcher Mel Clark smoking. Near the end of the film, Al, the angel who has been communicating with the boy, Roger (the only person in the film to actually see the angels), appears in the California Angels' dugout. He is there, he says, to check on Mel, who will soon be "one of us." "He smoked for years," Al tells Roger. "It's always a mistake. He's got 6 months left, doesn't know anything's wrong yet."

Interestingly, in light of the popular history of chewing tobacco in baseball, baseball films virtually never show ballplayers chewing tobacco, or make any reference at all to this vice. One film which does broach this touchy subject is *The Sandlot* (1993). The team leader, Benny Martinez, manages to get some chewing tobacco and gives a wad to each of his teammates. They then go to a carnival and, while riding the ferris wheel, proceed to get sick to their stomachs, raining this lesson in clean living down on innocent bystanders on the ground below. The audience is left assured that chewing tobacco is not a habit these kids will be likely to adopt.

Although baseball films have consistently adhered to the moral decree that true baseball heroes do not smoke or drink, noticeably lacking in these films has been any reference at all to drugs other than alcohol or tobacco; marijuana, LSD, crack, cocaine, speed. As far as baseball films are concerned, these drugs do not even exist. And, to date, steroids have yet to be mentioned as well. While one might argue that the complete avoidance of mentioning these drugs in baseball films serves to deliver the message that, obviously, real ballplayers don't do drugs, the failure of baseball films to even refer to this issue — in light of the attention focused on this issue within the culture at large, not to mention the well-publicized drug problems of a number of real-life players—is curious, at best. As far as drugs other than alcohol or tobacco are concerned, the moral vision contained within baseball films is one shielded by blinders. In the idealized community constructed by these films, such problems do not even exist.

> *"Without you, I'm just half a man, waiting to black out. God*
> *sure must think a lot of me, to have given me you."*
> — Grover Cleveland Alexander,
> *The Winning Team*, 1952

Grover Cleveland Alexander's loving devotion to his wife, and her equally powerful and unwavering devotion to him, represent another crucial moral imperative in baseball's cultural vision. The true baseball hero is married — and monogamous. Indeed, a common theme in baseball films is that marriage to a good and loving wife is one of the rewards of maturity; of acquiring the other characteristics of the baseball hero, such as honesty, humility, and selflessness. In *Alibi Ike* (1935) for example, Cubs' pitcher Ike Farrell initially jeopardizes his romance with the manager's daughter, Dolly, by his tendency to concoct alibis for everything. When he shows up late for spring training, he claims it is because his calendar didn't work. After losing a game, his excuse is that he doesn't pitch his best on Wednesdays. When Dolly overhears Ike explaining to his teammates that he's only marrying Dolly because he feels sorry for her, because he is too embarrassed to admit he really loves her, she walks out on him. All is resolved, however, and at the end of the film, as Ike and Dolly stand at the alter, Ike, having matured enough to win back Dolly's love, vows never to tell another alibi. Similarly, it is only when Babe Ruth abandons not only his nightlife, but also his self-centeredness and arrogance, that he is rewarded with the hand of his long-love, Claire (*The Babe Ruth Story*, 1948). In the 1951 version of *Angels in the Outfield*, when Pirates manager Guffy McGovern, known for his tendency to swear at and abuse his players, sports writers, and just about anyone else, finally overcomes his anger and bitterness, he is rewarded with the love of and eventual marriage to reporter Jennifer Page. Together, they adopt the orphan, Bridget White who, as the only person to actually see the angels, served as the vehicle for both the Pirates' and McGovern's transformations. At the end of the film, McGovern is shown standing with new wife and daughter, proudly proclaiming, "Look at what I got."

The list of such examples of true love and marriage as the ultimate reward for the acquisition of moral virtue goes on and on. In virtually every baseball film the hero settles down, at least by the end of the film if not before, with his true love. By the end of *Take Me Out to the Ball Game* (1949), for example, shortstop Eddie O'Brien, notorious for his way with the ladies, eventually finds true love and marriage with the Wolves' new owner, K.C. Higgins. Although he wakes up at the beginning of the film in what appears to be a teen-age girl's bedroom, once *Mr. Baseball*'s (1992) Jack Elliot learns to replace his arrogance and self-centeredness with humility and a commitment to the team, he is rewarded with the love and hand of his manager's daughter, Hiroto.

A subtle variation on the theme of true love as the reward for maturity is the theme of regaining lost love through that same process. In *The Pride of St. Louis* (1952), for example, it is only when Dizzy Dean quits wallowing in self-pity at the end of his career, gives up the accompanying drinking and gambling and begins a more responsible and respectable life as a broadcaster, that his wife, Pat — who had finally walked out on him — returns, and their marital bliss is restored. In *Major League* (1989), catcher Jake Taylor is able to win back the love of his ex-wife by demonstrating that he is no longer the irresponsible and unfaithful adolescent she divorced. And, of course, *The Natural* (1984) Roy Hobbs is able to regain the long-lost love of his childhood sweetheart only when he abandons both his nightlife with Memo Paris and his own self-pity. With his lessons finally learned, Hobbs is able to not only lead the Knights to the pennant, but finish the film back on the farm, united with his life's true love, and the son he never knew he had. In *For Love of the Game* (1999), Billy Chapel's often stormy, on-again off-again relationship with Jane Aubrey finally comes to a happy resolution, with the two finally getting back together for good, only after Chapel realizes he needs her more than anything else in his life, including the game of baseball.

Consistent with baseball cinema's definition of true love and marriage as the ultimate rewards for the baseball hero's moral maturation, the related concepts of marital loyalty and fidelity are, not surprisingly, particularly important in the moral code of baseball films. Once he has found his true love, the ideal baseball hero does not violate his life-long commitment. Real baseball heroes do not sleep around. The ideal marriage of course, is that of Lou and Eleanor Gehrig (*The Pride of the Yankees*, 1942). In fact, the film was originally billed as a love story. This film serves as the model relationship and moral order to which other baseball couples will aspire. The Gehrig marriage is so perfect, in fact, that the film makes a point of scoffing at the slightest possibility of disharmony or infidelity. In a scene that takes place not long after Lou and Eleanor are married, Lou is late for his own birthday celebration, a quiet dinner with Eleanor and his pal, sportswriter Sam Blake. Eleanor informs Sam she knows where the tardy Lou is, that this has happened before and that she intends to go get him. Sam, wondering if Lou might be up to something indiscreet, begs her not to go ("you can't just bust in on him this way"), but she will not relent. To drive home the seriousness of such a transgression, on the way to Gehrig's secret rendezvous, Blake threatens to bash the superstar's head in with a baseball bat for the wrong he has done to the "true-blue" Eleanor. And find him they do, just where Eleanor knew he would be — umpiring a children's baseball game on a sandlot. Eleanor makes a fool of Sam and anyone in the audience who might for a moment entertain the notion that Lou Gehrig is anything less than thoroughly virtuous and faithful to Eleanor or that Eleanor is anything less than utterly trusting of Lou.

So powerful is baseball ideology's commitment to the moral values of monogamy and marital fidelity, the commitment to one's partner is considered more important than even the game itself. In *Damn Yankees* (1958), when the devil, Applegate, attempts to seduce Joe Hardy with the temptress Lola, Hardy does not succumb. Even though he is now 20 years younger, as a result of his pact with the devil, Hardy still loves and is still loyal to his wife, Meg. Eventually, Hardy breaks his pact with the devil, deciding to give up his life as Joe Hardy, superstar for the Washington Senators, and return to his life as middle-aged real estate salesman Joe Boyd. In the end, he comes to understand that the love of his wife, Meg, is the most important thing in his life. The film ends with the devil foiled; his final temptation avoided by Joe and Meg holding one another, singing about their life together.

Even in difficult times during a marriage, the true baseball hero remains faithful. In *The Slugger's Wife* (1985), for example, when Darryl Palmer's wife walks out on him, because he is not willing to allow her to continue her own career, the Braves' manager, Burley, decides that some good sex might help pull Palmer out of his depression. He orders two Braves players to set Palmer up for the night. The two players and Palmer go out drinking, and eventually end up back at Palmer's house, with three women all willing to do their part to help the Braves win the pennant. Palmer is unable to have sex with any of them, however, because every room in the house that he and one of the women go to, including the kitchen, reminds him of his beloved Debbie.

As *The Slugger's Wife* (1985) demonstrates, while some more recent films, on the surface at least, may appear to challenge traditional moral values, these values are eventually upheld and preserved. No film serves as a better example of this pattern than *Bull Durham* (1988). Despite the film's explicit language and sex, and apparent initial endorsement of a much looser set of sexual values, in every important respect both the baseball hero of this film, Crash Davis, and the independent Annie Savoy eventually embrace the same conservative moral virtue of earlier cinematic baseball heroes. Early in the film Annie Savoy takes both Crash Davis and Nuke Laloosh home with her. She explains to them both that she chooses one player to hook up with every season, that they appear to be the most likely prospects, and that she would like to know a little more about them. She is immediately challenged by Crash Davis, who wants to know why she gets to choose. Crash leaves, explaining that after 12 years in the minors he does not try out. He will not play the game by her rules. As he leaves, however, he delivers a long soliloquy on what he believes in. Despite the explicitness of some of the language, the sermon is a recitation of rather conservative and traditional values. Annie's "Oh my," as he walks out the door is a clear indication of what is to come. Indeed, it is precisely this outburst of a traditional and nostalgic view of life which seems to attract the feminist Savoy to Crash Davis. At the end of the film, they sit side-by-side on the front porch swing, making plans for their life together. In the end, they too discover and choose baseball's ideal. They, too, do what true cinematic baseball heroes have done for more than 70 years. They settle down with their one, true love.

Subsequent films, of course, have been even freer and more open in their portrayals of sexual relationships, reflecting to a degree the changing values and standards of American culture. But even in later films such as *For Love of the* Game (1999) and *Summer Catch* (2000), in which casual and/or multiple sexual relationships are portrayed as a common, natural part of life for single men and women, the central plot line is still that of the film's baseball hero discovering and eventually settling down with his one true love. Monogamy is still the norm — the ideal to which all baseball heroes aspire.

Since the 1930s, the cinematic image of the true baseball hero has remained strikingly consistent — a testament to the enduring appeal of that vision. Hardworking, courageous, yet also humble, honest and clean living, free from vice, the cinematic baseball hero reflects unambiguously traditional Puritan values. In film, at least, baseball's ideal community is populated with heroes who conform to traditional values without question. And, most significantly, such moral virtues are not simply qualities that true baseball heroes possess and live, they are the qualities that *make* them heroes. In baseball films, a player who beats his wife, uses drugs, or carries a concealed weapon would never be accorded heroic status. For in baseball films, being a true baseball hero means much more than being a great player, or posting record-breaking statistics. It also means reflecting in every way the personal characteristics and moral values that are so much a part of baseball's cultural vision. Ultimately, it is the humble, virtuous, devoted and hardworking family man, rather than the arrogant, undisciplined, morally uncontrolled loner, who is more suitable to the needs of industrial civilization. It is the model husband Lou Gehrig, the reformed Babe Ruth, and the matured Crash Davis and Billy Chapel who are, within the ideology of baseball, deemed most suitable as role models for American youth.

The ability of contemporary film makers to preserve the heroic images of their characters, however, has become more difficult given the nature of contemporary sports journalism. Unlike sports writers of earlier eras, modern sports writers do not hesitate to detail the less than heroic aspects of the private lives of today's stars. Thus, cinematic portrayals of modern players in the same heroic mold as Babe Ruth or Lou Gehrig become more difficult to sell to an increasingly cynical public. The result has been a marked shift to the use of fictionalized, heroes in modern films. Contemporary baseball films have adopted the "designated" hero. While eight of the 21 baseball films produced between 1940 and 1962 were either biographies of, or starred, real baseball players of that era, only five of the 35 baseball films made since 1973 have been about real baseball players. And of those, four were stories not of contemporary baseball heroes, but of historical figures. *Eight Men Out*, produced in 1988, told the story of the 1919 Chicago "Black Sox" scandal. *The Babe*, released in 1992, was another version of the Babe Ruth story. *A League of Their Own* (1992) told the story of players in the women's professional baseball league in the 1940s, and *Cobb* (1996) finally attempted to portray the real Ty Cobb. The only recent film to tell the story of a real-life, contemporary baseball player was *The Rookie*, released in 2001. And, this film did not tell the story of one of the game's modern-day superstars, but rather of an unknown high-school baseball coach who made the Tampa Bay Devil Rays roster as a relief pitcher. The truly big-name stars of the modern era have not seen their careers reflected on the silver screen, and for good reason.

As Wenner (1989) suggests, the contemporary media focus on the escalating salaries of modern athletes undermines the traditional association of sports with such values as unselfishness and self-sacrifice. Humility and devotion to the game are characteristics which many fans find increasingly difficult to attribute to the modern sports star. In addition, the increasing proliferation of media sports coverage, particularly on television, has brought more focused attention to such off-the-field activities as gambling, alleged drug or steroid use, and other unseemly behavior by such well known stars as Pete Rose, Darryl Strawberry, Jose Canseco, Jason Giambi, Mark McGwire, and Barry Bonds. While the press of the early 1900s tended to portray all players as virtuous (Riess, 1980) and attempted to whitewash the less virtuous activities of heroes such as Babe Ruth (Voigt, 1976), contemporary journalists provide full, and often critical, coverage of the transgressions of current stars. Thus, even though the heroes of the early 1900s engaged in many of the same sorts of behaviors as current stars, the lack of a constant media focus on such activities made it easier for proponents of the baseball ideology to maintain the illusion and made the heroic cinematic portrayals of these players more believable.

The glare of an increasingly critical media spotlight renders the manufactured images of heroes in the mold of Babe Ruth and Lou Gehrig less and less plausible. The image of the baseball hero painted in baseball's preferred ideology, and the images of the modern, real-life baseball star painted daily in the press, are simply too divergent to permit contemporary film audiences to accept as credible a modern cinematic portrayal of a "real" player in the mold of Roy Hobbs or even Crash Davis. While the popularity of films about real baseball stars in the 1940s and 1950s may also be reflective of a greater trend toward biographies in general during that era, we suggest that the dominance of fictionalized heroes in contemporary baseball films, and the complete absence of more contemporary stars, is also in response to the increasing contradiction between the ideology of baseball and the realities of baseball in contemporary America. The shift to fictionalized heroes in contemporary films reflects an attempt to legitimize that ideology in the face of this contradiction. Rather than abandoning an ideology of baseball which is inconsistent with the realities of the sport in contemporary society, however, Hollywood film makers and their audiences have abandoned contemporary athletes, who are inconsistent with the ideology. Given the inability to mesh reality with ideology, modern-day America has chosen to hang on to the ideology. Films such as *The Natural* (1984), *Bull Durham* (1988), *Mr. Baseball* (1992), *Little Big League* (1994) and *Ed* (1996), whose heroes continue to reflect the traditional values and characteristics of the cinematic Lou Gehrig and Babe Ruth of the 1950s, permit us to believe that, indeed, the one constant through all the years in America, is the game of baseball and all that it stands for. Contemporary baseball films, like their predecessors, attempt to reconcile the contradiction between the ideology and the reality of baseball, and thus, the contradiction between the ideology and reality of contemporary America itself. The fictionalized heroes of contemporary films permit us, as a culture, to maintain the belief that despite the momentary domination of the game by men whose personalities and actions both on and off the field suggest otherwise, the *game* of baseball continues to embody traditional American values such as honesty, selflessness, humility, teamwork, and devotion to the game. At the same time, these films continue to comfort us with the assurance that these values do, indeed, reflect the true America, and offer audiences longing for a return to these more basic and purer values the hope that such a return is indeed possible.

5

For Love of the Game

"You mean I'm gonna get paid to play baseball?"
— Babe Ruth, *The Babe Ruth Story*

It is a cold winter's day in 1914 when Brother Matthias calls a young George Herman Ruth into his office at the St. Mary's Industrial School for Boys in Baltimore. Brother Matthias introduces the young Babe to Jack Dunn, manager of the Baltimore Orioles, who offers Babe a $600 contract to sign with the Orioles. "You mean I'm gonna get paid to play baseball?" the wide-eyed Babe exclaims. "Yeah," says Dunn, "ain't we the crazy ones?" "$600!" whistles the Babe. "There ain't that much money in the whole world" (*The Babe Ruth Story*, 1948).

One of baseball's most enduring myths is that those who play the game, even professionally, do so for no other reason than a pure love of the game itself. This has also been one of baseball's most challenged myths in recent years, as baseball salaries have escalated to over $20 million a year. In baseball films, however, the real-life contradictions between the game as business and the game as a game disappear. Love of baseball is the only motivation, and the true baseball player will play whenever and wherever he can.

The true baseball player is driven by something inside, an essential part of his or her being. From the early days of childhood, the heroes of baseball cinema have wanted to do only one thing — play baseball. The opening scene of *The Babe Ruth Story* (1948) for example, shows the young Ruth playing ball in the streets of Baltimore. When he is chased back to his saloon-home by an irate businessman whose window he has just broken, his father threatens him with a return to the orphanage in which he has

100

William Frawley as Jack Dunn (right) and William Bendix as Babe Ruth in *The Babe Ruth Story* (Allied Artists, 1948).

already done time, if he doesn't learn to behave. Fortuitously, Father Matthias, from the orphanage, appears at that moment to see how the young Ruth is doing. When he learns that he would have the opportunity to again play baseball back at the orphange, the young George Ruth literally pleads with Father Mathias to take him back then and there.

The opening scene in *Pride of the Yankees* (1942) shows Lou Gehrig as a boy attempting to buy his way into a sandlot baseball game with his meager collection of baseball cards. Later in the film, Gehrig will tell his mother that he is a ballplayer, and no one can make anything else out of him. We are told in the opening narration of *The Jackie Robinson Story* (1950) that, like all boys, the young Jackie Robinson looked forward to spending his summers playing baseball. And for young Benny Martinez (*The Sandlot*, 1993), who goes on to a career with the Los Angeles Dodgers, baseball, as we are told in the film, "is his life."

But it is not just as children that baseball players can think of nothing other than finding a game. In *The Winning Team* (1952), a young Grover

Cleveland Alexander decides at the last minute to go pitch in a local semi-pro game, forgetting about his promise to meet his fiancée, Aimee, and future father-in-law at the farm he and Aimee hoped to buy. Aimee's father had intended to surprise the couple with the down-payment on the farm as a wedding gift, but withdraws the offer after being stood up. He further tries to convince Aimee to dump the irresponsible Alex, saying Alexander doesn't want to do anything but play games all his life. Like the young Grover Alexander, Monty Stratton (*The Stratton Story*, 1949) also was clearly meant to be a ballplayer and not a farmer, regularly walking several miles to pitch for a local team, and then the several miles home again to do the chores.

The conflict between the baseball player's drive to do what she or he was meant to be and the expectations by others that the ballplayer pursue more "responsible" pursuits is a theme central to a number of baseball films. Grover Cleveland Alexander (*The Winning Team*, 1952) and Monty Stratton (*The Stratton Story*, 1949) are expected to become farmers. Adam Polachuk (*The Big Leaguer*, 1953) is expected by his father to become a lawyer. In fact, Adam deceives his father, who thinks his son is at law school, when he is actually at the New York Giants' spring tryout camp. The idea that the drive to play baseball is natural and inborn is perhaps most succinctly expressed in *The Pride of the Yankees* (1942), when Lou Gehrig explains to his mother, who had envisioned her son as an engineer and not a ballplayer, "Mom, people have to live their own lives, nobody can live it for you ... nobody can make anything but a ballplayer out of me." Fifty years later, manager Jimmy Dugan tells catcher Dottie Henson, who has decided to leave the team just before the AAGPBL World Series to go home to Oregon with her husband, who has just returned wounded from the war, "Baseball is what gets inside you. It's what lights you up. You can't deny that" (*A League of Their Own*, 1992). Henson proves him correct, by returning for the seventh and final game against the Racine Belles.

The cinematic baseball hero's deep devotion to baseball is just as persistent, even at the end of his or her career. In *Bull Durham* (1988), Crash Davis' initial reaction to his demotion to the Class A Bulls, so he can help tutor rookie pitcher Nuke LaLoosh in both baseball and life in general, is to storm out of the manager's office, proclaiming in a flurry of expletives his intention to quit. But, he returns seconds later to ask, "Who do we play tomorrow?" Soon after the Bulls release him near the end of the season, Crash is on the road to another minor league city, chasing a possible opportunity to catch on with another club. As his lover, Annie Savoy, puts it, "You have to respect a ballplayer who's just trying to finish the season." Davis' devotion to the game is further emphasized through his lack of patience with those who do not share his reverence for baseball. When he is asked by Nuke why he does not like him, Crash replies, "Because you don't respect yourself, which is your problem. But you don't respect the game, and that's my problem."

The true rewards of the game, at least according to the official ideology of baseball, are not monetary, but rather the fulfillment of pursuing one's true passion. Indeed, the issue of money is made to seem almost irrelevant in these films. An example is the scene described at the beginning of this chapter, in which an awestruck Babe Ruth, when offered $600 a season to play in the minors, gasps, "You mean, I'm gonna get paid to play baseball?" (*The Babe Ruth Story*, 1948). In *The Natural* (1984), Roy Hobbs responds to the team owner's offer of a new contract with the comment, "If you want to pay me more money, that's up to you." Lou Gehrig (*The Pride of the Yankees*, 1942) signs his initial player contract with the Yankees without bothering to read it. Although his decision to leave engineering school and sign with the Yankees is presumably promoted by his desire to help pay for his mother's hospital expenses, it is clear that Gehrig is little concerned with how much he will actually be paid. And, in *Field of Dreams* (1989), the returned spirit of Shoeless Joe Jackson, banned from baseball for life as a member of the 1919 Chicago "Black Sox," tells Ray Kinsella, "Man, I did love this game. I'd have played for food money. It was a game. The sounds, the smells ... I'd have played for nothing." This juxtapositioning of a pure devotion to the game against individual material interest is even further accentuated in the portrayals of gambling, and of baseball's ownership, which we address in the following chapters.

Even when abused by the corporate interests of baseball, the cinematic baseball hero never abandons his devotion to the game. Although the New York Knights' corrupt majority owner attempts to have him bribed, poisoned, seduced and blackmailed, Roy Hobbs refuses to quit before the crucial playoff game with the utterance, "God, I love baseball" (*The Natural*, 1984). And when Babe Ruth is callously fired from his position as club vicepresident by the Boston Braves when he decides to retire as a player, a young teammate suggests he file a lawsuit. Babe replies incredulously, "Sue baseball? Why, that would be like suin' the church" (*The Babe Ruth Story*, 1948).

The most striking portrayal of players who play not for love of the game, but for the money, is *Eight Men Out* (1988), the story of the 1919 Black Sox scandal, in which self-interest and materialism lead to tragedy for all. What sets this film apart from other contemporary baseball films is the unbridled greed and the absence of devotion to the game evidenced by the players. The consequences are nothing short of tragic. In failing to adhere to baseball's moral code, these players not only fail to overcome their wealthy, exploitative owner, Charles Comiskey; their greed destroys their own careers, diminishes their lives, and threatens the national pastime.

In more recent films, in response, no doubt, to the controversies over modern player salaries, the theme of playing the game for love rather than money is developed through an even more explicit juxtapositioning of the two values. In *Major League II* (1994), the heroic figures of the miraculous season in the original *Major League* (1989) have, during the off-season, all signed million dollar contracts, and become caught up in their own success. Star pitcher Rick Vauhgn has abandoned his motorcycle, leather jackets, and punk hair style for a limousine and business suits—and lost his fastball. Speedster Wille Mays Hayes has starred in a movie, taken to wearing gold chains, and doesn't want to play, because of a sore leg resulting from stunts for his movie. No one is having fun, the team is losing, and the stands are empty; until, following an on-field brawl amongst themselves in the first game of a double header — precipitated by a clash between Vaughn and Hayes—the Indians are lectured by their new catcher, Rube. "I love to play baseball," he tells them. "And I'll bet, somewhere along the line, you all did too" Even though he can barely walk, a result of being hit in the foot by a pitch in the first game, Rube tells acting manager Jake Taylor to put him in the lineup for the second game. "A day of playing ball is better than whatever most people have to do for a living."

Although greeted with cynical groans and grimaces from most of the players, Rube's speech is, in fact, the turning point for the Indians. In the bottom of the ninth in the second game, Rube hits a single and hobbles to first base, barely making it with a head-first slide. Willie Mays Hayes, who has spent much of the season on the bench nursing his sore leg, takes off his gold chains and hands them to interim manager Jake Taylor, symbolically giving up the superficial adornments, and his obsession with image and money, to return to the game, purified and committed. He immediately steals second, third and home to score the tying run, revitalizing the entire team. Following this, slugger Pedro Cerrano, whose new devotion to Buddhism has, until now, replaced his devotion to baseball, rekindles his spirit for the game, and hits the game winning home run. The Indians finally begin playing as a team, having fun, and focusing on the game itself. Once they abandon their concerns with the tangential aspects of the game, most notably the obsessions with status and money, they are able to once again "love playing baseball," and, once again, succeed. In an especially interesting twist, in the final game of the championship playoffs against the New York Yankees, reliever Rick Vaughn abandons the clean-cut corporate image he has maintained throughout the film, and returns to his true, essential being as the "wild thing," just in time to get the crucial final strike-out, and win the American League Championship for the Indians.

While the conflict between the values of greed and love of the game has not been as central to the plot lines of baseball films since *Major League II*, it has become somewhat of a standard feature; an ongoing undercurrent helping to define the desired values and characteristics of the true baseball hero. In *Summer Catch* (2000), for example, the egocentric Eric Van Leemer, who is obsessed with the size of his anticipated signing bonus, is contrasted with the humbler, working-class star of the film, Ryan Dunne, who plays the game simply for the love of it. The tension between these values is presented much more subtly in *For Love of the Game* (1999), when Billy Chapel chides his friend and former teammate Davis Burch for leaving the Detroit Tigers for free agency and the New York Yankees. "It's your team, too," Chapel tells Burch. "How much money we gotta make?" In *Hardball* (2001), the seemingly outlandish contract provisions of modern-day major leaguers is satirized when Kofi, the team's shortstop who left the team after being yelled at by his coach for fighting with a teammate, says he will come back to the team if his contract demands, which include a free pizza if he hits a ball over the gate in the outfield fence, are met. Contemporary films thus continue to reflect an awareness of the fiscal realities of the modern game, while at the same time letting viewers know this is not the way of the true baseball hero.

In their history of American sports, Gorn and Goldstein (1993) chronicle the rise of "the amateur ideal" in the late 1800s. "The amateur ideal," they write, "purported to defend sport as a realm of pure competition that money-grubbing professionalism threatened to destroy. True sport was sullied by those who played for pay, because they were not motivated by uncontaminated love of the game" (p. 133). It is this ideal, of course, that is reflected in the "devotion to the game" ethic that is so central to baseball's value system. And, just as in the late 1800s, contemporary controversies over sport reflect the tensions between this ideal and the impetus to use sports as means of material gain. Stylistic differences notwithstanding, the remarks expressed in this letter from a veteran baseball player to a baseball weekly paper, in 1868, could just as well have been written last week:

> Somehow or other they don't play ball nowadays as they used to some eight or ten years ago.... I mean that they don't play with the same kinds of feelings or for the same objects they used to.... But it's no use talking like a father to you fellows, you're in for "biz" now, and have forgotten the time when your club's name stood higher as a fair and square club than it does now" [Gorn and Goldstein, 1993, p. 223].

Baseball films consistently adhere to the amateur ideal. Clearly, the players in these cinematic visions of the game are professionals; they do get paid, and often plenty, for what they do. But, in baseball films, at least, we are allowed to believe that true baseball heroes do what they do—play the game — simply out of love for the game itself. The money, we are told, really doesn't matter. And, when it does matter, the fabric of the baseball community itself is threatened.

As Riess (1980), Betts (1974), Jhally (1984) and other historians and social theorists have observed, the lessons of baseball were intended not simply to teach one how to play the game, but also how to live within an urban, industrialized American culture. The "true" baseball hero is an ideal citizen, as well. One of the critical functions of baseball's ideology, as it was constructed during the early years of the 20th century, was to temper the increasing individualism in American culture which accompanied the processes of industrialization and urbanization, and to locate that individualism within the context of the larger community. It is in the interests of protection of the larger community that "devotion to the game" has been elevated to commandment status in baseball's ideology. Greed — playing the game motivated primarily by the pursuit of wealth — is viewed through baseball's ideological lens as essentially a selfish impulse, incompatible with the ideals of team and community. The individual who plays the game out of love, rather than in hopes of furthering his or her own individual financial interests, is more likely to be willing to sacrifice his or her own interests for the greater good of the team/community. Additionally, the individual who plays out of devotion to the game, rather than devotion to self, is presumed to be less susceptible to corruption from gamblers or other sources of evil that might threaten the integrity, and financial stability, of the game. In baseball's cultural vision, the dangers are clear; when players become concerned about money, when they become motivated by their own financial self-interest, they tend to place those interests above those of the larger community. The result is not simply a violation of the integrity of the game at the individual level, but a breakdown of the harmony of that larger community. This is why the incompatibility of baseball and greed is such an enduring theme in baseball cinema, and why the moral imperative so consistent. The true baseball hero plays for the joy of playing and has little interest in the monetary rewards baseball might have to offer.

There is a second significant ideological function served by this emphasis on "playing the game for its own sake," in these films, however. Playing simply for love of the game, rather than for any material rewards, provides a justification for continuing to "play the game" even when success is not guaranteed. In his analysis of the similarity between the ideological values of the workplace and those of baseball, Gelber (1983) cites Max Weber's definition of the capitalist work ethic as labor "performed as if it were an end in itself, a calling" (Weber, 1958, p. 62). Like baseball players, those workers who are motivated by this work ethic value the process of work itself more than the reward (Gelber, 1983). They, too, "play the game for its own sake." Gelber argues that the promotion of such a work ethic serves to legitimize and protect an economic system in which success is not guaranteed, no matter how hard one works. Given the increased likelihood of failure in a complex economy, an ethic emphasizing work for its own sake, rather than the financial rewards it offers, functions to "buffer psyches against the shocks of an increasingly volatile marketplace. When work was its own reward, failure was less important" (Gelber, 1983, p. 11). From this perspective, the value of "devotion to the game," playing the game for its own sake, can be viewed as providing a rationalization for continuing to work within an economic system which is neither necessarily fair nor democratic in terms of its rewards, thus ameliorating the incentive to challenge dominant interests within that economic system.

> *"Maybe the problem is you guys forgot how much fun this is ...*
> *You guys get to play baseball every day ... From now on, let's stop*
> *worrying about winning and losing. Just go out and play and*
> *have fun."*
> — Billy Heywood, *Little*
> *Big League*, 1994

As we noted in Chapter 4, baseball films have always emphasized the importance of hard work. Lou Gehrig, the "iron-man of baseball," epitomized this ethic with his constant hard work, and philosophy that "you can never try too hard" (*Pride of the Yankees*, 1942). Babe Ruth revived his career by buckling down, getting back in shape, and focusing on the game of baseball, rather than on his nightlife (*The Babe Ruth Story*, 1948). Christy Cooper, the "kid from left field," stayed up well past his bedtime, developing strategies for the next day's game (*The Kid from Left Field*, 1953). And big-leaguer wannabes at the New York Giants' tryout camp were advised to "give it all you've got," whether 4 runs ahead or 10 runs behind (*The Big Leaguer*, 1953). *Mr. Baseball*'s (1992) Jack Elliot revived his sagging career by lifting weights and running wind sprints up and down the stadium steps. More recent baseball films, however, have tended to emphasize a somewhat different dimension of baseball's ideological vision — the idea that the game should be fun. While it was always clear that Lou Gehrig (*Pride of the Yankees*, 1942), Babe Ruth (*The Babe Ruth Story*, 1948), Monty Stratton (*The Stratton Story*, 1949) and Grover Cleveland Alexander (*The Pride of St. Louis*, 1952) all truly loved playing the game of baseball, the idea that baseball should be fun received explicit attention in the 1980s and 90s, emerging as a central theme in a number of films. Even Jack Elliot (*Mr. Baseball*, 1992), who had to re-learn the value of hard work, also realized that baseball was still supposed to be fun. Indeed, while it is his manager's re-instilling of the work ethic in Elliot that helps salvage Elliot's career, it is Elliot's teaching his manager, Uchiyama, that he needs to lighten up and let his players have some fun, that helps the manager succeed as well. When Uchiyama learns to not be so strict and to allow his players to enjoy the game, the team begins to play better. Together, Elliot's hard work and Uchiyama's willingness to allow his players to have some fun produce the championship-winning success of the Dragons. And, while Lou Gehrig proclaimed that "you can never try too hard" (*The Pride of the Yankees*, 1942), the lesson that young pitcher Jack Cooper (*Ed*, 1996) learns, along with he understanding that there are more important things in life than baseball, is precisely the opposite; yes, you can try too hard.

As Cooper leaves the family farm for a tryout with the Santa Rosa Rockets, he asks his dad if he has any advice. His dad tells him, "Work hard," to which Jack responds, "Aw, dad!" Dad smiles, and says, "Have fun." "It's baseball," Jack tells him. "How can I not have fun?" Despite this theoretical commitment to the joy of baseball, however, Jack proceeds to have anything but fun. After being signed by the Rockets, Cooper begins to struggle. His control is lousy; he hangs his curve ball. Driven by the desire to succeed, Jack dedicates himself to nothing but baseball — even spending his time away from the park reading books on pitching by Nolan Ryan, and throwing baseballs through a tire outside his apartment. When Liz, Jack's neighbor, asks him why he hasn't asked her mom out, yet, Jack tells her playing baseball is like doing homework. "There's stuff you have to do before you can have fun." Liz tells him his "priorities suck," but Jack doesn't listen. In a later scene, the day after the team has been out drinking, toasting those who didn't make the cut, their manager, Chubb, tells his seriously hung-over ball players to forget practice, and go home and sleep it off. Cooper, however, heads out to the mound anyway, telling Chubb he needs the work. Chubb tells him to lighten up and to take the day off and have some fun. Cooper finally takes this advice, goes home and begins a romance with Liz's mom. It is at this point that his career finally begins to turn around.

In *Ed* (1996), Jack Cooper's problem was that he was taking the game itself too seriously; he was working too hard to succeed. It was only when he realized that, as his manager told him, it's only a game, and that he needed to allow himself to have fun both on the field and off, that he achieved the balance in his life that allowed him to finally succeed. In this sense, the lesson Jack Cooper learns is similar to that learned by earlier cinematic baseball heroes, such as Monty Stratton (*The Stratton Story*, 1949) and Dizzy Dean (*The Pride of St. Louis*, 1952). What separates *Ed* from these earlier films is the explicit critique of working too hard at the game itself. The problems faced by Stratton and Dean were not a result of working too hard to play the game well. Indeed, they both loved playing baseball and were successful from the very beginnings of their careers. Rather, these earlier heroes had to learn what the paradigm example of baseball heroes, Lou Gehrig (*The Pride of the Yankees*, 1942) knew all along: there is more to life than baseball. Jack Cooper (*Ed*, 1996) was forced to confront this philosophical truth as well, but also the New Age insights of the 1990s; all work and no play makes Jack a dull boy, and a mediocre baseball player, at best. A similar lesson is delivered to the young Scotty Smalls, by mentor Benny Martinez (*The Sandlot*, 1993), who instructs the serious young academic to stop thinking so much, and to just have fun.

In *Little Big League* (1994), having more fun is presented as the antidote to the intrusion of materialistic values into the game. When Billy Heywood, who inherited the team from his grandfather, takes over as manager of the Minnesota Twins, the team is struggling, to say the least. They are in last place. The stands are empty. Furthermore, they've just gone from being managed by an abusive jerk, to being managed by a 12 year old kid, who also happens to own the team. There's not much life on the field or in the clubhouse, where players seem more concerned about multi-year contracts than anything else. In short, their attitude is about as negative as it can get. That's when Billy Heywood delivers the speech. The problem with the Minnesota Twins, he tells them, is that they have forgotten how to have fun. But all that is going to change. Win or lose, they are just going to try and have a good time. It works. They try a few trick plays, the players loosen up, and the Minnesota Twins are suddenly pennant contenders. When Heywood re-introduces the concept of fun, the negativity, cynicism, and selfish concern with the material rewards of the game all disappear. The Twins begin playing as a team, and they begin winning. Later in the film, when Heywood forgets his own lessons, and begins taking himself and the game too seriously, becoming precisely the same type of abusive manager he replaced, the Twins once again stop having fun, and stop winning.

Baseball, at least according to its ideologists, is a game of balances between the conflicting values of individualism and teamwork; and of competition and cooperation. It is also, as baseball films of the 1980s and 1990s especially suggest, a balance between hard work and having fun. Within these films it is often the failure to have fun which results in the individual's inability to play well, and the team/community's inability to succeed. Hard work is essential to success, these films tell us. But, so too is the enjoyment of one's work. Like all workers, baseball players are supposed to work hard, but they are also supposed to have a good time doing it. In giving voice to this vision, these films also uphold the notion that pure devotion to the game is the only reason to play baseball. In baseball's cultural vision work provides its own, intrinsic satisfactions and rewards, not simply a paycheck. There is no alienation of labor in this world view. When one ceases to play the game for any other reason than the pure love and enjoyment of it, one fails. And no amount of money, no long-term contract or guarantee of endorsements, can compensate for that failure.

This emphasis on the importance of having fun in more recent films serves as a response to the increasing intrusion of material values into the game; an intrusion which has tarnished the image of purity and innocence associated with the game which baseball's ideologists have long sought to preserve, and in which millions of fans desire to believe. Issues such as the labor strife between owners and players, the escalating costs of attending a baseball game, the multi-million dollar salaries of individual players and the $100 million dollar (and climbing) payrolls offered by owners seeking to buy a pennant, have dominated much of the public discourse about the game in recent years. These conflicts challenge the most fundamental value of baseball's ideology; people play the game solely out of devotion to and love of the game itself, and for no other reason. It is the centrality of this value in baseball's ideology that accounts for the depth of the reaction against both players and owners by fans who increasingly feel the individual financial interests of both parties have diminished the integrity of the game. Increasingly, many have come to feel that a devotion to the game has been replaced by a commitment to individual self-interest. To many Americans, this is a violation of all that the game stands for. In a culture dominated by the values of capital exchange, baseball *films*— if not so much the game itself — offer the vision of a world in which people are driven by other, more pure and more human, motives. Beyond serving to legitimize and reinforce these fundamental values, these films may also function to dramatize the gap between the "true" values of the game and the values which seem to motivate many of today's superstars.

> *"I mean, come on. Let's be real here, you know? What are we doing? We're not curing cancer, you know? We're playing a game. That's all. It's just a game"*
> — Bobby Rayburn, *The Fan*, 1996

At the same time that baseball films teach an ethic of pure and complete devotion to the game, they temper that commitment with a healthy recognition that there are even more important things in life than baseball. Indeed, one of the most common lessons learned by that cinematic baseball hero, who so often proclaims "no one can make anything but a ballplayer out of me," is that there are other aspects of his life and his community that also deserve his attention and commitment.

Most important among those, of course, as noted in Chapter 4, is the love of a devoted wife and family. In *The Pride of St. Louis* (1952), it is only when Dizzy Dean is able to accept the end of his baseball career, and realize that there is meaningful life after baseball, that he is able to quit drinking and pull his life back together. Similarly, Monty Stratton (*The Stratton Story*, 1949), whose short career is ended in a hunting accident, spends a good part of the film sitting around the house feeling sorry for himself — withdrawing from his mother, wife and young son — until he is able to recognize and appreciate that his family has even more to offer him than did the game of baseball. Pirates manager Guffy McGovern comes to this same appreciation when, at the end of the 1951 version of *Angels in the Outfield*, he is shown standing with his new bride and their adopted daughter, proclaiming joyfully, "Look at what I got." Manager Chuck Knox learns a similar lesson in the 1994 remake of *Angels in the Outfield*, as he is transformed from an angry, bitter and failing manager, to a kind, caring, and much softer father figure, who ends up adopting the two foster children in the film. In *Damn Yankees* (1958), Joe Boyd decides to give up his pact with the devil, and his career as a star of the New York Yankees, and return to his life as a middle-aged real estate salesman, realizing that his life with his loving wife is much more fulfilling than any baseball career could ever be. In *For Love of the Game* (1999), Detroit Tigers' superstar Billy Chapel spends the time between innings during the final game of his career coming to the realization that the perfect game he is pitching means little to him without the presence of his lover, Jane Aubrey, in his life forever.

One of the most dramatic expressions of the "it's only a game" theme is the 1996 psycho-thriller, *The Fan*. At the film's open, life is looking good for Bobby Rayburn — a National League MVP, coming home to play for his boyhood idols, the San Francisco Giants, with a $40 million salary. Expectations are high all round. But, things soon begin to unravel for the cocky, arrogant Rayburn. He can't get "his" uniform number 11 from Juan Primo, the Giants' other superstar. He starts the season in a massive slump. The press and fans are getting ugly. In steps superfan Gil. He knows what will get Rayburn back on track — his uniform number. So Gil murders Primo in a sauna, solving the problem. Rayburn gets his number back and, sure enough, begins hitting. But Gil's work is not finished; a little thank you from Bobby would be nice. In a fortuitous opportunity available only to the most dedicated stalker, he finds himself in a position to save Rayburn's young son from drowning in the ocean, at the player's beach house. The grateful Rayburn invites Gil in and offers him a change of clothes. How can he thank the man who saved his son's life? He can let him hang around the house all day. He can give him his old Braves' uniform and a Giants' hat. He can let Gil pitch to him on the beach. He can thank Gil for knocking off Juan Primo, perhaps. Fishing for a bit of recognition on Bobby's part that it was his timely execution of the rival Primo that made the difference, Gil asks Rayburn why he thinks he's suddenly hitting again. Rayburn, unfortunately, does not give the answer Gil seeks. Rayburn says he just stopped caring — caring about being the best, about trying to be a perfectionist.

Primo's death did indeed make a difference. It changed Rayburn's whole perspective. "There's more to life than just baseball," he tells Gil. The agitated Gil presses Rayburn. "Like your house? Like your big-ass car? Like your forty-fucking million?" What does Rayburn care about? Gil wants to know. "I care about my son," Rayburn tells him. "That's what I care about." It is not the answer Gil was looking for. He promptly kidnaps Rayburn's son.

While true love, marriage, and a family are the most common goals portrayed in baseball films as more deserving of the true baseball hero's commitment than the game itself, there are others, as well, which have served to provide a healthy balance to the baseball player's devotion to the game. In the film *Ed* (1996), pitcher Jack Cooper must learn to not only take time for romance and to "smell the roses," but he must also learn that being there for his friends—in this case rescuing the team's chimpanzee mascot and third baseman, Ed—are more important than his own career. In fact, it is only when he does come to these realizations that he begins to achieve real success as a pitcher, and as a human being. He is signed by the Los Angeles Dodgers, and is shown in the final scene driving to L.A. with his new wife, daughter and, of course, Ed.

In *Field of Dreams* (1989), Ray Kinsella goes back in time to the 1970s, to meet Doc "Moonlight" Graham, who had played half an inning for the New York Giants in 1922, in the final game of the season. He then left baseball to become a small-town doctor in Minnesota. While he had only been a major leaguer for five minutes, and never had an at-bat in a major league game, he refused to feel any regrets, telling Kinsella "If I'd only gotten to be a doctor for five minutes, that would have been a tragedy." His contributions to his community as a doctor far outshone anything he might have achieved as a ball player. This greater commitment to serving others as a doctor dominates Graham's life once again, when he is given a second chance at a baseball career on Kinsella's field of dreams. Having been transformed back to his youth to join the other spirits playing ball on Kinsella's magical baseball field, Graham chooses to give up his dream when he steps across the foul line—and becomes an old man once again—in order to save the life of Kinsella's daughter.

Even leading a "normal" life is presented in baseball films as being more important and desirable than the status or rewards of being a baseball hero. In both *Rookie of the Year* (1993) and *Little Big League* (1994), the two children who have been central to their teams' success—Cubs pitcher

Henry Rowengardner and Twins manager Billy Heywood — decide to give up their baseball careers (although Heywood does retain ownership of the Twins), because they simply want to spend time with their friends, doing the things kids normally do.

While the admonition that "it's only a game," might at first glance seem contradictory with baseball ideology's emphasis on devotion to the game, the recognition that there is more to life than baseball serves much the same function as the devotion-to-the-game ideal — subordinating the interests of the individual to the community. While the value of devotion to the game emphasizes the proper motivations for playing the game of baseball, the recognition that baseball is still, in the end, *only* a game locates the individual baseball hero within the even larger community beyond the game of baseball. Emphasizing the importance of family, service to the larger community, even participation in the "normal" socializations of childhood, baseball films reinforce the centrality of community, and selfless devotion to that community, in the life of the ideal baseball hero/citizen. More specifically, recognition that "it's only a game," serves to promote a sense of humility in baseball players, who are often the center of cultural attention, and who are often among the most highly rewarded, in American society. As we noted in Chapter 4 humility, because of its role in tempering excessive individualism and its value in promoting a greater awareness of and commitment to the larger community, is a principle quality of the ideal baseball hero. The oft-repeated mantra "it's only a game" humbly reminds the baseball hero that what he does is, in the larger scheme of things, really not so important after all. Together, devotion to the game, accompanied by the awareness that baseball is still *only* a game, remind us all that both the game itself and the larger community in which it is played are more important than the individual; and it is there, in that larger community, rather than with the self, that one's loyalties should reside.

6

Don't Bet on It

"Are you gonna let a bunch of racketeers and gamblers step in and say America can't have baseball?"
— Pop Clark, *Death on the Diamond*

Members of the St. Louis Cardinals baseball team have been meeting mysterious ends. Shot. Strangled. Poisoned. Someone doesn't want them to win the pennant. And no one has any doubts about who that "someone" is. After all, gamblers will stop at nothing. In baseball's mythology, they are the greatest threat America's national pastime has ever faced.

In Chapter 4 we discussed baseball's moral code, which has been a central theme of baseball films since the 1930s. As we noted then, the idealized baseball hero represented in baseball films adheres to a strong, Puritanical moral code, refraining from such vices as smoking, drinking, and womanizing. In Chapter 5, we examined the ways baseball films have presented another central component of baseball ideology, devotion to the game. In this chapter, we focus on an issue related to both of these concerns which was particularly troublesome for baseball during the late 19th and early part of the 20th century; an issue which has been seen as a threat to baseball's strong moral code, and to the integrity of the game itself. Through the years gambling, more than any other issue, has served as a flash point around which the conflicting values of playing the game for love and playing the game for money have exploded into public consciousness. No issue has been more consistently troublesome to the preservation of baseball's moral order.

Wagering on ball games is considered the most serious transgression a player can commit — the one transgression for which players are banished from the game for life. No offense threatens the economic interests of the

David Landau (far left) as Pop Clark in *Death on the Diamond* (MGM, 1934).

game quite like gambling. However, although the issue of gambling is, ultimately, an economic one, threatening the economic stability of the game
and the profit margins of baseball's ownership, it has regularly been defined
by baseball's ideologists as a moral issue. In doing so—in re-casting what
is essentially a financial concern as a moral imperative—the authors of
baseball's cultural vision have authored not only a significant component
of baseball's ideology, but of American cultural ideology, as well. No mass
medium has been a more conscientious ally in baseball's war on gambling
than American film. For more than half a century, baseball films have consistently framed gambling as an absolute evil. Before we explore these cinematic portrayals, however, we provide a brief history of the economic
underpinnings of baseball's war on gambling.

> "Any player, umpire, or club or league official or employee, who shall bet
> any sum whatsoever upon any baseball game in connection with which the
> bettor has a duty to perform shall be permanently ineligible."
> — Rule 21(d)

Gambling *is* baseball's ultimate sin. And baseball's war on gambling has been a long campaign. While for many people the first, and most notable, scandal involving gamblers and baseball occurred in 1919, when several members of the Chicago White Sox threw the World Series against the Cincinnati Reds, the struggle between professional baseball and gambling is almost as old as the game itself. As early as 1867, for example, *Harper's Weekly* told readers that baseball betting was common practice and warned that even "the most respectable clubs" not only participated in the wagering but also in the fixing of the outcome of games "for the benefit of gamblers" ("The Base-ball Championship," 1867, p. 685). Suspicions and allegations about gambling and corruption in baseball were heard with increasing frequency in the 1870s, when there were even predictions that gambling would lead to the game's demise (Seymour, 1990). Gambling and the fixing of games were already fixtures in professional baseball (Voigt, 1983), and in 1875 baseball writer Henry Chadwick called for reform — including the banishment of dishonest players — as a sound business remedy for declining attendance.

Concern over the economic future of the game motivated professional baseball's all-out war on gambling. In 1876, baseball's National League was formed, dedicated to bringing a more businesslike approach to the game. Among their strategies to attract more paying spectators, owners and league officials sought to present the game in a fashion more consistent with middle-class values. Affecting a high moral posture, the National League no longer scheduled games on Sundays and banned betting in league ball parks. And, the league took a hard stand on players who sold their services to gamblers, expelling from major league baseball for life four players on the Louisville Grays club who were accused of throwing games and intentionally losing the 1877 pennant race in return for a share of a New York gambler's winnings. The 1877 scandal spurred National League officials to undertake even more substantive actions to control the game, restore credibility, and to protect their business interests. The league owners placed new strictures on player behavior and agreed that all clubs in the league would respect the blacklisting of players found guilty of collusion with gamblers (thus giving teeth to the penalty of lifetime banishment).

During the next two decades — the so-called Golden Age of baseball — the game gained greater respectability, popularity, and prosperity. Baseball clubs, sensitive to criticism from moralists and more eager than ever to present the game as a wholesome and honest diversion, adopted strict codes of conduct for players and worked to construct an image of the game which would appeal to middle class audiences. Journalists and sports writers of the time, seeking to build the game's appeal as a means of furthering their own professional interests, similarly promoted baseball as a wholesome amusement for the American middle and working classes (Riess, 1980). Professional baseball players began to take on heroic status, due to both growing public interest in the competition and sports writers' idolizing accounts of player heroics (Voigt, 1983). And while fan betting on baseball continued during the Golden Age — especially by means of the increasingly popular betting "pools" — the game itself managed to avoid any serious taint from gambling and scandal. As a result, baseball's stature as the national pastime — pure, pastoral, untouched by base motivations — had become firmly cemented in the American consciousness by the turn of the century. William Howard Taft called baseball "a clean, straight game" and Theodore Roosevelt admired what he called the "rugged honesty" of professional ball players (Seymour, 1971, p. 274). Baseball officials and their publicists cultivated this image, taking every available opportunity to remind the public just how pure and uncorrupted the game was.

Despite the game's popular image, however, gambling and gamblers were common fixtures in professional baseball during this time. Gamblers frequented ball parks and players' hotels. Many baseball insiders were aware regular season games were being "sold" for the benefit of gamblers who often boasted openly of fixing games (Dickey, 1980). Rumors of bribery and corruption, even in World Series play, were frequent (Voigt, 1970) and some of the game's most prominent figures were implicated (Dickey, 1980; Seymour, 1971). While publicly deploring the evils of gambling, denying the rumors of wagering in baseball, and insisting that the game was utterly clean and straight, ownership pursued a "policy of concealment" (Seymour, 1971, p. 283), intentionally ignoring or suppressing evidence of corruption and misconduct. Baseball officials demonstrated little interest in aggressively pursuing the eradication of gambling and game fixing.

Baseball leadership's lack of enthusiasm for purging gambling might be explained by their own involvement in it. Baseball's management enjoyed wagering on a variety of sports, including their own. Several owners, including Jacob Ruppert of the Yankees and Charles Stoneham of the Giants, owned and bet on thoroughbred racehorses (Riess, 1980). Stoneham and Giants manager John McGraw were gambling partners of the notorious Arnold Rothstein, the racketeer who engineered the game's worst gambling scandal; American League president Ban Johnson bet on baseball with Reds' president Garry Herrmann; Cubs president Charles Weegham laid down thousands of dollars in baseball wagers, sometimes with professional gamblers (Seymour, 1971). New York Highlanders (later Yankees) owner Frank Ferrell was a member of the New York gambling syndicate (Riess, 1980).

In 1920, however, a betting scandal broke that even baseball ownership could not conceal. Several members of the Chicago White Sox confessed to conspiring with gamblers to throw the 1919 World Series to the underdog Cincinnati Reds. Amidst tremendous public outcry, and desperate to save their "blighted business" (Seymour, 1971, p. 310), baseball leadership loudly feigned shock and dismay that gamblers had compromised the game and proclaimed the Black Sox scandal an ugly but isolated incident. In addition to the usual tactic of denial, the owners assured the public steps would be taken to separate baseball from gambling and corruption once and for all.

Just as concern over their economic interests promoted owners in the late 1870s to undertake reorganization and launch a public image campaign dedicated to establishing the purity of that game, their fear of the potential economic impact of the Black Sox scandal moved ownership to once again reorganize the game itself, and to renew the ideological work of assuring middle-class America that the game was, in fact, a reflection and embodiment of traditional, moral values. The first step for ownership was to scrap the governing organization of baseball — the National Commission — in favor of a commissioner system headed by a strong leader who could restore public confidence in organized baseball (Seymour, 1971). The owners chose as their symbol of the game's renewed righteousness Federal Judge Kenesaw Mountain Landis. The hiring of a Commissioner of Baseball was but one step in the attempt to rebuild the idealized view of baseball as America's national pastime. Along with the new commissioner came increased efforts to rebuild the game's image as a reflection of traditional American values. It is a process that has continued through modern times, the most notable recent example being the lifetime suspension from baseball of Cincinnati Reds superstar Pete Rose for betting on major league games.

As suggested earlier, a central strategy in this effort to protect the game from gambling and to preserve the game's image has been the redefinition of gambling as a moral issue, rather than an economic issue. While the ongoing attempts to eliminate gambling from baseball, as well as the effort to construct an image of the game as pure and untainted by undesirable influences, were motivated by concerns over the economic future of the business of baseball, baseball's war on gambling has, since the 1870s, been defined not as a campaign dedicated to protecting the economic interests of its wealthy ownership, but rather as an effort to preserve the basic moral values of American culture.

Reflective of that general strategy, baseball films have regularly portrayed gambling as a moral transgression, rather than as an economic concern. They have accomplished this through the development of two principal themes. First, consistent with baseball's idealized image of those who play the game, these films define the ideal baseball hero in moral terms, as someone who is free from such vices as smoking, drinking, womanizing — and gambling. The true baseball hero, in contrast to lesser beings, these films exclaim, would never consider selling himself or the game to gamblers. Second, these films associate gambling with a wide range of other, more serious evils. The descent into moral turpitude never stops just at gambling in baseball films. This transgression almost always leads to a host of other, even more problematic and threatening behaviors.

> "I wouldn't throw a game if my mother was playing
> on the other team."
> — Ike Farrell, *Alibi Ike*, 1935

The true baseball hero, as characterized by baseball's ideology, is the embodiment of moral virtue, free from all vices— including gambling (Riess, 1980). In cinematic images of the game, the true baseball hero is defined, in no uncertain terms, as one who resists without hesitation the advances of gamblers. And the response of baseball heroes who are approached by gamblers has been consistent throughout the years. In *Elmer the Great* (1933) star hitter Elmer Kane, offended by the suggestion that he throw the World Series, starts a fight with the crooked gamblers who made the offer. Fifteen years later in *The Babe Ruth Story* (1948), when gamblers approach a despondent Babe with a lucrative invitation to have a bad game, the great Bambino similarly responds by punching them out. The equally mythic, although fictional, Roy Hobbs (*The Natural*, 1984) serves as a more recent example of such moral virtue when, even at the risk of his own life, he first refuses the monetary inducements, and later ignores the threats to his life, from gamblers seeking to keep him out of a crucial playoff game for the National League pennant.

While Ruth and Hobbs serve as the idealized examples of moral virtue — true heroes who would never even consider responding to the advances of gamblers— this normative characteristic of the baseball hero is also developed through cinematic portrayals of more negative examples as well; players who do respond, or are suspected of responding, to the overtures of professional gamblers. In several early films (*Elmer the Great*, 1933; *Death on the Diamond*, 1932; *Alibi Ike*, 1935) there are portrayals of players who are thought to have sold out to gamblers. The suspected players are quickly denounced and ostracized by management and their fellow players, and are able to regain the respect of their teammates only when they finally prove their innocence — usually by single-handedly winning the crucial game and thus thwarting the gamblers' interests. Elmer Kane (*Elmer the Great*, 1933) and Frank Ferrell (*Alibi Ike*, 1935) are threatened with the end of their baseball careers, and even jail in the latter film, when their managers mistakenly suspect them of selling their services to gamblers. Both, however, prove their innocence and go on to win the championships for their respective teams. Larry Kelly (*Death on the Diamond*, 1932) is nearly lynched by his teammates when they see him picking up a $10,000 attempted payoff from gamblers. Kelly goes out the following day and pitches a no-hitter, providing, in the words of his manager, "the best kind of an answer to a lot of crooked gamblers."

It was not until 1987 that a baseball film finally portrayed what has been an undeniable fact of life in baseball's history — the player who actually sells his services to gamblers seeking to fix the outcome of games. Prior to *Eight Men Out* (1988), baseball cinema had faithfully conformed to the idealized image of the baseball hero. While *The Natural* (1984) made brief reference to players on the take, *Eight Men Out* (1988) is the first baseball film to directly focus on baseball's greatest sin, and the game's greatest scandal. Not surprisingly, it does so in a way that serves to reaffirm the idealized characteristics of the true baseball hero, while at the same time prioritizing moral virtue over economic considerations. In an early scene in the film, when the gamblers are going through the White Sox line-up to identify possible targets for bribery, they quickly dismiss third baseman Bucky Weaver and catcher Ray Shalk, both of whom "hate to lose too much." Genuine baseball heroes, these players put the game above all else, including the opportunity to get rich quick.

At the same time, the film seems to redeem some of the players who did sell out, such as pitcher Eddie Cicotte, by suggesting that they were driven by financial desperation as a result of the refusal of miserly owner Charlie Comiskey to keep his promises of financial bonuses, or to even pay a living wage to his players. This cinematic redemption of the game's most famous transgressors is carried even further in *Field of Dreams* (1989). In a remarkable attempt to salvage the heroic persona of "Shoeless" Joe Jackson, the greatest talent among the 1919 Black Sox players, the film returns the ghost of Jackson to baseball in the fashion of the true baseball hero. Born again on a contemporary ballfield carved from a stand of Iowa corn, Jackson (along with his banished teammates) plays ethereal innings of baseball for the sheer love of the game. "I'da played for nothin,'" says Jackson.

Such a portrayal reflects the long-standing image of the cinematic baseball hero as one who plays the game not for money, but simply for the love of the game itself. As noted in Chapter 5, in a number of baseball films the hero is portrayed as not caring at all about what he is, or is not, getting paid. *Eight Men Out* (1988) makes clear that it is when players do become motivated by economic concerns, that they and the game become vulnerable to the corruption of professional gamblers. This is an interesting ideological twist, which serves to ground the resistance to gambling in the moral character of the hero rather than the economic concerns of the owners, which have been the real motivation behind baseball's attack on gambling. At the same time, it also serves to further reinforce the idealized image of the true baseball hero as someone who is not concerned at all with what he is paid, but who plays the game only out of a commitment to the game itself.

In a more recent variation on baseball's anti-gambling theme, the 2001 film *Hardball* tells the story of Connor O'Neal, a small-time gambler who, in order to try to pay off his gambling debts before he has his thumbs broken, accepts an offer to coach an inner-city little-league team for $500 a week. While O'Neal bets only on basketball games in the film, the consequences are just as tragic as for those cinematic heroes in other films who have bet on the national pastime. Gambling is controlling, and ruining, O'Neal's life. During the course of the film, just like the heroes of earlier baseball films, O'Neal undergoes the moral transformation which enables him to recognize and appreciate those things that truly matter in life, and quits gambling.

Whether it be through the idealized portrayal of the true baseball hero in the mold of Babe Ruth and Roy Hobbs, or through the moral condemnation of those even suspected of being guilty of baseball's greatest sin, baseball films construct an image of the baseball hero as someone who reflects the highest moral virtue, who abstains from all moral vices, including gambling, and, of course, who would never even consider selling himself or the game to gamblers. In the end, these films suggest, it is a question of character and moral virtue, not economics. And real baseball heroes don't gamble.

> *"I don't like to be disappointed."*
> — Gus Sands, *The Natural*, 1984

The second central strategy in cinematic definitions of gambling as the ultimate moral transgression against the game is the linkage of gamblers with a range of other evils. The characterizations of gamblers in baseball films are not subtle. It is not enough to simply show the gambler as one who wagers on and awaits the outcome of an honest game of baseball, since many fans probably do the same thing. Without exception, every gambler portrayed in baseball films attempts to fix a baseball game. In other words, there is no such thing as simple, honest wagering on baseball games. And, to dramatize the magnitude of the sin, the games to be fixed are usually important, even championship, contests. But, lest the moral message still be too subtle, game-fixing is only the beginning. Gambling itself is always associated with other, more serious legal and moral transgressions, as well. Indeed, gamblers in baseball films are portrayed as the embodiment of evil — all kinds of evil.

In 1984's *The Natural*, that evil takes the form of Gus Sands. In one scene, a few of the New York Knights and friends have gathered to celebrate the Knights' victory on the last day of the season, which tied them for first place, and put them into a one-game playoff the next day for the pennant. Gambler Gus Sands casually approaches Knights star slugger Roy Hobbs at the hors d'ouevres table for some casual small talk. He expresses his genuine concern for Roy — his low salary, what a shame it would be to lose a beautiful woman like Memo Paris to a better provider, things like that. Roy is not concerned about any of that, however. He has turned his life, and his game, around. And, he intends to win the pennant. As he tells Gus Sands, "Tomorrow, I wouldn't bet against me." Unfortunately, Roy has missed the point of the whole conversation. For, as Sands tells him, "I already have." After a rather awkward parting, Sands approaches Memo Paris. He doesn't have to say much. "I misjudged your boy," he tells her. "I don't like to be disappointed." There is a brief nod — a final, murmured "um hmm" in her direction. Paris knows what to do. For though her heart belongs to Roy Hobbs, her soul, and everything else she owns, belong to Gus Sands. She goes and gets a special treat for Hobbs. One intended to keep him out of tomorrow's game.

Gus Sands' attempts to ruin the New York Knights pennant-deciding playoff game through bribery, blackmail, seduction and poisoning are far from unusual in the cinematic war on gambling. Threats of violence and mayhem are common fare. In two early films (*Elmer the Great*, 1933; *Alibi Ike*, 1935), the leading character in each is portrayed as a naive country-boy who is entrapped by gamblers in the city. In *Elmer the Great* (1933), star hitter Elmer Kane goes to a speakeasy with a teammate to drown his sorrows in soda, after an argument with his hometown girlfriend. Elmer begins playing dice, and losing. Thinking that he is playing only for poker chips and not real money, Elmer continues to get more chips, and continues to lose. At the end of the evening, the crooked gamblers who run the casino present Elmer with a $5,000 tab, and tell him he can pay it off by losing the World Series. Kane does what any true baseball hero would — he tries to punch the gamblers out. In *Alibi Ike* (1935), pitcher Frank Farrell is lured to a hotel room full of gamblers by a crook who tells Farrell he wants him to come speak to a Young Men's High Ideals Club. Once there, Farrell is propositioned, and threatened, by the gamblers.

If the offer of bribes or simple entrapment does not work, however, gamblers— at least in baseball films— have no hesitation to resort to more serious means to achieve their ends. In *Death on the Diamond* (1932), it is suggested that gamblers are killing members of the St. Louis Cardinals to keep them from winning the pennant. Although, in a bizarre twist at the end of the film, the gamblers turn out to be innocent of the murders, the message throughout the film is clear — gamblers are certainly *capable* of resorting to murder to serve their own interests. In *Alibi Ike* (1935), once the naive Frank Farrell finally grasps what is going on, and refuses to go along, he is threatened, and later kidnapped by the gamblers, in an attempt to keep him out of the World Series. In the 1949 film *Take Me Out to the Ballgame*, gamblers resort again to deceit, hiring Wolves' star Eddie O'Brien for a theater production, which keeps him up late at night for rehearsals, thus draining his energy and abilities as a ball player. And in *Eight Men Out* (1988), the gamblers who engineered the fix of the 1919 World Series are able to ensure the continued participation of pitcher Lefty Williams only by threatening to kill his wife if he fails to live up to his agreement to throw the 9th game of the World Series. The World Series is also on the line in

Rhubarb (1951), as desperate gamblers try to kill the Brooklyn Loons' lucky cat

As evidenced by the various means of terror at their disposal, the gamblers presented in these films are not loners or small-time operators. They are usually portrayed as gangsters, professional criminals, or crime bosses who only a person of great fortitude — like a baseball hero—could stand up to. Stillman of *Elmer the Great* (1933) runs a large casino operation. Joseph "Con" McAvoy is described as "one of the biggest gamblers in the country" in *Death on the Diamond* (1932) and sits in council with a nationwide gaming syndicate. In *Alibi Ike* (1935), the gambler Crawford heads a large gang of thugs. Arnold Rothstein is accurately portrayed in *Eight Men Out* (1988) as a racketeer of enormous wealth and influence. And there clearly are no limits to what gamblers in these films will resort to in their attempts to corrupt baseball and the men who play it. The message of baseball films is unambiguous. Gambling is always accompanied by other serious threats to the moral order, and is on the same moral plane as assault, extortion, bribery, and animal cruelty.

As observed in our discussions of baseball's moral code in Chapter 4, the moral values embraced within baseball's ideology in the early years of the 20th century reflected the needs and interests of a corporate/industrial economy. The purpose of these values was to help create a disciplined workforce, suited to the structure and rhythms of industrial life, and which would not pose a threat to the emerging economic and social order. What were then presented, and continue to be presented today, as universal moral values were in reality values and behavioral norms which expressed the economic interests of a particular economic/political class. So too, the definition of gambling as a violation of baseball's moral code served to protect the economic interests of baseball owners.

Most obviously, it protected those owners whose financial share for winning the pennant and getting into the World Series, and perhaps their winner's share from the Series itself, might be threatened by players throwing games in return for payments from gamblers, as was the case with the Chicago White Sox in the 1919 World Series. And, owners also faced a tremendous loss of revenue from fans who would likely stop attending games if they believed those games were fixed. The ongoing war on gambling has served to assure fans the games they play to see are honest contests.

The motivations for baseball's war on gambling go much further than these two immediate concerns, however. As Riess (1980) observes, the image — indeed, the very justification of the game of baseball constructed during the early 20th century — was built around a moral code intended to appeal to middle-class audiences. As noted in Chapter 1, baseball's Puritan ideology has, since the early 1900s, presented the national pastime as an embodiment of the basic, rural values upon which the nation was presumably founded. Particularly stressed in baseball's ideology is the moral virtue of the baseball hero who, we are told, is a hard worker, a devoted husband and family man, and does not smoke, drink, or gamble.

It is this broader ideological function of baseball which serves as perhaps the most compelling reason for baseball's war on gambling. The concern of ownership is not simply that players associating with gamblers may end up fixing games. The more dramatic concern is that the failure of players to adhere to the strict moral code embodied in baseball's ideology may threaten the appeal of the game to middle-class audiences; not simply because those audiences may fear the games are fixed, but because they may come to believe the game no longer reflects their own middle-class, Puritan moral values. Having made the value of the baseball hero as a role model for America's youth a central component of the game's appeal and justification, ownership must work continuously to not only ensure the players themselves abide by that moral code, but to ensure as well that middle-class America believes that players are doing so.

Baseball films have served as an important ally in baseball's war on gambling, articulating, along with baseball owners and journalists, a moral vision which among other things defines gambling as the ultimate transgression against America's national pastime. The existence of this shared cultural vision, however, does not necessarily reflect a conspiratorial collusion amongst these various groups. It would be overly simplistic, and inaccurate, to suggest that sports writers and filmmakers have themselves been directly dominated by the economic interests of team owners. Indeed, each of these groups has had their own economic incentives to uphold baseball's idealized moral vision. Sports writers, notes Riess, "cared about the success of baseball because their own personal careers were wrapped up in it. By promoting baseball they were advancing themselves professionally and helping their papers compete for readers" (1980, p. 17). Similarly, filmmakers have reflected an idealized view of the game and its values because such themes resonate with the middle-class audiences that fill the theaters. Owners, journalists and filmmakers have each had their own interests in promoting baseball's ideology. The result of the convergence of these interests has been a consistent image of the game which has permeated American culture from a range of different sources, including baseball films. In light of the seemingly steady stream of negative publicity associated with contemporary real-life players who violate that code, this ongoing ideological work becomes even more noteworthy. For despite the activities of players in the real world, even the most recent of films have continued to assure us that the game itself continues to embody the Puritan values of its origins; the strong moral code on which the game and the nation, at least according to the official ideology, were founded. And, baseball films continue to define for audiences the ideal baseball hero/citizen of American culture.

7

I Hate This #*%# Song

"I hate this fucking song."
— Rachel Phelps, *Major League*

It is the final game of the season, a one-shot playoff between the Cleveland Indians and the New York Yankees to determine the championship of the American League Eastern Division. The Cleveland Indians have not been in post-season play for over 50 years. The game is tied, in the top of the ninth. The bases are loaded with Yankees. Through the bullpen doors in center field emerges ace reliever Rick Vaughn. The ominous, opening slide of the electric guitar leads into Vaughn's theme song. The stadium explodes. A community of thousands of cheering fans— ecstatic over the possibility of the first championship team in Cleveland in some 50 years— dance and scream along, "Wild Thing, I think I love you." It is an electrifying moment. Cleveland Indians owner Rachel Phelps sits alone, sullen and isolated in her private box. There is little else she can say: "I hate this fucking song."

In the prologue to their analysis of the future of America's national pastime, Jack Sands and Peter Gammons (1993) write, "No one — player, owner, or fan — seems to enjoy the game anymore. The simple confrontation between a pitcher and a batter is today far less significant than confrontations over huge sums of money" (p. 12). The financial controversies of baseball, those confrontations over huge sums of money, have increasingly been at the center of media and public attention in recent decades, often overshadowing the game between the lines. Much has been written of the increasing disgust directed at players and owners by fans, and many, like Sands and Gammons, feel that these controversies, if not resolved, threaten the viability of major league baseball.

Margaret Whitton as Rachel Phelps in *Major League* (Paramount Pictures, 1989).

Whether it be the decision by an owner to try and move the local team to a more lucrative market, or a star player to sign with another team for a higher salary, there has emerged a growing perception amongst the public that players and owners alike no longer care about the fans or the game; just the money. And the reaction by the public against this intrusion of financial concerns into the game has been vehement, for such motivations violate the basic ideals of the game itself. And because, as the national pastime, the game of baseball is thought to embody the ideal values of American culture at large, this violation of the game's fundamental values is perceived not just as a sullying of the game of baseball, but also as a violation of the central values of American culture.

As discussed in Chapter 5, a central value in baseball's ideology is "devotion to the game." Since the 1930s, baseball films have religiously recited the traditional baseball value of devotion to the game for its own sake. In direct opposition to the monetary motivations that often seem to dominate the game in the real world, baseball films, without exception, articulate the view that both players and owners should value the game in and of itself, and that their involvement and activities in the game should be driven by a love of the game — not by any consideration of the possible financial rewards the game might offer. Indeed, it is when financial motivations intervene that the harmony of the idealized baseball community often begins to break down.

In this chapter, we examine the ways baseball films serve to uphold the ideal of "devotion to the game " through their depictions of baseball's owners. For although a number of recent films have reflected in varying degrees on the problem of players who seem more motivated by the financial benefits of their careers than by a pure love of the game (*Eight Men Out*, 1988; *Major League*, 1991; *Little Big League*, 1994; *Major League II*, 1994; *The Fan*, 1996), the intrusion of commercial considerations into the game, and the subsequent damage to the game and the baseball community that result, have been more frequently and more powerfully associated with owners and their functionaries in upper management. Indeed, in three of the films just cited which do include negative portrayals of player greed, *Eight Men Out*, *Major League* and *Major League II*, the evil of these players is far overshadowed by the even greedier and more morally bankrupt owners portrayed in these films. The representations of owners in baseball films give powerful expression to the fundamental value of devotion to the game. They serve as a means of contrasting the "true" baseball person, who reflects a pure, honest commitment to the game itself with the individual who views the game simply as an opportunity to pursue his or her own financial self-interest.

> *"But, Hazel, that was before the bankers took over."*
> — Marianna DeAngelo, *Ladies' Day*, 1943

The most significant distinction drawn between good and evil in cinematic portrayals of baseball owners is the principal motivation that underlies their actions. Consistently, those owners portrayed negatively are seen as being primarily concerned about profit and their own material gain. Occasionally, this single-minded focus on the bottom line has been ridiculed in a humorous way, as in the 1943 farce *Ladies' Day*. In this film, the Sox have been taken over by new owners— a group of bankers. Their interests are represented by a ridiculous character named Updyke who, among other things, instructs the team's manager, Dan Hannigan, to have his team slide less, so that the owners will not have to pay to have uniforms cleaned as frequently. He then sets up a booth for film star Pepita Zorita to sell war bonds during a game — right on top of home plate, so it will be clearly visible. And if all of that's not enough, players' wives no longer get into the games free, but have to pay 25¢ admission. As one of the wives, Marianna DeAngelo, remarks, what can you expect from a bunch of bankers anyway?

For the most part, however, the character and activities of financially driven owners have been portrayed as much more sinister. Owners Sallison Porter (*The Bingo Long Travelling All-Stars and Motor Kings*, 1976), Charles Comiskey (*Eight Men Out*, 1988), and Rachel Phelps (*Major League*, 1989; *Major League II*, 1994) are more typical of the greedy antagonist of baseball films. Rather than the absurdly humorous Updyke of *Ladies' Day*, these are mean, vindictive, selfish individuals who will stop at nothing to further their own financial interests. Humorous or sinister, however, common to all of the negative depictions of owners in baseball films is a central preoccupation with profit and material gain.

In contrast, owners portrayed in a desirable light share the common characteristic of a love for and devotion to the game of baseball itself. These owners seem to have no concern either for their own financial interests, or even the profitability of the teams they own. Owners K.C. Higgins (*Take Me Out to the Ball Game*, 1949), Van Buren (*Damn Yankees*, 1958) and Thomas Heywood (*Little Big League*, 1994) are three typical examples of owners who reflect a love of the game itself and, in contrast to those owners who seem to care about nothing but their own financial gain, express no interest at all in the business or financial aspects of baseball. While those owners focused solely on their own gain are often willing to sacrifice the team's success on the field to serve their own individual financial interests, the idealized owners of baseball films care only about building a winning ball club. Their devotion to the game is perhaps expressed most succinctly by Washington Senators owner Van Buren who, while defending his star player Joe Hardy to the press, proclaims "these newspaper people don't know what it's like to have your heart in the ball club" (*Damn Yankees*, 1958).

Not only are the ideal owners envisioned by baseball films seemingly unconcerned with either their own material gain or the financial success of their teams, in several films they react against the blatant greed and self-interest of those around them. In *Rhubarb* (1951), for example, Thaddeus J. Bannister leaves his entire multi-million dollar estate, including the Brooklyn Loons, to his cat Rhubarb, rather than allowing his selfish daughter, Myra, to inherit it all. In *Rookie of the Year* (1993), when Cubs owner Bob Carson, who is initially portrayed as almost senile, discovers that his greedy nephew Larry Fischer, who has been running the team, tried to sell the Cubs' young pitching phenom Henry Rowengardner to the Yankees for $25 million, he takes back control of the team and relegates Fischer to hawking hot dogs in the stands.

While the contrast between the ideal owner, devoted to the game for its own sake, and those who are motivated by greed and self interest is more often drawn between different films, with the owner in a particular film being portrayed either positively or negatively, there are some films, as the above two examples suggest, in which the values of honest devotion to the game and financial greed are contrasted within different elements of ownership in the same film. In *Rookie of the Year* (1993) and *Ed* (1996), an older owner's benevolence and love of the game of is contrasted with the excessive materialism and greed of a younger family member (nephew and son, respectively) who has assumed control of the team. In *Death on the Diamond* (1934) and *The Natural* (1984), the long-time co-owner/ managers of the St. Louis Cardinals and the New York Knights are threatened with the loss of their teams to their scheming business partners.

In *For Love of the Game* (1999), long-time owner Gary Wheeler sells the Detroit Tiger to a group whom he refers to as "sons-of-bitches," for announcing at the last minute that they want to trade 19- year veteran Billy Chapel, who has been a Tiger all his life, to the Giants. Wheeler, who has treated Chapel almost like his own son, is sickened by what the game has become. "Everything's changed, Billy," he tells Chapel. "The players, the fans, TV rights, arbitration. It isn't the same. The game stinks, and I can't be part of it anymore." Although we never actually see the new owners in this film, the implication is clear. The Detroit Tigers are about to be taken over by owners of the modern era; owners whose motivations and values are very different ... who do not view the team as family in the same way that Gary Wheeler did.

Regardless of whether the contrast between idealized and evil owners is drawn within the same film or through the portrayals of ownership in different films, the common denominator of their difference is the same. Ideal owners, like ideal players, are driven by a love for and commitment to the game of baseball in and of itself. They reflect the older, purer values of the game, the way it used to be. Those owners depicted negatively in these films are universally motivated by financial greed, and little else. Love of the game is not among their limited repertoire of values. They are not "real" baseball people.

> *"...not even baseball people. You know the kind."*
> — Christi Lober, *The Big Leaguer*, 1953

A second common characteristic shared by many of baseball cinema's evil owners is that they are almost always "non" baseball people. At one level, this epithet refers simply to the fact that the owner, or owners, of a team have not been part of the game of baseball themselves, but have somehow acquired the team either through inheritance or as an investment. *Major League*'s (1989) Rachel Phelps, for example, inherited the team in the estate of her late husband. In *Ladies' Day* (1943), as noted above, the Sox are owned by a group of bankers.

Beyond the reference to the fact that an owner may never have actually been part of the game of baseball him/herself, however, the derisive label "not even baseball people," refers to a much more sinister quality; a failure to love and appreciate the game of baseball for its own sake. In *The Big Leaguer* (1953), Hans Lober, manager of the New York Giants' spring tryout camp, is portrayed as someone who has devoted his life to the team. But, it has been awhile since the camp has turned out any superstars, and he learns that some people in the front office are starting to grumble. Some are even saying perhaps its time he was replaced. Who are these people, who would turn out the devoted Lober after all these years? They are, his niece tells him, "...not even baseball people. You know the kind. The ones that are always hanging around and telling you how to run your ball club" (*The Big Leaguer*, 1953).

The owner for whom baseball, in some way, has not always been a part of his or her life not only presumably lacks the knowledge of the game to be a quality owner, but also lacks the philosophical commitment to the game of the "true" baseball person. Owners who "are not even baseball people," who have not come to appreciate the game in and of itself through their own involvement in baseball, value the game primarily for its potential to satisfy their own financial interests rather than simply loving the game of baseball for its own sake, and thus are most likely to sacrifice the team and its fans to serve those selfish interests. In *Major League* (1989) for example, new owner Rachel Phelps clearly has no interest in or love of the game itself, and certainly no loyalty to the fans of Cleveland or the team. She simply seeks to use the Cleveland Indians as a means of pursuing her own financial gain. And, as noted above, the sole concern of the bankers who own the Sox in *Ladies' Day* (1943) seems to be keeping down costs for such things as the cleaning of team uniforms.

In contrast to those owners for whom baseball has only recently become a part of their lives, baseball films suggest that the best owners are those for whom baseball has always been a central part of his or her life. Pop Kelley, long-time manager of the St. Louis Cardinals (*Death on the Diamond*, 1934), for example, is prototypical of the true baseball person, who has devoted his life and love the game. However, unless he can win the pennant, he loses the team to shady businessman Henry Ainsely. A similar scenario is played out in *The Natural* (1984), in which baseball old-timer and New York Knights manager Pop Fisher faces loss of his team to crooked co-owner Judge Goodwill Banner. In stark contrast to Pop Fisher's love of the game and his team, and life-long desire to win the pennant, the judge's motivations are purely monetary. Deeply involved with gamblers, the judge actually wants the Knights to lose the pennant, and will stop at nothing, even the poisoning of the Knights' star player, Roy Hobbs, to insure his own success.

In *Take Me Out to the Ball Game* (1948), K.C. Higgins inherits the 1906 World Series champion Wolves from "a distant relative." When the team learns the new owner is on the way to their spring training camp, to "actively participate" in the operation of the club, the players are outraged. "You mean we gotta take orders from someone who never even swung a bat?" When they discover K.C. is a woman, they are in even further despair. Unlike *Major League*'s (1989) Rachel Phelps, however, K.C. Higgins is a true baseball person who obviously grew up with the game, possesses a great love and understanding of the game, and is even able to field ground balls. A true baseball person, she proves herself to be a competent owner, and quickly wins the team over. Even 12-year-old Billy Heywood, who inherits the Minnesota Twins from his grandfather (*Little Big League*, 1994), has already established himself as a life-long fan and player of the game and, as a result of this complete love for and devotion to the game, possesses such an incredible knowledge of both the history and strategy of baseball that he is able, as owner/manager, to miraculously pull the Twins out of last place and turn them into pennant contenders. In baseball cinema's vision of the way things should be, the best owners are those who have been deeply involved with the game all their lives, and who thus possess not only the knowledge, but the commitment to the game, as well, to serve the interests of the team and the fans.

These two dimensions of the non-baseball person, a lack of historical involvement with the game and a lack of love and appreciation of the game for its own sake, are typically related in baseball films. Those owners who have had little or no involvement with the game throughout their lives are virtually always portrayed as lacking a love and appreciation for the game, and thus have no hesitation in sacrificing the team, the fans, and the game itself to serve their own financial interests. The fact that an owner does have a history of prior involvement in the game, however, is no guarantee that he or she will not similarly abuse the game for her or his own gain. Although, according to baseball films, persons for whom the game has been a central part of their lives are more likely to be "true" baseball people, and thus the best owners, there are exceptions; most notably, Charles Comiskey of the 1919 Chicago White Sox (*Eight Men Out*, 1988). Despite his own history as a hall-of-fame player and manager, as an owner Comiskey repeatedly cheats and abuses his players. Similarly, the owner's nephew in *Rookie of the Year* (1993) and son in *Ed* (1996), both of whom presumably "grew up" with baseball as a result of their close family connections with the game, are focused solely on the financial bottom line and their own potential gain. These exceptions, however, serve only to re-enforce the central theme in cinematic portrayals of baseball ownership. In the end, the critical characteristic of a "true" baseball person is a deep commitment to the game of baseball for its own sake. Owners who lack that commitment, regardless of the degree of their prior involvement with the game, are likely to abuse their team, the fans, and even the game itself—and in the end, pay a heavy price for that abuse.

> "He's a circus act. A sideshow... What the hell can I say? Keep
> him on, let him think he's going to manage."
> — Boston Braves' owner, Mr. Fuchs, *The Babe*, 1992

Driven by their own greed and self-interest, it is not surprising that the evil owners of baseball films are evidently willing to do whatever it takes to satisfy those interests. Again, the essential structure of these portrayals is remarkably consistent, and the linkages clearly drawn. In film after film, those owners who are motivated principally by financial interests are also engaged in a range of morally reprehensible conduct. Mean, vindictive, and ruthless, they do not hesitate to use players for their own purposes, and then cruelly discard them; or, if necessary, attempt to destroy them.

In the original *Babe Ruth Story* (1948), the Babe is signed by the Boston

Braves as a vice-president/assistant manager, and player. As it turns out, however, the Braves have taken cruel advantage of the naive Bambino who, like most true baseball heroes, did not take the time to read the fine print of his contract. When the tired and physically struggling Babe finally hangs up his spikes, after hitting three home runs against the Pittsburgh Pirates, he learns that his tenure as "vice-president/assistant manager" was good only as long as he continued playing. Once he quits playing, he is fired by the Braves for breach of contract.

The portrayal of ownership in the original *Babe Ruth Story* (1948) is extremely temperate, however, when compared to the portrayal of the Yankees and Braves owners in the 1992 version, *The Babe*. In this film, the deceit and abuse of the respective owners are much more graphic. Yankees owner Colonel Ruppert, for example, promises Babe he can manage the Yankees, and then reneges on that promise. After being released from the Yankees, Ruth signs on with the last place Boston Braves as a player and assistant manager. When he's finished playing, the Braves have told him, he'll manage the team. But, even as assistant manager, the Babe doesn't get much respect. In a game against the Pirates, he tries to convince the Braves' manager not to have the runner on first steal. The manager ignores Ruth, and the runner is thrown out at second. Ruth has had enough. He's supposed to be the assistant manager. He walks back through the dugout, down the tunnel toward the team offices, to take his case to the Braves owner. As he reaches the office, he overhears the Braves' owner, Fuchs, talking to the General Manager, describing the greatest player in the history of the game as a circus act. The owners have been lying to him all along, just to squeeze a little more out of him at the gate. When they are finished with him, they'll toss him aside. In baseball films, that is what evil owners do.

Ebony Aces owner Sallison Porter (*Bingo Long*, 1976) is portrayed as equally despicable. In the opening scene of the film, he banishes a destitute, disabled panhandler from in front of his ball park; the panhandler was once a star player for Porter. Later, he fires a player who was seriously injured when hit in the head by a pitched ball, and then charges the rest of the team for the player's bus fare home. And, when Bingo Long leaves the Ebony Aces and forms a barnstorming team of his own with other players from around the league, Porter and the other owners do everything they can to put the team out of business, including having their thugs critically wound one of Long's players, Charlie Snow, with a razor. In *The Natural* (1984) the evil judge, the co-partner who stands to gain complete control of the Knights if they fail to win the pennant, poisons his own star player, Roy Hobbs, in an attempt to keep him from playing.

Indeed, miserly owners who sacrifice their teams, and even the game itself, to foster their own financial well-being is a common theme in baseball films. *Major League's* Rachel Phelps purposely puts together a rag-tag team of losers, in hopes of drawing such low attendance she can break her stadium lease and move the Indians from Cleveland to Florida — where she has been offered all sorts of inducements, including her own membership in an exclusive club. Walter Harvey and the other owners initially plan to simply disband the All-American Girls Professional Baseball League they created after the first year, and discard the players who have committed themselves to that league, when it becomes evident the major leagues will not have to cease play during World War II (*A League of Their Own*, 1992). And White Sox owner Charlie Comiskey (*Eight Men Out*, 1988) is portrayed as treating his players so badly that his actions in many ways serve to justify the decision by several players to sell-out to gamblers, and throw the World Series.

In sharp and unmistakable contrast to those owners motivated solely by greed, and who will do whatever it takes to satisfy that greed, are the idealized owners of baseball's cinematic vision. As noted previously, these owners are true baseball people, who love the game and all it stands for. The ideal owners in baseball films, consistent with their devotion to the game and the values it embodies, are portrayed as kind, generous souls who genuinely care about the game, the fans, and their players. Often, the ideal owner is a grandfatherly type, symbolic of the older, traditional values that the game of baseball represents. The most noble of this breed of owner is Los Angeles Dodgers owner Branch Rickey in *The Jackie Robinson Story* (1950), who repeatedly throughout the film reminds us of the basic values the game of baseball presumably embodies, and finally breaks baseball's color barrier by bringing Jackie Robinson to the big leagues. In the film, at least, Rickey is portrayed as being motivated only by the purest of values; the desire to bring to the game the equality of opportunity its ideologists have so long proclaimed, and to make baseball the all-inclusive community envisioned by the American dream.

Also typical of the owner favored in baseball films, Minnesota Twins owner Thomas Heywood (*Little Big League*, 1994) is a kind, gentle, grandfather with a genuine love of family and the game of baseball. That love and appreciation for the game has clearly been instilled in his 12 year old grandson Billy, who inherits the team upon his grandfather's death. It is young Billy, as owner and manager, who re-instills in the team a love of and excitement for the game. With his message that baseball is supposed to be fun, Billy transforms the team from a collection of jaded losers into a team that once again plays the game for the joy of it, and begins to win.

While those owners driven by materialistic concerns typically abuse their players in a variety of ways, and thus invite the justified animosity and derision directed at them by their players (*Eight Men Out*, 1988; *Major League*, 1989; *Major League II*, 1994), the ideal owners presented in baseball films exhibit a sense of caring and generosity that earns them the respect of their players and those around them. When Cubs owner Philip Wrigley, for example, who has just acquired pitcher Grover Cleveland Alexander, offers to send Aimee Alexander $500 every other month while Alex is off fighting the war, and $10,000 if he doesn't return, a gushing Alexander proclaims, "he's a swell guy" (*The Winning Team*, 1952). In *The Kid from Left Field* (1953), Bisons owner Fred Whacker is another kindly, grandfatherly sort. When Pete Cooper is fired from his job as a concessionaire by a disagreeable supervisor, Whacker promises Cooper's son Christy, who has come to plead his father's case, that he will give his father his job back. In addition, he gives young Billy a job as batboy, and later, at the request of the team, makes young Billy the manager. As noted earlier, when Cubs owner Bob Carson discovers his nephew has tried to sell star young pitcher Henry Rowengardner to the Yankees, he demotes his nephew to selling hot dogs in the stands. Then, when young Rowengardner informs Carson he does not plan to return to the Cubs the following season, because he'd rather spend his time being a kid, Carson fully understands, and happily agrees that's probably the best choice (*Rookie of the Year*, 1993).

The pattern, over the years, has been consistent. "Good" owners, baseball films teach us, are motivated by a love and devotion to the game. They are usually true "baseball" people who know baseball and who have been a part of the game for much of their lives, and are frequently portrayed in films as kindly, gentle individuals who genuinely care about other people. "Evil" owners on the other hand, are driven principally by their desire for profit and their own financial gain. They are usually "non-baseball" people who know and care little about the game itself. To compound their evil, they are often represented as mean, vindictive individuals who care little about others, and frequently use baseball players to serve their own interests—and then simply discard them. It is they who suck the joy and innocence from America's national pastime. However, in more recent years, the distinction between good and evil in baseball owners has been drawn increasingly through negative depictions of ownership. In one film after another since 1973, professional baseball's ownership or management has been cast as a greedy, often malevolent force preoccupied with the material rewards the game might generate for them. Not since the 1930s have baseball's owners been portrayed so negatively in film.

From 1934 through 1938, owners were generally presented in a negative light, in films such as *Death on the Diamond* (1934), *Alibi Ike* (1935), *Ladies' Day* (1943) and *The Babe Ruth Story* (1948). However, even these portrayals were not nearly so menacing as those in films of more recent years. As already noted, in *Death on the Diamond* (1934), the ideal owner/manager Pop Clark was contrasted with the shady investor and businessman Henry Ainsley, who stood to gain the team if the Cardinals failed to win the pennant. In *Alibi Ike* (1935), the negative portrayal consists simply of a warning to Cap that if he fails to win the pennant, the "stockholders" are likely to demand a change. And, as noted earlier, the negative depiction of owners in *Ladies' Day* (1943) was done in a humorous way.

From 1949 through 1958, however, portrayals of owners in baseball films were strikingly positive. Owners in *Take Me Out to the Ballgame* (1949), *The Jackie Robinson Story* (1950), *Rhubarb* (1951), *The Winning Team* (1952), *The Kid from Left Field* (1953), and *Damn Yankees* (1958) were all consistent with the principal characteristics of the ideal owner. The only negative reference to ownership during this era came in *The Big Leaguer* (1953), in which lifetime baseball man Hans Lobert faced replacement as director of the New York Giants spring tryout camp by those "non-baseball people ... who are always hanging around and telling you how to run your ball club."

In the most recent era of baseball films, however, beginning with *Bang the Drum Slowly* in 1973, portrayals of owners have been much more negative — both quantitatively and qualitatively. Films such as *Bang the Drum Slowly* (1973), *The Bingo Long Traveling All-Stars and Motor Kings* (1976), *The Natural* (1984), *Eight Men Out* (1988), *Bull Durham* (1988), *Major League* (1989), *A League of Their Own* (1992), *The Babe* (1992), *Rookie of the Year* (1993), *The Scout* (1994), *Major League II* (1994), *Ed* (1996) and *Mr. 3000* (2005) all contain negative portrayals of owners. These representations became more pronouncedly negative during the 1980s and 90s. For example, although the owners in *Bang the Drum Slowly* (1973) are portrayed as hard-edged business people, seeking to keep costs down by limiting player salaries, they also exhibit some human emotion, briefly, when they finally learn of catcher Bruce Pearson's terminal illness. There are no such traces of humanity in the Judge (*The Natural*, 1984), Yankee or Boston Braves owners in *The Babe* (1992), or Indians owner Rachel Phelps (*Major League*, 1989; *Major League II*). In contrast to the numerous negative portrayals of owners since 1973, only a handful of films have offered positive representations of owners during the past four decades. *Rookie of the Year* (1993), as discussed earlier, presents both types of ownership, contrasting the ideal, older owner of the Cubs with his greedy nephew. Both *Angels in the Outfield* (1994) and *Little Big League* (1994) offer viewers kindly, grandfatherly-type figures as owners, as well as a 12 year old phenom who teaches the Minnesota Twins how to enjoy the game for its own rewards, and how to have fun playing once again (*Little Big League*). And 1999's *For Love of the Game* portrays an old-school owner, Gary Wheeler, whose father bought the Detroit Tigers when Wheeler was only 7, who is now selling the Tigers, because he can no longer stand to be a part of what the game has become.

That the focus on selfishness and greed in baseball films during recent decades is a response to the emergence of these values as major issues within the game itself seems obvious. Given the tremendous attention and publicity devoted to player salaries, the multi-million dollar prices for franchises, the constant threats by owners to move their teams to more lucrative locales, the labor strife between players and owners etc., it is not surprising that issues of money, greed and self-interest — and the threats they pose to the game — should emerge as central themes within baseball films. What is more significant is that owners, much more than players, have been cast as the real villains in cinematic treatments of these issues.

One reason why baseball films tend to single out owners instead of players as being driven more by self-interest and greed, and as being more sinister in their efforts to fulfill those desires, may simply be that such portrayals reflect public perceptions that owners are more guilty of tarnishing the game in pursuit of their own financial interests than are players. Popular filmmakers typically find it easier to appeal to a broader audience by echoing dominant public values and perceptions rather than challenging them. The producers of baseball films may simply be attempting to remain consistent with what they judge to be popular sentiment. At the same time, however, we would argue that the consistent negative portrayals of owners, particularly since 1984, may have helped to shape those public perceptions. At the very least, such films may serve to reinforce a public sense that, while both players and owners are guilty of violating the essential values of the game, the greater sin lies with the owners.

Another possible explanation for the recent tendency to depict owners negatively may lie in the changes in the nature of ownership within major league baseball itself. In their analysis of how financial issues threaten the game, Sands and Gammons (1993) discuss the shift from family to corporate ownership.

> The sale of the Phillies by the Carpenter family and of the Chicago Cubs by the Wrigley family in 1981 were perfect examples of the changes that were rapidly occurring in the makeup of the ownership of major league clubs in the early 1980s. The days of family-and-business-owned baseball clubs were over. The new breed of owner were either entrepreneurs backed by a syndicate of investors or a Fortune 500 corporation interested in a club for promotional and marketing value to enhance the corporation's primary business [p. 31–32].

This new breed of owner is typical of the "non-baseball person" derisively referred to in *The Big Leaguer* (1954). The owners portrayed in the films of the 1950s were typically family owners who owned their teams because they loved the game of baseball itself. The owners depicted in films since the 1980s reflect the reality that contemporary owners are more often investors, who view their teams as simply another element in their corporate mix. They serve as a commentary on what, in the vision of traditional baseball ideologists, the game has now become.

Undoubtedly, both the negative public perceptions of baseball ownership, as well as the actual changes in the types of owners getting into the baseball business, have contributed to the nature of the portrayals of ownership in baseball films. However, there is more at work here. We believe that the tendency to vilify owners more than players for threatening the game with their own greed reflects a desire, in film at least, to preserve the integrity and image of the baseball hero, and the attempt to continue attracting audiences who seem to prefer their baseball icons unsullied. After all, within baseball's cultural vision, it is the baseball player, not the owner, who serves as the role model for American youth. As we have argued throughout this book, one of the central appeals of baseball films for their audiences is their vision of an ideal community; a community in which, among other things, members of the community are motivated by something more noble and pure than simple self-interest and greed. By associating owners, more than players with the threat of greed and self-interest, baseball films have been able to confront what has become a central public issue in a way that reaffirms the traditional values of the game, and still preserves the image of the "true" baseball hero. As we see in the news and sports programs everyday, the increasing obsession with money threatens the basic values, even the very fabric of the game (and our culture) itself. But, despite these realities, these films assure us, there are still those who do not fall victim to such temptations. Somewhere within our cultural vision, true baseball heroes still exist.

8

The Back of the Dugout

"It ain't the color and all. It's the smoke, it's the hummer...
What you do with your God-given gift."
— Roy Dean Bream, *Pastime*

Aging minor-leaguer Roy Dean Bream has a wealth of baseball knowledge to impart to his new teammate, teen pitching phenom Tyrone DeBray. But in broaching the subject of race, Roy Dean has stumbled upon a matter as disconcerting for him to talk about as it has been for baseball to deal with. Tyrone happens to be the only African American player on the 1957 Tri-City Steamers of the California D-league. In a clumsy attempt to explain to the youngster that he can go as far as his talent and hard work take him despite the bigotry he faces, Roy Dean blurts out the unfortunate phrase "credit to your people." After a bit more fumbling about, Roy Dean finally finds the words to express baseball's myopic vision of the subject of race.

The makers of baseball films would probably sympathize with Roy Dean. As awkward and inadequate as it may be, "it ain't the color and all" is about all baseball and the proponents of its ideology in the American film industry have to offer on the subject. And even that is a recognition of racial issues and divisions rare in baseball films, past or present.

Central to any discussion of baseball's ability to bridge differences and construct a sense of community is the issue of race. Baseball's history in this regard is not a proud one. With the exception of Fleet Walker's one season with the Toledo Blue Stockings of the American Association in 1884, no African American player was allowed to play major league baseball until Jackie Robinson entered the line-up for the Brooklyn Dodgers in 1947. For most of the game's history, overt racism was endemic to professional base-

William Russ (left) as Roy Dean Bream and Glenn Plummer as Tyrone Debray in *Pastime* (Bullpen Productions/Open Road Ltd./Miramax, 1991.

ball. And even today, undertones of racism exist at the highest levels of the game. As Voigt (1976) succinctly observed, " ... the historical evidence mocks baseball's claim to being a lighthouse guiding the way to full social equality for all Americans."

Although the sport itself has been riddled with racism and racial conflict throughout its history, baseball films—past and present—tend to depict a world in which race is not even an issue. In films produced prior to *The Jackie Robinson Story* (1950), racial issues—including segregation in both the game and the larger culture—are never acknowledged and portrayals of racial minorities, particularly African Americans, are distorted and unflattering at best. While those portrayals largely fell away after the release of *The Jackie Robinson Story*, baseball films of the next two decades otherwise ignored issues of race. Teams depicted in baseball films of the 50s and 60s are typically all-white, and the integration of baseball—an ongoing phenomenon that was revolutionizing the game at the time—goes unmentioned, as does any other matter of race. This silence continues in recent baseball films (those produced in the past twenty-five years), but with a twist: these films depict a national pastime that is as racially diverse as it is devoid of racial tensions.

When the American film industry began in the 1890s, pioneers in the new medium captured short scenes of everyday life, including brief images of baseball. Films made during the early 1900s were one-reel features, and some included diverse, often authentic depictions of racial minorities, including images of black U.S. soldiers overseas and anthropological vignettes of Caribbean natives (Cripps, 1979). These unadorned and authentic motion picture portrayals of minorities soon gave way to commercial film makers' pandering to the widest audience and lowest common denominator and by 1917, the movie industry was churning out the feature-length, commercially-successful narratives that would define the American film industry. Racial stereotypes, particularly caricatures of African Americans borrowed from Southern popular culture, emerged as the standard portrayals of people of color in seminal American film (Cripps, 1979). Perhaps the most renowned of these early films is D.W. Griffith's appallingly racist epic *The Birth of a Nation* (1915), a picture in no way atypical of the way blacks were depicted by Hollywood over the next thirty years. Like baseball and the culture in general, the film industry was largely a segregated enterprise until the mid-twentieth century. The major leagues banned black ballplayers and Hollywood contributed a veneer of naturalness to this situation, reinforcing the "absurdity" of the notion of black men playing major league baseball by employing the grossest cinematic stereotypes of African Americans. When people of color appeared on screen at all, it was usually for some grotesque comic purpose. By the 1930s, the cinematic practices of ignoring or stereotyping racial minorities were well entrenched in popular film, and baseball movies were no exception. In the 1933 Joe E. Brown comedy *Elmer the Great*, for example, Chicago Cubs star Elmer Kane is jailed for his involvement in a brawl with crooked gamblers seeking to fix the World Series. The only other men in the lock-up are both black. They are the only people of color seen in the film. When Elmer, embittered at what he perceives to be his team's duplicity in his predicament, insists on staying in jail even after his bail is posted, one of the black inmates turns to the other and says, "Is he fightin' to stay in jail, or is I conscious?" Another Brown comedy, *Alibi Ike* (1935) depicts a single person of color — A dull-witted, wide-eyed black doorman who is duped into helping crooked gamblers kidnap the film's protagonist. Similar depictions of African American train porters and bootblacks in *The Pride of the Yankees* (1942), the film biography of Hall of Fame first baseman Lou Gehrig, are the only time we see any other than white faces in the film. These are the sort of portrayals of

African American men — incarcerated, illiterate menial laborers, too dumb to be dangerous— often used for comic effect in the era. But as the only images of black people many white Americans might encounter, it also served to justify segregation (Orbe and Harris, 2001), both in the broader culture and in specific institutions like major league baseball.

Latino ballplayers, if sufficiently light-skinned, could slip past major league baseball's color barrier prior to the game's integration, but they were not portrayed in baseball films until the 1950s. The 1942 comedy *Ladies Day* may be the only baseball film prior to 1973 to feature a person of Latin descent in the same film as African Americans (who are cast as train porters and maids). In the film, pitcher Wacky Waters marries a Latina movie star named Pepita Zorita. Pepita is not particularly bright, and at times seems spoiled and egotistical — in short, not a particularly flattering portrait of a Latina woman. But in fairness it must be said that the players' Anglo wives are even less appealing characters. Asian Americans were nearly invisible in American film until the arrival of anti–Japanese propaganda films during World War II. Moreover, even when a film role called for an Asian character, the role often went to a European American in "yellow face" (Orbe and Harris, 2001). One of the few portrayals of an Asian character in a baseball film is seen in *The Babe Ruth Story* (1948). At the beginning of the film, a young George "Babe" Ruth is chased into his father's saloon by a business man whose window George has broken while playing baseball. The man is Chinese, and his business is, of course, a laundry. Excitable and jabbering, he speaks no English and a helpful white sailor translates that the man hit himself in the head when attempting to take the bat away from George. The man is placated by George's fafther only when given a free beer.

> *"The box score is democratic. It's all that ought to count!"*
> — Branch Rickey, *The Jackie Robinson Story*, 1950

When Jackie Robinson stepped onto the Ebbets Field infield on April 15, 1947, and stepped over baseball's color line, he did not, as many now believe, open the floodgates for black ballplayers. Rather, Robinson pried open a door that would not swing wide for several years. It would take even longer for baseball films to fully integrate their teams. Motion pictures like *It Happens Every Spring* (1949) *Angels in the Outfield* (1951), *Rhubarb* (1951), *Roogie's Bump* (1954), and *Safe at Home* (1962) continued to feature all-white teams. Occasionally a team with one Latino or African American player would appear, e.g., *Damn Yankees* (1958), or *The Kid from Cleveland* (1949), which offers a brief appearance by Hall of Famer Satchell Paige. It should also be noted that many of the baseball films produced during this period were set in baseball's segregated past, including *The Babe Ruth Story* (1948), *Take Me Out to the Ballgame* (1949), *The Stratton Story* (1949), *The Pride of St. Louis* (1952), *The Winning Team* (1952) and *Fear Strikes Out* (1957).* However, none of these films, regardless of their chronological setting, includes racial minorities on their teams, nor do they make any mention of the exclusion of black players from major league baseball. It is as if segregation never existed, and integration made little difference.

Despite the ideology of baseball's claims to inclusiveness and bonding citizens, both the game and the films that portray and promote it remained essentially white from 1947 through 1962. The exceptions are few. The most notable is, of course, *The Jackie Robinson Story* (1950). Starring Jackie Robinson himself, this film chronicles Robinson's breaking of baseball's color barrier. While the film does contain scenes hinting at the types of abuses Robinson was forced to endure — an exhibition game being canceled due to a city ordinance banning games against blacks and whites, harassment by white fans, a barrage of racial insults — these depictions are relatively mild. Full of platitudes from Dodger owner Branch Rickey about baseball and the American way, the film offers the illusion that Robinson's success solved not only the problem of racism in baseball, but even within American culture at large. For example, in a final scene of the film, one of the most racist fans who has taunted Robinson throughout the film is converted by Robinson's great play into a vocal supporter and is even shown warmly shaking hands with a black fan after Robinson scores the run that wins the pennant for the Dodgers. The racism that confronted Robinson has suddenly disappeared, and baseball's myth of equality and diversity is affirmed.

In addition to proclaiming baseball's sordid racist history to be at an end, *The Jackie Robinson Story* also delivers an unambiguous message about how the fight for racial equality should be conducted. Robinson is told by Branch Rickey that he must never respond to the taunts and assaults he will endure, but must remain quiet and humble, and prove himself through the quality of his play on the field, and his demeanor off the field. Rickey tells

---

*Fear Strikes Out, released in 1957, portrays the early playing career of Jimmy Piersall, who played for a Boston Red Sox organization that did not have an African American player on the major league roster until the year of the film's release.

Robinson he wants a ballplayer tough enough not to fight back, declaring "You *can't* fight back."

This is not to detract from the significance of Robinson's historic achievement. It was Jackie Robinson who, with a remarkable combination of courage, talent and intelligence, finally broke the color barrier in major league baseball. In so doing, he did much to force an entire culture to rethink policies of racial segregation. But the ideological dimensions of the film chronicling that achievement are significant. *The Jackie Robinson Story* serves to reaffirm baseball's myth of racial equality, a myth still not fully achieved in the early twenty-first century. Perhaps more significantly, the film defines in a very narrow way — and for dominant elements in our society, a very "safe" way — the types of activity that are considered acceptable and productive in the fight for racial equality. Racism is just another obstacle the baseball hero can overcome through hard work, devotion to the game, humility, allegiance to the community. The unmistakable message of this Cold War film is that "the system works for everyone," a message that more than 50 years after the film's making, many Americans find dubious at best.

Another exception — albeit a less significant one — is the portrayal of a Latino player in a supporting role in *The Big Leaguer* (1953). In the film, the New York Giants' latest prospects gather in the off-season at the team's tryout camp in Melbourne, Florida and a collection of young men vie to make an impression that will keep them in professional baseball. One of them is a Cuban player, Chuy Ramon Santiago Aguilar, who struggles with his limited understanding of English. But we are assured that this will not matter in how he is evaluated at the Giants' tryout camp — he will be judged on his baseball skills alone. Aguilar is the only racial minority we see in the Giants' camp. Ironically, the final act of the film features a game between the Giants prospects and the Brooklyn Dodgers' rookies. Despite the Dodgers' relatively advanced integration of their organization at the time the film was made, including the presence of great African American players like Jackie Robinson, Joe Black, and Roy Campanella on the parent club, not a single black ballplayer is seen on the Dodgers' team in the film.

A third exception to the almost all-white baseball films of the 1950s is *The Great American Pastime* (1956). A modest comedy about little league baseball in suburbia, the teams feature multiple black players and parents. In this regard, *The Great American Pastime* was forty years ahead of its time. However, race is never an issue and segregation is never mentioned in the film.

"Well, what do you expect? All we got on this team's Jews,
spics, niggers, pansies and a booger-eatin' moron."
— Tanner Boyle, *The Bad News Bears*, 1976

Although Hollywood released at least a dozen baseball films in the 1950s, and half that number in the 1970s, only one (*Safe at Home*) was produced during the 1960s. And eleven years would pass between the release of *Safe at Home* in 1962 and the next baseball film, *Bang the Drum Slowly* in 1973. In other words, at the height of the civil rights movement in the United States, Hollywood simply stopped making baseball movies. Whether this is an ironic coincidence or result of some correlation between the two may never be understood, and is beyond the scope of this discussion.

Given the social upheaval of the 1970s, it is perhaps easier to understand why that decade produced films that were at least willing to make attempts, even if rather tepid ones, to address issues of racism in the game of baseball. The first baseball film to acknowledge issues of racial tension in the aftermath of baseball's integration was *Bang the Drum Slowly* (1973). The fictional New York Mammoths baseball club features more than one black player as well as Latino players. During the playing of the Star Spangled Banner on opening day, the camera pans down the Mammoths as they stand in line for the anthem. The players are grouped by race. The Latino players stand together, as do the three African Americans on the team. Sandwiched between two of them, who are singing the anthem, is the third black player, his facial expression betraying his disdain for the ceremony while he holds his cap over his heart with the middle finger of his right hand displayed against the bill. It is a gesture reminiscent of the black-gloved fist raised in protest by African American track athletes John Carlos and Tommy Smith at the 1968 Olympic Games. Early in the film, protagonist-pitcher Henry Wiggin tells us in a voice-over that the Mammoths are "a strong club," and "I didn't think there was anyone who could beat us— except maybe ourselves. We started raggin' on each other... We weren't pullin' like a club." Much of the clubhouse discontent that afflicts the Mammoths is racially motivated. In one scene, an Italian American player accuses his Latino teammates of criticizing him in Spanish, a charge they hotly deny. Later, the same player scuffles with a black teammate after a tough loss. In mid-season, manager Dutch Schnell gathers the team to discuss "people who can't control their feelings toward their teammates." He tells them "Rule one (is) no dissension," but then lists the reasons for the Mammoth's internal strife and the erratic play it causes, including members of the team who "don't agree with the color of their (teammates') skin." As mild as these references may seem, they were the first mention in any baseball film of race as an issue in the clubhouse since *The Jackie Robinson Story* twenty-three years earlier.

Another baseball film which attempts to deal with issues of race on a more substantive level is *The Bingo Long Travelling All-Stars and Motor Kings* (1976), the story of a barnstorming black baseball team in the years when baseball was still segregated. As baseball film historian Hal Erickson (2002) notes, racism is taken as a given in this film, and the numerous incidents of racism faced by black players in this era are not focused on to nearly the degree they might have been. Still, Bingo Long and his teammates confront racism at every turn. They are not permitted to play in the white leagues, they are not permitted to consort with white prostitutes, they earn half of what white workers are paid for picking potatoes. In order to win the support of white audiences— and in one case, to avoid being assaulted by a group of racist fans— they must resort to clowning and showboating. In many ways, this film provides a fuller picture of what black baseball players had to endure in 1939 America. Interestingly enough, when the white professional leagues sign one of the black All-Stars at the end of the film, the reactions amongst the other black players is mixed. Along with the joy of finally having a black player signed, there is some skepticism. In the final scene, All-Star catcher Leon Carter tells Bingo Long the white men are moving in, and it will eventually be the end of the Negro leagues. In Carter's view, the whites are about to take over black baseball, just as they have taken over everything else. Unlike most baseball films, *Bingo Long* does not reaffirm baseball's myth of equality. While the team of the All-Stars is within itself a wonderful example of a community of tolerance and equality, the larger culture in which it exists is clearly not.

The Bad News Bears (1976) is remembered by many for the obscenities and racial slurs uttered by the youngsters on the Bears team. In the film, the ultra-competitive and very white suburban North County League is threatened with legal action if they do not allow the Bears, a team as racially diverse as they are initially inept, to play in the league. Early in the story, one of the Bears players, Tanner Boyle, laments the disparate composition of the team, describing them as a bunch of "Jews, spics, niggers, pansies." It appears to be the sort of foul-mouthed, macho experimentation with emotive language used by a child who does not fully comprehend its hurtful potential. No overt racist behaviors manifest themselves to suggest otherwise, and throughout the film Tanner stands up for everyone on his team. The real conflict in the film is created not by internal racial tension, but by a struggle of the "have-not" Bears scrapping it out against the "haves," the more affluent teams in the league.

> "He can't speak much English, but that's the beauty of baseball — if he can go to his right and hit the broad side of a barn, that'll do all his talking for him."
> — *The Big Leaguer*, 1953

While baseball films through the 1950s and 60s reflected a baseball world which was all-white and made virtually no mention of the issue of racism in any way, and films of the 1970s made diffident attempts to come to grips with racial issues, baseball films of the past two and a half decades have tended to go in a quite different direction. With few exceptions, contemporary baseball films pay homage to the value of equality contained within baseball's ideology to the degree that race in these films is never even an issue and seldom even mentioned. These films do not confront either the decades of segregation in the game, nor present-day issues of race. In films since the 1980s, in stark contrast to the real world of baseball, we see baseball communities of great diversity in which the values of tolerance and equality have been so fully achieved that racial issues never emerge.

Perhaps no better example exists than *Major League* (1989). The film makers who assembled the Cleveland Indians team of *Major League* went to great lengths to construct the most motley collection of players imaginable — veterans and rookies, dedicated players and greedy prima donnas, convicts and innocents, a Fundamentalist Christian and a Voodoo practitioner — to create every sort of conflict imaginable. The divisions that create the heterogeneity and the discord the Cleveland Indians of *Major League* must overcome to form a winning team are many: ego, women, religion, status, age, money — but never race. Despite the fact that racial divisions are among the most salient of difficulties faced by American culture (and in turn, by the game of baseball), race is the one difference that never arises and is never mentioned.

An occasional brief, "tip of the cap" reference to the segregated era of baseball occurs in a few films of recent years. In the film *Eight Men Out* (1988), for example, Chicago sportswriters Ring Lardner and Hugh Fullerton sit in an empty Comiskey Park after watching the 1919 Chicago White Sox clinch the American League pennant. Winslow, a black stadium attendant, is picking up trash in the seats around them. "Hey, Winslow, your boys look sharp," Fullerton tells him. "Yeah, they the best I seen yet," Winslow replies. "Best white folks team, anyways."

A similar brief reference to segregation is seen in *A League of Their Own* (1992). The teams in the 1940s All-American Girls Professional Baseball League were, of course, all white. In one short scene, a ball gets away during pre-game warmups and bounces to a group of fans standing at the edge of the playing field. A black woman picks it up and throws it, with considerable force, past catcher Dottie Hinson to the pitcher. The brief exchange of glances between the woman and Hinson is clear — Were it not for the color of her skin, she could have played in this league, too.

It is a powerful scene, but it loses some of its moral impact when compared to an earlier incident in the film. While Dottie Hinson and her sister Kit Keller are traveling from their home in Oregon to the league's tryout camp in Chicago with scout Ernie Capadino, they make a stop in Colorado so Capadino can evaluate a hitting prospect named Marla Hooch. In a tryout, Hooch proves to be a switch-hitter of extraordinary ability, but Capadino deems her to be too unattractive to play for the new women's league. When he tells Hinson and Keller that Hooch will not be coming with them to Chicago, the sisters drop their suitcases, fold their arms and refuse to budge, a clear indication that if Marla Hooch is not allowed to play, they are not interested in joining the league. When compared, the latter scene weakens the noble intent of the former, unintentionally advancing the dubious premise that racial discrimination may be inevitable and acceptable, but prejudice based on perceived prettiness is not.

A third and perhaps more honest acknowledgment of racial discrimination occurs in the film *Pastime* (1991). Set in 1957, *Pastime* is about aging minor-leaguer Roy Dean Bream's final season. Bream clings to the lowest rung of the professional baseball ladder as a marginal relief pitcher for the D-league Tri-City Steamers. He is joined in the role of team outcast by the only black player on the Steamers, a teenage rookie pitcher of great promise named Tyrone DeBray. Their common antagonist is pitcher Randy Keever, an arrogant bigot who is openly hostile toward both Tyrone and Roy Dean and subtly racist in his comments to others about Tyrone. As noted in the opening paragraph of this chapter, Roy Dean makes a well-meaning but clumsy attempt to assure his young teammate that dedication, talent and hard work matter more than race. The scene is played with an awkwardness that exemplifies the reluctance of baseball and baseball cinema to confront the issue. And while *Pastime* advances baseball's standard ideological reply to any threat to community — differences don't matter, working hard and playing the game to the best of your ability are what matter — it is a recognition of racial attitudes rare in baseball films of the recent past.

A film which does appear to present a tension between different races is *Mr. Baseball* (1992). The conflict is resolved when Jack Elliot, the white American player, learns the Japanese virtues of humility, acceptance of others, and putting the good of the community/team above his own self-interest. However, even in this instance, the tension is far more cultural than racial, and Jack overcomes it not so much by accepting Japanese culture as by finally embracing the ideology of American baseball and its virtues of hard work, clean living, modesty and team play. The one recent film that can rightly be called an exception to baseball cinema's neglect of the subject of race is *Hardball* (2001). In its portrayal of the Kekambas, an African American little league team from the Cabrini Green housing project of Chicago coached by an aimless young man from the white underclass, it is the first baseball film to depict the desperate circumstances of many of America's minority citizens. The players on the Kekambas team are not the middle-class minority kids featured in films like the *Bad News Bears* and the *Sandlot*. These children are surrounded by the abject poverty, crime, drug abuse and routine violence of life in the projects. One player is mugged when he returns from baseball practice after dark, another is recruited into a gang when he is forced to leave the Kekambas team on an eligibility technicality, yet another is killed by a gang-banger's errant bullet not long after helping the Kekambas reach the league championship game. Hope for these youngsters comes from few sources; one is their mothers, depicted as strong women and good parents deeply concerned about the welfare and future of their children. Another is their parochial school education. But the film makes clear the real source of their salvation is baseball.

There is certainly a greater emphasis on racial inequality in *Hardball* — as it is visually constructed, if not explicitly developed in the film's dialogue — than in any other film in our sample. Yet *Hardball* breaks little new ground beyond this more-realistic portrayal of the black underclass. The film inevitably returns to the same message baseball films have broadcast since *The Jackie Robinson Story* fifty years earlier: baseball offers salvation for those willing to play the game the right way. For the members of the Kekambas team, playing baseball is positively associated with all the things that will get them out of the projects: Getting an education, involvement with a supportive community, staying away from gangs, guns and drugs. Even when the smallest player on the team, "G-Baby" Evans is killed, it is baseball, and the chance to play for a championship, that will give meaning to his death. The film offers the strongest endorsement of baseball's promise of hope and possibility, even in the face of racial discrimination, since *The Jackie Robinson Story*.

Aside from these few exceptions, baseball film makers have opted to avoid the issue of race altogether. In most baseball films, the issue of race receives not even a brief reference. In the mystic tale *Field of Dreams* (1988), the spirits of ballplayers past who haunt Ray Kinsella's Iowa baseball diamond are, without exception, white. One might have thought at least a single Negro League or Cuban or Japanese baseball player in need of redemption might have appeared. However, ethereal voices ordering one to destroy the season's cash crop to construct a baseball field are one thing. Minority athletes joining players of the segregated era, particularly Southerners like Shoeless Joe Jackson, in a friendly game of baseball would have been to stretch suspended disbelief to the breaking point. More importantly, it might have required the film's makers to deal directly with the issue of race, and that is subject matter contemporary baseball films choose not to broach.

And in those films which do feature multi-cultural teams, the value of equality contained within baseball's ideology seems to be taken as an unproblematic given — to the degree that race in these films is never even an issue. In *The Sandlot* (1993), which takes place in the 1950s, we see a kids' baseball team with an Hispanic leader and a black player, in which all of the kids are part of a close, tight-knit community, and in which the issue of race never emerges. In other contemporary baseball films like *Bull Durham* (1988), *Major League* (1989), *Major League II* (1994), *Little Big League* (1994), *Ed* (1996), and *The Fan* (1996), we are shown multi-racial teams in which racial differences and issues are not even referred to. In *Rookie of the Year* (1993) and *Angels in the Outfield* (1994), the racially heterogeneous Chicago Cubs and California Angels have black managers— still something of a rarity in the real world of major league baseball. Yet the rarity, and the history which explains it, are never mentioned.

The idea that baseball might serve as a site for the integration of peoples of diverse backgrounds and experiences into a common community has long been a central theme of baseball's ideology (Riess, 1980). As the above examples illustrate, that theme remains a prominent element of baseball's cultural vision. However, it is impossible to overlook the duplicity of baseball and the proponents of its ideological vision in ignoring the systematic exclusion of an entire race of people from the national pastime before its integration, and the racial divisions in American and in baseball that persist half a century later.

As if embarrassed that the national pastime's definition of equality did not extend much beyond white European immigrants, Hollywood has chosen to remain essentially silent on the issue. Without an adequate explanation for the segregation that violated one of the central canons of baseball ideology, contemporary baseball films confront neither the decades of segregation in the game, nor contemporary issues of race. Instead, we are assured in baseball films of the past twenty-five years that our racial troubles are behind us, and our diverse society, like a multiracial baseball team, need no longer concern itself with issues of race. Yet during this same period, a number of popular and/or critically-acclaimed films representing a wide range of other genres openly discussed, even focused on, racial issues—*Malcolm X, Do the Right Thing, Jungle Fever*, and others by Spike Lee; *Mississippi Masala, White Men Can't Jump, The Color Purple*, and *The Long Walk Home* by other filmmakers.

Jhally and Lewis (1992) have coined the phrase "enlightened racism" to describe the wishful belief that racism is no longer an issue in America, that society has advanced to the point that effort, optimism and perseverance hold the keys to success for all. Enlightened racism acknowledges the historical significance of racial issues, but insists those are in the past, and that racial barriers no longer impede those willing to work to achieve the American dream.

Baseball films have found in enlightened racism a way to reconcile the reality of a racially divided society with the ideology of the national pastime. Racism is no longer advocated in baseball films, as it was in the first half of the Twentieth Century. Instead, it is now denied. At best, we may see the very occasional, brief acknowledgment of baseball's segregated past in contemporary baseball films, such as *Eight Men Out, A League of Their Own*, and *Pastime*. Much more consistently, we see racially diverse communities of people who seem utterly oblivious to issues of race, past or present. And in those very rare films which have more directly confronted issues of racial inequality in both baseball and the larger culture, in every one of these films, including *Hardball*, we are presented with an ideological vision that hard work, devotion to the game, subordination of the individual to

155

the team, and adherence to baseball's moral order will inevitably lead to success for all within those communities, regardless of race. The message is clear: The way outcasts—from Jackie Robinson to Bingo Long, from the Bad News Bears to the Kekambas—fight back is by collectively embracing the values of the game.

In an era marked by conflict and tensions between various cultures and ideologies, baseball films of the past two and a half decades have offered audiences a comforting vision of cultural harmony. The communities they portray are not communities in which everyone is the same, but rather are communities in which people who are often very different from one another come together to achieve common goals and in so doing, form bonds of acceptance, caring and friendship. They are clearly idyllic communities; reflective of the fact that baseball films are not so much about the reality of baseball, as the myths of its ideological vision.

9

Girls Don't Play Baseball

*"I haven't got ballplayers! I've got girls! Girls are what you
sleep with after the game, not what you coach during the game."*
— Jimmy Dugan, *A League of Their Own*

Jimmy Dugan, ex–major leaguer and current alcoholic, has, in his view, sunk about as far as one can go. He has been reduced to managing one of the teams in the new All-American Girls Professional Baseball League. In his view, and in the view of many within American culture, women have only a very limited role to play in professional baseball. And that role isn't on the field. Although in this particular film, *A League of Their Own* (1992), Dugan quickly learns otherwise, and redeems his own life in the process, his enlightenment remains an exception in baseball lore. The reality, even today, is that the role of women within baseball's cultural vision remains extremely limited.

In her analysis of the construction of gender in baseball, Ferrante (1994) contends that baseball is "an expression of the naturalness of a patriarchal order that regularly associates positive meanings with men and negative meanings with women" (p. 238). "Baseball," she continues, "embodies a nostalgia for a pure and perfect experience of individual, masculine achievement," and "the sacredness of that ideal is protected against the mundane by a taboo against women." Accordingly, women have traditionally been restricted to auxiliary roles in baseball, argues Ferrante, primarily as providers of comfort and support to men. In the idealized community constructed within baseball's cultural vision, the positions assigned to women remain anything but ideal.

Consistent with Ferrante's analysis of the vision of women as defined

Tom Hanks (far right) as Jimmy Dugan in *A League of Their Own* (Columbia Pictures, 1992).

within baseball's patriarchal order, Solomon (1985), in his review of the roles of women characters in baseball literature, found that women generally do not appear in baseball novels. When they do appear, women are portrayed as "either complaisant wives, stupid bimbos—or sexual threats" (p. 19). In baseball films, however, women have been accorded a somewhat more central and positive role. In numerous baseball films, women are central, and often positive characters, playing significant roles in constructing the ideal community and moral order envisioned in baseball's ideology. Nevertheless, the nature of those roles remains narrowly defined.

Dickerson (1991) identifies two principal roles for women in baseball films. The first is the evil "vamp" who interferes with and threatens the hero's success. The second is the loyal, wholesome, hometown girl who serves as a source of strength and power for the male hero, and with whom the hero eventually settles down. Together, these two representations construct a vision of the proper role and place for women within baseball's cultural vision.

> *"Women are Wacky's downfall." "Every time he falls for a
> dame, his pitching average falls to pieces."*
> — Kitty McGowan and Hazel Jones,
> *Ladies Day,* 1943

Although not as typical as women who serve as sources of strength and support for their heroic counterparts, women as a threat to the baseball hero are not uncommon in baseball films. Occasionally, this theme has been treated lightheartedly, as in the 1943 comedy *Ladies Day*. In this film, pitcher Wacky Waters tends to lose his focus— and his control — every time he falls in love, which is quite frequently. When he falls in love with and marries the alluring Pepita Zurita late in the season, thus threatening the Sox's chances in the World Series, a group of Sox wives conspire to keep the two apart until after the series, even kidnapping Pepita and holding her hostage in a hotel for a week. Ultimately, however, the value of true love and marriage is upheld. In a sudden switch, Wacky falters in the final game of the World Series, until Pepita escapes and makes her way to the ball park. Her sudden appearance, rather than distracting Waters, revives the struggling star, who not only regains his pitching form, but even drives in the winning runs. Thus, the "threat" posed by women to the Sox's star pitcher is, in the final reel, dissolved in favor of the more common role of women as supporters and nurturers.

Typically, women who threaten the success and well-being of the baseball hero are portrayed as significantly more sinister. In *Rhubarb* (1951), for example, the sole human survivor of Brooklyn Loons owner Thaddeus J. Banner, daughter Myra, is portrayed as so evil that, upon his death, Banner leaves the team to his cat Rhubarb, rather than his spoiled, disagreeable daughter. She responds true to character by trying to kill the cat, among other schemes. This selfish pursuit of their own material interests is the common thread characterizing the "evil" women of baseball films. In *Bang the Drum Slowly* (1973), "mercenary good time girl Katie" (Erickson, 2002, p.88) convinces the dying and gullible Bruce Pearson that she loves him, in hopes he will make her the beneficiary of his insurance policy — a plan thwarted by Pearson's best-friend, roommate, and insurance agent, Henry Wiggen. In *The Natural* (1984), even though she has fallen in love with New York Knights' star Roy Hobbs, the sultry seductress Memo Paris eventually poisons Hobbs, at the behest of her keeper, gambler Gus Sands, to try and keep Hobbs out of the championship game. In *Major League* (1989), owner Rachel Phelps does not resort to quite such drastic means, but still does everything within her power to destroy the Cleveland Indians, so she can break her stadium lease and move the team to Florida. And, in *Major League II* (1994), pitcher Rick Vauhgn allows himself to be transformed into a selfish jerk by his agent/lover, Flannery, who then callously makes plans to dump him when his career begins going downhill — only to return once his career begins taking off once again.

In these films, the baseball hero is confronted by the traditional temptress; the woman who seeks to use him solely for her own, selfish interests and who, in doing so, threatens not only his career, but even his life. Contrasting with the greed and selfishness of the Myra Banners and Memo Parises, however, is the much more dominant stereotype in baseball films; the supportive, nurturing savior of the baseball hero. Where the vamp represents the sinister potential of women in baseball's moral order, the nurturer and redeemer represents the idealized role of women within baseball's cultural vision.

> *"Whether you asked for it or not, you represent the dreams and ambitions of millions of American kids. How you act, they act."*
>
> — Claire Hodgson, *The Babe Ruth Story*, 1948

As we have noted previously, the Lou Gehrig of *Pride of the Yankees* (1942) is the epitome of the ideal baseball hero — humble, hardworking, morally virtuous, and one of the game's greatest players. But while it is Lou's talent and character which make him a baseball hero, it is Eleanor Gehrig's nurturing and support which, in the film, enable him to fulfill that role. Eleanor Gehrig's presence, from the very beginning of his career, ensures Lou will be a "hero of the peaceful paths of everyday life," rather than just an ordinary ball player.

Eleanor ensures Lou's virtue by being everything this baseball hero could want. When Lou apologetically reminds her that they honeymooned in Yankee Stadium, Eleanor replies, "we've never had anything but (a honeymoon)." After he is honored for playing in his 2000th consecutive game, Lou thanks Eleanor for "being the greatest fan a man ever had," "for not letting me quit" and for nursing him through injury and illness. She is the perfect wife of traditional marriage vows: she loves, honors and cherishes Lou for better or worse (richer and poorer are never an issue for the Gehrigs), in sickness and in health, till death does them part. The Gehrigs, in baseball cinema's cultural view, are the ideal — the perfect hero and his perfect wife; the model relationship and moral order to which other baseball couples will aspire.

The early Babe Ruth of *The Babe Ruth Story* (1948) is not so virtuous as the cinematic Lou Gehrig, and much of this film's narrative follows Babe's attainment of the moral characteristics of the baseball hero, which were so much a part of Lou Gehrig's essential character. The Babe and his future savior/wife, Claire, meet early in the film in a restaurant, where Claire proves to a struggling Ruth that the reason he has lost four in a row, and been knocked out of the game early in his last five pitching starts, is that he is telegraphing his curve ball to opposing batters by sticking his tongue out during his windup. As a result of this knowledge she saves Babe Ruth's baseball career. And, it is in this early scene that a central subplot of the film is established — the great Bambino's pursuit of the love of his life, Claire.

Winning Claire's affections is not an easy task for the Babe, however; an arrogant, self-indulgent individual who likes to spend his evenings throwing money around in night clubs. A number of early scenes, depicting Claire's continual rejection of Babe, establish in no uncertain terms that the reason for Ruth's failure to impress Claire is that at this stage in his life/career he has not yet acquired the qualities of humility or moral virtue that are characteristic of the true baseball hero. As a result of his conceit and his lack of moral discipline, Babe not only fails to win over the object of his affections, but his life on and off the field begins to decline. His playing has begun to slump. A constant discipline problem, he is finally suspended by the Yankees for two weeks. And there is also the matter of his drinking. It is at this point in Babe's life that Claire intervenes again. Although she has been avoiding Ruth as much as possible, not wanting to get involved with someone as immature and irresponsible as Ruth has proven — time and again — to be, Claire finds herself face-to-face with the Great Bambino on Christmas Eve, decked out as Santa Claus, a bag of presents over his shoulder, stumbling up the steps of the children's hospital. The Babe has had a bit too much to drink. His ever-present friend, Phil, recognizing Ruth is in no condition to be around small children, is pleading with him not to go in. At Phil's urging, Claire convinces Ruth not to go into the hospital. After telling him the story of a young urchin who had begged her for a quarter on the street, so he could buy a Babe Ruth hat, just like all the other kids have, she reminds the Babe of his position as role model for America's youth. "How you act, they act," she tells him. This moment is a turning point in Ruth's life and career. The contrite, humbled Ruth allows Claire to take him home, and begins the transition from great ballplayer to true baseball hero.

In *The Babe Ruth Story* (1948), Claire Ruth serves as a source of knowledge, virtue and inspiration for the great Bambino. While it may have been

Babe Ruth who saved baseball, it was Claire who saved Babe Ruth —first by spotting the flaw in the delivery of his curve ball, then as the source of moral virtue in convincing Babe to reform his personal life, and finally as the source of inspiration, whose love gives Babe the strength and determination to redeem both his career and his life. While perhaps not quite as dramatically as the original, the Claire of the 1992 production of *The Babe* performs a similar role over 40 years later, serving once again as a source of knowledge, support, and virtue for baseball's best-known hero.

Claire Ruth is not a unique figure in baseball cinema, a mythic realm in which saviors abound. In baseball films, at least, it is often women who perceive what the hero needs at any given moment in his life, and fulfills that need. It is Adam Paluchek's romantic interest Christy Lobert, also the daughter of the Giants' tryout camp director, Hans Lobert, who delivers the crucial lecture at the crucial moment in *The Big Leaguer* (1953). When top prospect Adam Paluchek, feeling guilty about deceiving his father, who believed Paluchek was at law school, decides to leave camp in the middle of the night, Christy tells him that "running out on your father is not as bad as running out on yourself." Paluchek learns the lesson of being true to himself, and is eventually signed by the Giants. In the early Joe E. Brown comedy *Elmer the Great* (1933), Gentryville's star pitcher, Elmer Kane, is offered a contract by the Chicago Cubs. Kane, however, declares he does not intend to go to Chicago, but plans to remain in Gentryville, to be near his beloved Nellie. Nellie, recognizing that being signed by the Cubs is the greatest opportunity in Kane's life, professes that she has no similar feelings for Kane, and fires him from his job as a delivery man for her general store. Kane, of course, becomes a star pitcher for the Cubs. But, her role as Kane's guardian angel does not end there. Later in the season, when the naive Kane becomes involved with gamblers, she pays off his debts, bails him out of jail, and convinces him to return to the Cubs for the final game of the World Series against the Yankees, which Kane naturally wins. He and Nellie are, of course, married at the end of the film.

In *The Stratton Story* (1949), Ethel Stratton not only remains devotedly and lovingly by her bitter husband's side, following the hunting accident which ended his career, but inspires him to begin rebuilding his life by reminding him of his own words, "a man's got to know where he's going." When Aimee Alexander, who walked out on her husband, Grover, because of his drinking, learns that he actually suffered from a neurological disorder, she searches the country for him, finally tracking him down in a seedy carnival. With the aid of friend and Cardinals manager Rogers Hornsby, she helps Alexander rebuild his life, marriage, and his career. Near the end of the film, Alexander credits his wife as being the source of his strength and inspiration, telling her, "without you, I'm just half a man, waiting to black out" (*The Winning Team*, 1952).

The Natural's (1984) Roy Hobbs is not unlike the Babe Ruth of *The Babe Ruth Story* (1948): a basically good man who succumbs to temptation, but returns to virtue with the help of a good woman. It is not until the reappearance of Iris Gaines— Roy's childhood sweetheart and the woman he had proposed to, and then abandoned, sixteen years before — that Roy can achieve the mythic stature and virtue required of a baseball hero. After sixteen years, unable to watch him fail she later confesses, Iris attends a game at Wrigley Field where Roy and the Knights are suffering a typically dismal day. Roy strikes out three times. But during his final at-bat Iris, wearing a bright white dress and hat, backlit from the sun in an angelic glow, stands up in the crowd. Roy catches a glimpse of her through the late afternoon sun and returns to the batter's box to hit a massive game-winning home run that shatters the scoreboard clock. The following day Roy hits four home runs. Iris' reappearance is the inspiration for Roy's almost supernatural effort during the remainder of the season.

Later in the film, after Roy is poisoned by the evil Memo Paris (the classic Hollywood vamp stereotype juxtaposed against the angelic Iris), it is up to Iris again to provide inspiration and wisdom. She must provide Roy the strength to triumph over evil (as well as the Pirates) in the final playoff game for the pennant. As Roy lays in the hospital, wallowing in self-pity and trying to decide whether to risk his life by playing in the deciding playoff game against Pittsburgh, it is Iris Gaines who transforms Roy Hobbs into a true baseball hero, supplying the knowledge and wisdom Roy needs to emerge as moral exemplar. "I believe we have two lives," she tells him. "The one we learn with and the life we live with after that." And, reminiscent of Claire's speech to Babe, she tells him, "With or without the records, they'll remember you. Think of all those young boys you've influenced. There's so many of them." When his silent reflections lead him to summon the memory of his father and his love for baseball, rather than producing another statement of self-pity, we know Iris has taught the lesson well. With the words "God, I love baseball," Roy vows to play, and blasts a spectacular game-winning home run in the bottom of the ninth inning to win the pennant.

The savior role assigned to women by baseball films continued into the 1990s. In *Mr. Baseball* (1992), it is Hiroto, daughter of the Chunichi Dragons' manager who provides the wisdom, and the discipline, necessary for fading slugger Jack Elliot to rebuild his character and his career, and finally achieve happiness and fulfillment both on the field and off. And, in the 1996 film, *Ed*, it is Jack Cooper's love interest, Lydia, who delivers the wisdom and insight into his own character that enable Jack Cooper to succeed in both the game of baseball and the game of life. When Cooper's roommate and team mascot/third baseman, the chimp, Ed Sullivan, is sold to another team by the owner's greedy son, Lydia forces Cooper — who has a tendency to be concerned solely with his own pitching performance — to recognize his responsibility to others. "When Jack Cooper is in trouble, you work twice as hard. When it's someone else, it's just too much trouble," she tells him. "If you're best friend can't count on you, who can?" Lydia's daughter Liz reinforces the lesson, telling him, "Don't choke now, dude." Cooper finally learns the true meaning of one of baseball's core values — the willingness to sacrifice for others. His heroic character now firmly established, he rescues Ed from his abusive new owners, wins the final game, is signed by the Los Angeles Dodgers (Tommy Lasorda says to pay him whatever he wants), and in the final scene, drives off to Los Angeles with new family; wife Lydia, daughter Liz, and Ed.

In the 1999 release *For Love of the Game*, aging Detroit Tiger pitcher Billy Chapel's love interest Jane Aubrey is instrumental in Chapel's recovery from a terrible injury to his pitching hand, and from his inability to either give or accept true love. Chapel, frustrated by a lack of progress in his rehabilitation after cutting his hand in a table-saw during the off-season, accuses those around him of giving up on him. Jane, a single mother struggling up the career ladder in the New York publishing industry, tells him, "You need to let me teach you something about what I know. About how sometimes life seems like it's slamming you down, but it's really giving you a gift." It is one of the few scenes in which Jane, portrayed in much of the film as insecure and weepy, is shown as a strong, capable character. Her message, however, does not provide the immediate enlightenment that Iris Gaines' provided Roy Hobbs. Chapel sarcastically responds to her wisdom, saying, "If life gives you lemons, you make lemonade?" Chapel essentially kicks her out of his house and his life. But, eventually, as he pitches a perfect game in the final outing of his 19 year career, he comes to realize that he does need Jane Aubrey in his life, and that the love she offers is more important even than the game itself. After the game, on the biggest night of his career, a lonely Chapel, who learned earlier that day that Aubrey was moving to London, breaks down sobbing in his hotel room. Like so many saviors before her, Jane Aubrey has taught her baseball hero what life is really all about. The next morning, as he prepares to set off to London to pursue her, Chapel finds Aubrey still in the airport, where she missed her flight to watch the end of his perfect game, and the two are united once again; this time, presumably, forever. Like so many baseball heroes before him, Billy Chapel has been saved from himself.

The savior role for women continued into the 21st century, with *Summer Catch* (2000). In this romantic comedy, wealthy Cape Cod socialite Tenly Parrish helps blue-collar pitcher Ryan Dunn overcome his anger, and his fear. Telling him, among other things, to "let yourself be great," Tenly gives Ryan the insights into himself he needs to succeed in both love and baseball. Recognizing at last what matters most in his life, Dunn chooses not to even finish his no-hitter in the last game of the season in the Cape Cod League. He calls for the closer with two outs in the ninth, to pursue Tenly to the airport where she is scheduled to leave for San Francisco. Having proven he is now the pitcher, and the person, he was meant to be, however, Dunn is in turn pursued by a scout for the Philadelphia Phillies and immediately signed to a minor league contract at the airport. The film ends with Dunn's first appearance in the majors as a Phillie. His broad smile after giving up a home-run to the first batter he faces, Ken Griffey Jr., serves simply to confirm that he has learned his lessons well. Lessons which, in baseball films, are often imparted by women. And, in *Mr. 3000* (2005), it is Mo, an ESPN reporter and Stan Ross's love interest, who delivers the crucial lecture about his egotistical, self-interested nature which helps put him on the path to true baseball hero.

> *"These are the ground rules."*
> — Annie Savoy, *Bull Durham*, 1988

One film which initially appears to challenge many of the gendered assumptions of earlier baseball films is *Bull Durham* (1988). What seems to separate *Bull Durham* (1988) from the earlier stories of such epic heroes as Lou Gehrig, Babe Ruth and Roy Hobbs is the initially feminist character of Annie Savoy. On the surface, *Bull Durham* seems to counter the patriarchal order of these earlier films with an affirmation of feminist values of strength, independence, empowerment, and the control of women over their own sexuality. The film begins with Annie Savoy explaining that at the beginning of every baseball season she chooses one Bulls player to hook up with during the season. She gives the boys an education and makes them feel confident, she says, and in return they make her feel pretty. It is Annie Savoy who assumes the lead both in choosing her sexual relationships, as well as in directing the nature of her sexual encounters. It is Annie Savoy who confidently, almost swaggeringly, sets the ground rules.

In addition to her sexual independence and empowerment, Annie Savoy is seen as economically independent, living alone in a large older home in Durham. A part-time teacher at the local junior college, it is evident she is not dependent upon anyone for her financial support. And, perhaps most significantly, Annie Savoy is portrayed as knowing a great deal about the game of baseball. In an early scene, in rookie sensation Nuke LaLoosh's first pitching start with the Bulls, she sends a note to him in the dugout telling him he is not bending his back on his follow-through. This piece of advice enables the wild LaLoosh to regain his control. Throughout the film her advice to LaLoosh, from teaching him to breathe through his eyelids to having him wear garters to distract him and keep him from thinking too much about his pitching, dramatically improves his pitching performance. It is clear in the film that Annie Savoy knows a great deal about both the mechanics and the psychology of baseball.

Such images of an independent, knowledgeable and empowered woman are, however, only surface images. In the end, the independent Annie Savoy, in the mold of Eleanor Gehrig, Claire Ruth and Iris Gaines, devotes herself fully to the male hero of the film, Crash Davis. Indeed, the central storyline of the film centers around the romantic attraction of Annie Savoy and Crash Davis, and the domestication of them both. And, consistent with earlier films, *Bull Durham* (1988) offers a similar, though considerably more subtle and less mythic transformation of the male hero by a female savior. The independent loner Crash Davis, who has moved from one minor-league ballpark to the next for the past twelve years is, like an earlier Babe Ruth, tempered and domesticated by the film's female lead, Annie Savoy. Indeed, throughout the film she is portrayed as the only person who has anything to offer the aging loner. And it is Annie Savoy who emerges to provide a sense of purpose to his life at a most critical time for a baseball hero — the end of his playing career. After hitting the home run which gives him the record for minor league home runs Crash returns to Durham and to Annie Savoy. He tells her that he has quit playing baseball.

It is evident that, for the first time, there is more to life for Crash Davis than playing baseball. He is ready to settle, and to move on to the next stage of his life, hopefully as a manager, and clearly with Annie Savoy. Just as Claire served to help Babe Ruth "grow up," so too does Annie Savoy serve to teach Crash Davis that there is more to life than playing the game. By the end of the film, we see a more mature Crash Davis; one who for the first time seems to need what someone else has to offer, and who seeks to commit himself to something more than just finishing out the season.

Even more striking than the tempering and maturing of Crash Davis by Annie Savoy, however, is the transformation of Annie herself. Not only does she serve as the traditional savior/nurturer for the male hero in this film, but eventually abdicates her own independence and control, to accept a more traditional place in baseball's moral order, by the male hero's side. At the end of the film, sitting on the porch with Crash, who has just announced he has quit playing baseball, Annie Savoy announces she has given up boys. When Crash asks if she thinks he could make it as a manager, she is quick to assure him he could, and begins to expound on the nonlinear nature of baseball. Crash cuts her off, saying that he wants to hear all of her theories about baseball, and he will. But for the moment, he just wants to be. Tearfully, wide-eyed, Annie Savoy responds, "I can do that, too." The strong, independent Annie Savoy, who at the beginning of the film made it clear that she did the choosing, is no more.

In *Bull Durham* (1988), it is not only the male hero Crash Davis who is brought within the desired moral order. Annie Savoy herself is "redeemed," and also returned to the preferred moral order within the film. While films such as *The Babe Ruth Story* (1948) and *The Natural* (1984) have served principally to temper the excesses of masculinity in the male hero, and to reclaim him into a moral order more consistent with the needs and values of the modern industrial state, *Bull Durham* (1988) serves also to reclaim what contemporary patriarchal values perceive as the excesses of feminism into that same moral order. Like other Hollywood films of the 1980s (Ryan and Kellner, 1988), *Bull Durham* appears, in the end, as a reaction against feminism; a conservative return to a patriarchal vision of romance. In the end, the moral order which emerges in *Bull Durham* (1988) is very much the same as that which has emerged in baseball films before it. In the final scene, it is Annie Savoy, in the tradition of Eleanor Gehrig, Claire Ruth, and Iris Gaines, who offers support and encouragement to Crash Davis as he prepares to pursue his managerial career, and who gives up her career to commit to the relationship. It is Annie Savoy who tearfully assures Crash Davis, "I can do that, too."

This is not to suggest that there have been no changes in the portrayal of women in baseball films through the years. In several significant ways, contemporary films reflect changing roles of women within our culture, and offer — on the surface at least — a critique of the traditional, patriarchal values which have dominated our culture, as well as cinematic representations of women in earlier eras. The first notable change is in the representation of women baseball players. As Ferrante (1994) notes, historical records of the game have virtually ignored the fact that women have, since the Victorian era, played professional baseball. The tendency to ignore the role of women in baseball as *players* of the game has, obviously, been characteristic of baseball films, as well. The first film to feature a woman player was actually *The Bad News Bears* (1978), in which a pre-pubescent Amanda Wurlitzer, after first insisting she doesn't do "that tomboy stuff" anymore, puts her transition to womanhood on hold for another year to pitch for the Bears, in return for her coach's promise to pay for her ballet lessons. Despite shortstop Tanner Boyle's initial reaction of "Jews, spics, niggers and now a girl?" when Amanda is first introduced to the team, the issue of gender is not thematically significant in the film, however. She is immediately accepted as another member of the team and little more is made of the fact that she is a girl. It is noteworthy, however, that this equality of being is achieved as a result of Amanda agreeing to adopt the role of tomboy, rather than woman, for another season.

The issue of women as baseball players is more central to two films of the 1980s and 1990s, which portray women as professional ballplayers. The 1983 film *Blue Skies Again* tells the fictional story of Paula Fradkin, who becomes the first woman player to make it to the major leagues, and purports, in the process, to confront the range of sexist values which have inhibited women from achieving success not just in baseball, but throughout American culture. Unfortunately, as Erickson (2002) observes, the film's excellent premises are "laid low by muddled execution" (p. 100). More successful is *A League of Their Own* (1992), an historical look at the All-American Girls Professional Baseball League in 1943. This film not only portrays women as good, professional baseball players, it also ridicules some of the absurdities these players were forced to endure, such as attending charm school and wearing short skirts while playing, in order to assure the American culture that, even though they were playing baseball, they were still "ladies."

Beyond these two portrayals of women as professional baseball players, there has also been a modest shift in the representations of women in other professional roles, as well. For example, the 1996 film *The Fan* features a tough, aggressive sports reporter named Jewel Stern, known for asking hard questions and doing tough interviews. In stark contrast, for example, to the woman reporter featured in the 1951 version of *Angels in the Outfield*, who normally reported on household hints for her paper, and knew nothing about baseball, Stern is extremely knowledgeable about the game itself. And, even though Stern, like so many women before her, provides struggling Giants star Bobby Rayburn with some much needed insight into his own character, which helps him pull out of a horrendous slump and become a bit more of a human being, she does not become romantically involved with the star and does not, like Jennifer Page (*Angels in the Outfield*, 1951) or nearly all the other women who serve as a source of support and growth for baseball heroes, end up marrying him. *The Fan* (1996), at least, gives vision to the notion that it is possible for women to know a great deal about the game, to work as talented and successful professional sports reporters, and even offer some wisdom and insight to the baseball hero as a professional herself, without becoming romantically involved.

Another subtle change in the representation of women has occurred in the portrayal of single mothers. *Rookie of the Year* (1993), *Little Big League* (1994) and *Ed* (1996) all feature single mothers in strong, positive roles. These portrayals are particularly striking when contrasted with the portrayal of a single mother only 30 years earlier, in the 1954 film *Roogie's Bump*. Whereas Roogie Rigsby's mother, for example, essentially turned her son over to Boxey, the manager of the Brooklyn Dodgers, once the child became a baseball player, and continued to defer to Boxey's judgment regarding what would be best for Roogie, both Mary Rowengardner (*Rookie of the Year*, 1993) and Jenny Heywood (*Little Big League*, 1994) play strong and important roles in the development of their sons' careers and lives. Mary Rowengardner, for example, gets rid of her boyfriend, who was also Henry's agent, when it turns out he is simply trying to exploit the boy — flattening him with a right hook in the process. We also learn at the end of the film that she was once a baseball player herself. It is her old glove, not his father's, that Henry is wearing. And, all the stories she told him about his father as a baseball player were really about her own playing days. It is she who tells Henry what pitch to throw to get the final out in the division-winning game against the New York Mets. When Billy Heywood begins to take himself too seriously, Jenny Heywood grounds him for a day, forcing him to miss a game for swearing at an umpire. It is Jenny Heywood who helps her son understand what he is becoming, and to return to being the manager who told his team the only thing that mattered was that they have fun.

The third notable change in the representation of women in more recent films is that in at least three contemporary films there is some attention given to the ways women have been victimized by those patriarchal values which earlier films have consistently endorsed. In the 1992 version of the life and career of Babe Ruth (*The Babe*), for example, Ruth's first wife, Helen, is presented as a tragic victim of the early Ruth's immaturity and self-centeredness. Unable to play the role of dutiful, supportive wife to a sometimes abusive husband, who evidently would prefer partying with his teammates and other women rather than fulfill his responsibilities to his wife and child, Helen finally leaves Ruth. At the same time, however, the film, through its later redemption of Ruth, suggests that Helen was not victimized by "true" patriarchal values, but rather by Ruth's failure to live up to the genuine values of the idealized baseball hero. In other words, the expectations of women within a patriarchal order are not seriously challenged, as Ruth's cruel treatment of Helen is attributed not to the unquestioned, and often unstated, values of patriarchy itself, but rather to Ruth's individual deviances within what remains a conservative, patriarchal, moral order. Similarly, although audiences learn in *Major League* (1989) that Jake Taylor's wife, Lynn, left him as a result of Taylor's immaturity and infidelity, they also see her return to Taylor, resuming her rightful place as cheering supporter in the stands, when it is clear that Taylor has grown up, and forsaken his earlier ways. In *For Love of the Game* (1999), Jane Aubrey repeatedly suffers the emotional abuse inflicted by a common masculine stereotype, the emotionally withdrawn "old school" man. In this film, Billy Chapel seems incapable of expressing or receiving real love. More than once he lets Aubrey know that his career, not her, is the most important thing in his life. And that is a rejection which she cannot bear. "You don't need me," she tells him as she prepares to leave for a new job in London. It is Chapel's failure to recognize, or admit, that he does indeed need her which produces the emotional havoc wreaked on both of them in the course of the film. In the scene referred to earlier, for example, when he is attempting to recover from a potentially career-ending hand injury, Chapel cruelly tells Aubrey, "You make me feel distracted. You make me feel weak."

When Billy Chapel finally realizes that he needs something more than the game, and is able to accept, rather than smother his emotions, he and Jane Aubrey, the final scene of the film foreshadows, are both able to at last achieve lasting happiness as they continue their life together.

Perhaps the most explicit challenge to the usual expectations of a woman's role in the life of the baseball hero comes in the 1985 film, *The Slugger's Wife*. Like Grover Cleveland Alexander (*The Winning Team*, 1952) over 30 years before him, Atlanta Braves slugger Darryl Palmer receives his inspiration and power from having his wife Debbie sitting in the stands. The problem is, Debbie has her own career as a pop singer. Smothered by Palmer's possessiveness, and insistence she sacrifice her life for his, she finally leaves him. Although they do not completely reunite at the end of the film, audiences are left with the likely possibility of a reconciliation, as Palmer has evidently learned love means allowing one's partner the freedom to live her life, as well.

Despite these subtle changes in more recent films, we contend that the role of women within baseball's cultural vision remains essentially the same as it always has been. As Degler (1980) observed, the proper role of women within the patriarchal value system is to nurture and care for their husbands and children, as well as to shape and direct their husbands' moral behavior. That role is well defined within baseball's value system. As Ferrante (1994) noted, "Baseball as a cultural icon constructs woman as the Other, whose function is to bring comfort, meaning and identity to the One" (p. 247). Such is the role of the women in these films. The transformation from baseball player to baseball hero is, in these films, a process of tempering the excesses of masculinity — of containing the undisciplined dimensions of individualism and of redefining masculinity within a moral order more consistent with the needs of the modern bureaucratic and industrial society. Like women/saviors in other genres of Hollywood films, the central role of women in these films is to "civilize" the male hero, to temper his unbridled masculinity with the more "feminine" characteristics (at least according to cultural gender definitions) of moral virtue and humility, and thus assure his salvation. Their primary function is to inspire, to support, to nurture; to guide the baseball hero so he can achieve greatness on the field while maintaining a virtuous existence off the field (and after baseball).

Having thus completed the tasks of tempering the male jock's swaggering masculinity with a fierce moral fire, while at the same time inspiring his play and supporting his aspirations, the savior, in most films at least, then fades into relative obscurity and decided subordination, a mere spousal spectator to the continuing saga of a man now ready to assume the mantle of Baseball Hero. Eleanor Gehrig (*The Pride of the Yankees*, 1942) establishes the precedent for other women of baseball cinema to follow. Although she is a central facet of Lou's life, she has no life beyond his. Her function in the film is to maintain the ideal romantic marriage. After Claire marries Babe (*The Babe Ruth Story*, 1942) she abandons her own career on the stage, and we see her only in her role of caring and devoted wife — rooting for her Bambino at ball games, offering encouragement when he is down, and crying at his bedside as he is dying from cancer. And this is the role Iris Gaines (*The Natural*, 1984) and Annie Savoy (*Bull Durham*, 1988), to cite but two more examples, seem destined for at the conclusion of their film sagas, as well; Iris watching approvingly as father and son play catch, Annie sitting teary-eyed on the porch swing with Crash Davis.

On the surface, what is particularly noteworthy in many baseball films is the power of the central female characters, who play a prominent role in building the type of world envisioned in baseball's cultural ideology. Despite the influential role of women in transforming the male hero in these films, however, these films serve not as expressions of feminist values or a challenge to traditional patriarchal gender definitions, but rather as reflections of those values. These women serve not to challenge or redefine masculinity in a way which reflects feminist values, but rather in a way which adapts masculinity to the needs of the modern corporate/industrial state, while still preserving dominant, traditional patriarchal values. Indeed, when feminist values are present, as in *Bull Durham* (1988), they are incorporated back into the preferred moral order, just as the undisciplined excesses of masculine individuality are contained within these films.

A central function of ideology, of course, is to foster not only the illusion that the dominant social, political, economic, or, in this case, moral order serves the interests of those whom it actually oppresses, but also the illusion that this order is one which all have accepted freely, and which all have a voice in shaping. Baseball films serve as significant examples of this legitimizing process and function of ideology. In many cases, the world established in these films is presented as one which reflects feminine values and as one which is willingly acceded to and even constructed by women. It is a double twist that Hollywood's mirrors of illusion have offered to women here. Not only does this world serve your needs, they are told, but it is one which you have helped build, and which reflects your values.

Since the 1930s baseball films have expressed the dominant values which permeate our culture. The continued expression of these values, and the continuing popularity of these films, reflects how deeply ingrained these values remain. However, just as all media serve not only to reflect but to shape culture, as well, so too do these films work to legitimize, naturalize and perpetuate a moral order which embraces patriarchal values and power. What is most striking when these cinematic visions of American culture — which span more than 60 years — are placed side by side, is the realization of how little distance we have traveled.

10

The America That Was Meant to Be

"I needed him to be a hero."
— Al Stump, *Cobb*

The dilemma faced by writer Al Stump was difficult. Hired by baseball legend Ty Cobb to write his biography, Stump quickly discovers that, in Cobb's own words, "the greatest ballplayer who ever lived was also the greatest bastard." Stump would have to choose; to write the truth, and trash the mythic aura of one of baseball's greatest legends; or continue, as real-life sports writers had done during the era of Cobb's career, to preserve Cobb's image as a true baseball hero. In the end, Stump decides to publish the lie, and "put the truth in the closet." "I needed him to be a hero."

Claude Levi-Strauss (1969) writes that the principal function of myth is to reconcile the contradictions between conflicting values within a culture. For nearly 100 years, this has been the function of the myths of baseball. Since the early 20th century, the stories, legends and lessons of the game offered up by journalists, social reformers, story-tellers—and film makers—have addressed and offered reconciliation of the competing values of a changing America.

In the early 1900s, in response to the strains of urbanization and industrialization, these stories of the game offered an easing of tensions between the older, fundamental values of a passing rural America, and the newer demands of an urbanized society. Baseball, it was said, could show us how the long-held value of individualism could be smoothly incorporated into an appreciation of and commitment to the notion of teamwork, so critical to the functioning of the emerging industrialized economy. This game of rural origins played on a grassy field in an urban environment, it was said,

174

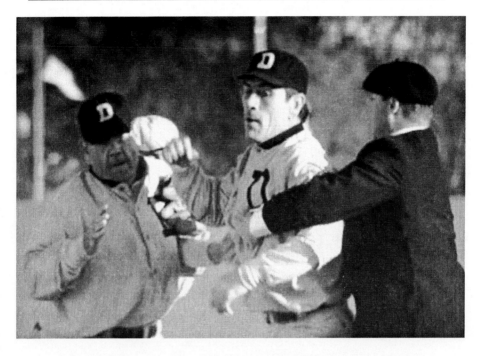

Tommy Lee Jones (center) as Ty Cobb in *Cobb* (Warner Bros., 1994).

could serve to bring the strong, religious-based moral values of rural America into the city; the conflict between the country and the city could become a balance, and America could take the best of what both had to offer. And a game which emphasized respect for authority and fair play, its advocates claimed, would serve to temper the potentially corruptive competitive energies of a rapidly advancing capitalism with self-restraint. America's youth would learn that there are rules to the game, and that playing fair is more important than winning.

These conflicts, between such values as individualism and teamwork, self-reliance and cooperation, urban and rural, competition and fair play, remain a part of the American struggle today. And America's national pastime, baseball films continue to assure us, can still show us the way. The vision of an ideal community, and the kinds of heroes/citizens which inhabit that community, are still the dreams of which baseball films are made. But perhaps the greatest contradiction confronted by baseball films is that between the vision and the reality. This is the contradiction confronted by Al Stump. This is the contradiction confronted by America, as well.

From one perspective, a critical one, the role of baseball, and baseball films, in addressing that contradiction is problematic. From this view, the game, and the films about that game, are seen as obscuring that contradiction, and as constructing support for the existing social order. Through the promotion of a particular set of social values, baseball and baseball films invite citizens to see the world, and their place in it, in ways that encourage acceptance of the existing social order, rather than leading them to challenge it. There is much evidence in the history of the construction baseball's ideology to support the argument that this is indeed a primary function of the national pastime. And, as discussions throughout this book have suggested, baseball films have consistently supported that ideological project. It is through such ideological work, argue critical theorists, that dominant interests are able to maintain their dominance.

Michel Foucault (1995) has traced the processes through which, in the modern era, the means of social control have shifted from coercion and punishment to socialization and normalization. While various forms of punishment certainly still exist, and always remain as the ultimate threat to those who would transgress against social norms and laws, Foucault argues that individual adherence to social norms, and maintenance of the social order, is achieved principally through education. This is not simply a matter of teaching citizens what those social norms are, says Foucault, but also of inculcating in them the practices of self-surveillance and self-discipline. For the most part, we obey the laws of society not simply because we fear punishment, writes Foucault, but because we accept them as "right;" because we have internalized the basic values which those laws seek to protect, and because we fear the discomfort of being seen, and seeing ourselves, as out of step with dominant social norms. We learn, says Foucault, to police ourselves.

Central to this disciplinary project is the concept of normalization; of communicating to individual subjects what constitutes acceptable thoughts, ideas, desires, values and behavior within a given culture. We learn, through the work of such interrelated social institutions as schools, churches and media, as well as the legal system, to recognize the "normal;" to value it, to monitor our own thoughts and behaviors, and to bring ourselves into compliance with it. Baseball, like most popular culture in America, has been a part of that socialization process. As Reiss (1999) has noted, professional baseball's ideology, which was constructed in the early years of the 20th century, "spoke directly to white Anglo-Saxon Americans and their need to secure order" (p. 7). A significant concern among white, middle-class Americans— the primary target audience of baseball's ideological message — was the prevention of "radicalism and anarchy by acculturating and exercising social control over the new immigrants and their children through such institutions as the public school and the national pastime..." (p. 7). In a time of tremendous social upheaval, and amidst widespread concerns about the stability of America's social order, baseball's ideologists represented the game as a means of binding together an increasingly stratified industrial society, of forging a sense of shared community in large, impersonal urban settings, and of teaching to both American youth and the thousands of immigrants coming to America's shores the basic values of American culture.

A large part of baseball's ideological work has been devoted to accommodating America's citizens to the needs and dangers of a corporate, industrial and urbanized economy. In the early part of the 20th century, amidst the social changes of a rapidly shifting economic and political landscape, the game's admonitions against such vices as drinking and smoking, for example, served as a reinforcement of traditional Puritanical values which were believed to be threatened by urbanization and its accompanying social and moral ills. The game's emphasis on teamwork, and putting the team's interests ahead of one's own, as Gelber (1983) observed, helped condition workers to the new realities of a corporate, industrialized workplace which not only required workers to cooperate and work together in the new processes of production, but which also required their loyalty in a changing economic and political sphere. And, as it has consistently through the years, baseball continues to embrace these same values even today, holding them up to American youth as central tenets to be followed both in the game of baseball, and the game of life. Indeed, it is because these values remain so central to baseball's and America's definitions of what is "normal," that the failure of contemporary ballplayers to adhere to these moral tenets themselves is the center of continued media attention and public consternation among American educators and political figures.

Since the 1930s, these have been the values celebrated in baseball films, as well. Unlike films of other genres, which have at times sought to challenge — or at least expose the inconsistencies between the real and the ideal — baseball films have remained true to the game's core cultural vision. Thus, from Elmer Kane (*Elmer the Great*, 1933), to Lou Gehrig (*Pride of the Yankees*, 1942), to Crash Davis (*Bull Durham*, 1988), to Jimmy Morris (*The*

Rookie, 2001), cinematic baseball heroes of all eras have exemplified such values as hard work, teamwork, humility, and moral virtue; the same essential values which are taught in American schools, churches, youth programs and other social institutions every day as "basic, American values." Through their definition of what constitutes both the ideal community and the ideal citizen within that community, baseball films are a part of the disciplinary project of modern American society. The idealized hero of baseball films is also the ideal citizen in America's ideal community. These films have sought to teach us the way we, and the world — at least according to baseball — are meant to be.

The history of baseball ideology, then, reveals a conscious and concerted effort to use the game as a means of smoothly acculturating America's citizens into the dominant order of industrial capitalism; to create, as Lipsky (1981) writes, "citizens of industrial civilization" (p. 112). And, baseball films have clearly played a supporting role in that ideological project. However, at the same time that the game, through the dissemination of values such as hard work, humility, and moral virtue, has functioned to socialize citizens into the dominant social order, it has also served to provide citizens an escape from the frustrations, hardships, and oppressive nature of that same social order. Recognizing the alienation of industrial labor, not to mention life in an impersonal and often grimy urban environment, the game's early proselytizers touted the ballpark as a space where city dwellers who spent their days toiling long hours in boring, repetitive jobs, could work off their anger and frustrations (Riess, 1999). At the same time, and much more significantly in terms of the game's socialization functions, baseball was presented as an activity which provided both players and fans opportunities for individual achievement often denied them in their daily working lives, as well as participation — if only vicariously — in a democratic, egalitarian community in which the values of hard work, moral virtue, and commitment to the team/community are rewarded. As Riess (1999) and others have noted, much was made in the Progressive era of the democratic nature of baseball. The game was said to be open to anyone who wanted to play. Presumably, any boy with the talent and dedication could grow up to become a major league ballplayer. (Baseball's ideologists, obviously, did not let the realities of racial segregation stand in the way of a good story.) Additionally, the ballpark itself was described as a place where fans of all social and economic classes could come together on an equal basis, to join in one united community rooting for the home team.

As Jhally (1984) observes, these two functions—the providing of an escape from the realities of the social order, and the socialization of individuals into that same social order — are related. The ability of sports in general to simultaneously serve both of these purposes, suggests Jhally, lies in their idealization of the dominant values and structures within American society. According to Jhally, sports mask the true nature of capitalism's authoritarian structures by making them appear as personal and human. Sports, and the mediated images of sports, present the dominant values and processes of social life in a preferred light, emphasizing the human and positive dimensions of modern social life, while deflecting attention away from the threatening and alienating characteristics of those same social, political and economic structures. Through sports, suggests Jhally, the cultural values and social processes that characterize and dominate American social life are portrayed as rewarding, fulfilling, and desirable. The institutions which dominate American culture are represented through sports as offering a true, human community, and as benefitting all who are members of that community. By celebrating idealized, rather than existent, structures of reality, by reflecting dominant values in an idealized way, sports, according to Jhally, have served to distort the realities of life in modern industrialized American society. And, in the end, the use of sports such as baseball as a means of establishing a sense of community, the linkage of sports with the development of good citizenship and democracy, the promotion through baseball of such values as teamwork and hard work, all serve, in this view, to promote the interests of contemporary capitalist society.

The hegemonic functions of baseball's ideology, and baseball films, is undeniable. At the same time that we recognize the hegemonic function of baseball ideology, however, we should also recognize that is not necessarily its only function. While it is clear that baseball's ideology was grounded, in part at least, in an effort to support and normalize the social relations of urban, industrial capitalism, it is important to keep in mind that opposition to the threats to community, to fundamental moral values, and to traditional ways of life posed by the new economic order were also part of the Progressive movement, and central concerns of many proponents of the "sporting republic" discussed in the first chapter of this book; a vision which helped to frame the construction of the ideology of baseball in later years. Fierce opposition to the new social order which came to dominate American culture is also a part of the heritage of baseball's cultural vision. Thus, while it may be that the audiences for baseball and baseball films accept as real these idealized images of social life, and are thus unlikely to challenge a social system which actually exploits, rather than engages, those same values, it may also be that these same audiences are, in fact, critically aware of the contradiction between baseball's idealized cultural vision and the world in which they live their daily lives. Viewing baseball films as part of the ideological project of dominant social, political and economic institutions and interests is clearly one, but only one, legitimate reading. Viewing them as an oppositional vision to the social order those interests have created, we would argue, is another.

"People," writes Sut Jhally, "choose and interact with social institutions that reflect their objective needs" (1984, p. 52). We believe that the popularity of baseball films is reflective, not of a blind, naive acceptance of the way society is, but of a desire for the way society ought to be. Baseball's cultural vision, as reflected in films from the 1930s into the 21st century, is one of an ideal community characterized by diversity, equality, tolerance, and nurturance; a community in which the individual, through commitment to the larger community, is able to achieve individual success and fulfillment at the same time that he or she contributes to the success and achievements of that community. It is a world in which individuals are motivated by a commitment to their team, family and community, and by a love of and devotion to the work they do for its own sake, rather than simple material greed. It is a world in which individuals work hard, but derive enormous joy and fulfillment from the work they do. It is a world in which people willingly adhere to a shared vision of morality. And it is a world in which these values are rewarded, rather than exploited; in which those who flaunt these values, whether they be baseball superstars or corporate executives, do not come out on top.

The popularity of baseball films and their heroes reflect a longing for a culture in which people such as Roy Hobbs and the cinematic Babe Ruth really do win; in which not only superstar athletes, but also the culture in which they perform and live, really do reflect the values of hard work, humility, and commitment to the greater good of the team/community. These cinematic portrayals of baseball and its heroes enable us to continue to hang on to a symbolic vision of what we would like our culture to become. It is a vision of the America that was meant to be. The challenge, it would seem, is not to make the ideology of baseball conform to reality, but to make reality conform to the ideology of baseball.

Filmography

1898 —*The Ball Game*† (Edison kinetoscope)
1899 —*Casey at the Bat*† (Edison kinetoscope)
1913 —*Breaking into the Big Leagues*† (Kalem Studios)
1915 —*Little Sunset*† (Paramount Pictures)
1915 —*Right Off the Bat*† (Mike Donlin Productions/Arrow Film Corp./All Features Booking)
1916 —*Somewhere in Georgia* † (Sunbeam Motion Pictures Corporation)
1916 —*Casey at the Bat*† (Fine Arts/Triangle)
1917 —*The Pinch Hitter*† (Triangle/Ince/Kay-Bee)
1917 —*One Touch of Nature*† (Edison/K-E-S-E Service)
1919 —*The Busher*† (Thomas H. Ince/Famous Players-Lasky/Paramount Pictures)
1920 —*Headin' Home*† (Kessel & Baumann/Yankee Photo Corporation)
1921 —*As the World Rolls On*† (Andlauer Productions/Elk Photo Plays)
1923 —*Trifling with Honor*† (Universal Pictures)
1924 —*Hit and Run*† (Universal Pictures)
1924 —*Life's Greatest Game*† (Emory Johnson Productions/Film Booking Offices of America)
1924 —*The Battling Orioles*† (Hal Roach Studios/Pathé Exchange)
1925 —*The Pinch Hitter*† (Associated Exhibitors)
1926 —*Out of the West* † (Robertson-Cole Pictures/Film Booking Offices of America)
1926 —*The New Klondike*† (Famous Players-Lasky/Paramount Pictures)
1927 —*Catch as Catch Can*† (Gotham Productions/Lumas Film Corporation)

1927 — *Babe Comes Home*† (First National)
1927 — *Slide, Kelly, Slide*† (Metro-Goldwyn Mayer)
1927 — *Casey at the Bat*† (Famous Players-Lasky/Paramount Pictures)
1927 — *The Bush Leaguer*† (Warner Bros.)
1928 — *Warming Up*† (Paramount/Famous/Lasky Corporation)
1929 — *Fast Company* (Paramount/Famous/Lasky Corporation)
1930 — *Hot Curves* (Tiffany Productions)
1930 — *They Learned About Women* (Metro-Goldwyn Mayer)
1932 — *Fireman, Save My Child* (Warner Bros.)
1933 — *Elmer the Great** (Warner Bros.)
1934 — *Death on the Diamond** (Metro-Goldwyn Mayer)
1935 — *Alibi Ike** (Warner Bros.)
1935 — *Swell Head* (Columbia Pictures)
1937 — *Girls Can Play* (Columbia Pictures)
1942 — *It Happened in Flatbush* (Twentieth Century Fox)
1942 — *Pride of the Yankees** (Samuel Goldwyn Co./RKO-Radio)
1943 — *Ladies Day** (RKO Radio)
1948 — *The Babe Ruth Story** (Allied Artists)
1949 — *It Happens Every Spring** (Twentieth Century Fox)
1949 — *Kid from Cleveland** (Republic)
1949 — *The Stratton Story** (Metro-Goldwyn Mayer)
1949 — *Take Me Out to the Ballgame** (Metro-Goldwyn Mayer)
1950 — *The Jackie Robinson Story** (Jewel Productions/Eagle-Lion Films)
1950 — *Kill the Umpire* (Columbia Pictures)
1951 — *Angels in the Outfield** (Metro-Goldwyn Mayer)
1951 — *Rhubarb** (Paramount Pictures)
1952 — *The Pride of St. Louis** (Twentieth Century Fox)
1952 — *The Winning Team** (Warner Bros.)
1953 — *The Big Leaguer** (Metro-Goldwyn Mayer)
1953 — *The Kid from Left Field** (Twentieth Century Fox)
1954 — *Roogie's Bump** (Republic Pictures)
1956 — *The Great American Pastime** (Metro-Goldwyn Mayer)
1957 — *Fear Strikes Out** (Paramount Pictures)
1958 — *Damn Yankees** (Warner Bros.)
1962 — *Safe at Home** (Columbia Pictures)
1973 — *Bang the Drum Slowly** (Paramount Pictures)
1976 — *The Bad News Bears** (Paramount Pictures)
1976 — *The Bingo Long Traveling All-Stars** (Universal Pictures)
1977 — *Bad News Bears in Breaking Training** (Paramount Pictures)
1978 — *The Bad News Bears Go to Japan** (Paramount Pictures)
1978 — *Here Come the Tigers* (Filmways Pictures/American International)
1983 — *Blue Skies Again** (Warner Bros.)

1984 — *The Natural** (Tri-Star Pictures)
1985 — *The Slugger's Wife** (Columbia Pictures)
1988 — *Bull Durham** (Orion Pictures)
1988 — *Eight Men Out** (Orion Pictures)
1989 — *Field of Dreams** (Universal Pictures)
1989 — *Major League** (Paramount Pictures)
1991 — *Talent for the Game** (Paramount Pictures)
1991 — *Pastime** (Bullpen Productions/Open Road Ltd./Miramax)
1992 — *A League of Their Own** (Columbia Pictures)
1992 — *Mr. Baseball** (Universal Pictures)
1992 — *The Babe** (Universal Pictures)
1993 — *The Sandlot** (Twentieth Century Fox)
1993 — *Rookie of the Year** (Twentieth Century Fox)
1994 — *Cobb** (Warner Brothers)
1994 — *The Scout** (Twentieth Century Fox)
1994 — *Major League II** (Warner Bros.)
1994 — *Little Big League** (Castle Rock Entertainment/Columbia Pictures)
1994 — *Angels in the Outfield** (Walt Disney Pictures)
1996 — *Ed** (Universal Pictures)
1996 — *The Fan** (Tri-Star Pictures)
1998 — *Major League: Back to the Minors** (Warner Bros.)
1999 — *For Love of the Game** (Universal Pictures)
2001 — *Summer Catch** (Warner Bros.)
2001 — *Hard Ball** (Paramount Pictures)
2002 — *The Rookie** (Walt Disney Pictures)
2004 — *Mr. 3000** (Spyglass Entertainment/Touchstone Pictures/Dimension Films)
2005 — *Fever Pitch** (Twentieth Century Fox)
2005 — *The Bad News Bears* (Paramount Pictures)

Works Cited

Aden, R.C. (1994). Back to the garden: Therapeutic place metaphor in *Field of Dreams. Southern Communication Journal, 59,* 307–317.

The Baseball Championship (1867). *Harper's Weekly,* October 26.

Bergan, R. (1982). *Sports in the Movies.* New York: Proteus.

Berger, P.L. Berger, B., and Kellner, H. (1973). *The Homeless Mind.* New York: Vintage.

Betts, J.R. (1974). *America's Sporting Heritage.* Reading, MA: Addison-Wesley.

Bruce, H.A. (1913). Baseball and the national life. *Outlook,* May.

Cripps, T. (1979). *Black Film as Genre.* Bloomington: Indiana University Press.

Degler, C.N. (1980). *At Odds: Women and the Family in America from the Revolution to the Present.* New York: Oxford University Press.

Dickerson, G. (1991). *The Cinema of Baseball.* Westport, CT: Meckler.

Dickey, G. (1980). *The History of American League Baseball Since 1901.* New York: Stein and Day.

Dryerson, M. (1997). Regulating the body and the body politic: American sport, bourgeois culture, and the language of progress, 1880–1920. In S.W. Pope (Ed.), *The New American Sport History.* Urbana: University of Illinois Press.

Edelman, R. (1994). *Great Baseball Films.* New York: Citadel.

Erickson, H. (2002). *The Baseball Filmography: 1915 through 2001,* 2nd ed. Jefferson, NC: McFarland.

Ewen, S. (1988). *All Consuming Images.* New York: Basic.

Ferrante, K. (1994). Baseball and the social construction of gender. In P.J. Creedon (Ed.), *Women, Media, and Sport: Challenging Gender Values.* Thousand Oaks, CA: Sage.

Fiske, J. (1989). *Understanding Popular Culture.* Boston: Unwin Hyman.

Foucault, M. (1995). *Discipline and Punish: The Birth of the Prison.* New York: Vintage.

Gelber, S.M. (1983). Working at playing: the culture of the workplace and the rise of baseball. *Journal of Social History, 16* (3), 3–24.

Gomery, D. (1991). *Movie History: A Survey.* Belmont, CA: Wadsworth.

185

Gorn, E.J., and Goldstein, W. (1993). *A Brief History of American Sports*. New York: Hill and Wang.

Guttman, A. (1978). *From Ritual to Record*. New York: Columbia University Press.

Jhally, S. (1984). The spectacle of accumulation: Material and cultural factors in the evolution of the sports/media complex. *Insurgent Sociologist, 12*, 41–57.

Jhally, S., and Lewis, J. (1992). *Enlightened Racism: "The Cosby Show," Audiences and the Myth of the American Dream*. San Francisco: Westview.

Levi-Strauss, C. (1969). *The Raw and the Cooked*. New York: Harper & Row.

Lipsky, R. (1981). *How We Play the Game*. Boston: Beacon Press.

Morris, T.M. (1997). *Making the Team: The Cultural Work of Baseball Fiction*. Urbana: University of Illinois Press.

Most, M., and Rudd, R. (2002). The America that was meant to be: Images of community in baseball films. In G. Gumpert and S. Drucker (Eds.), *Take Me Out to the Ballgame: Communicating Baseball*. Cresskill, NJ: Hampton.

Most, M.G., and Rudd, R. (1993). Don't Bet on It: The Representation of Gambling in Baseball Cinema. Paper presented to the Fifth Annual Symposium on Baseball and the American Culture, Cooperstown, NY.

Orbe, M., and Harris, T. (2001). *Interracial Communication*. Belmont, CA: Wadsworth.

Riess, S. (1991). *City Games: The Evolution of American Urban Society and the Rise of Sports*. Chicago: University of Illinois Press.

_____. (1980). *Touching Base: Professional Baseball and American Culture in the Progressive Era*. Westport, CT: Greenwood.

_____. (1999). _____. Rev. and expanded ed. Chicago: University of Illinois Press.

Ryan, M., and Kellner, D. (1988). *Camera Politica*. Bloomington: Indiana University Press.

Sands, J., and Gammons, P. (1993). *Coming Apart at the Seams*. New York: Macmillan.

Seymour, H. (1971). *Baseball: The Golden Age*. New York: Oxford University Press.

_____. (1990). *Baseball: The People's Game*. New York: Oxford University Press.

Solomon, E. (1985). "The bullpen of her mind": Women's baseball fiction and Sylvia Tannenbaum's *Rachel, the Rabbi's Wife*. *Arete, 3(1)*, 19–31.

Tonnies, F. (1963). *Community and Society*. (C.P. Loomis, trans. and ed.). New York: Harper & Row.

Voigt, D.Q. (1976). *America Through Baseball*. Chicago: Nelson-Hall.

_____. (1983). *American Baseball*, Volume I. University Park, PA: Penn State University Press.

_____. (1970). *American Baseball*, Volume II. Norman: University of Oklahoma Press.

Ward, G.C., and Burns, K. (1994). *Baseball: An Illustrated History*. New York: Alfred A. Knopf.

Weber, M. (1958). *The Protestant Ethic and the Spirit of Capitalism*. New York: Scribner.

Wenner, L.A. (1989). Media, sports and society: The research agenda. In L.A. Wenner (Ed.), *Media, Sports, and Society*. Newbury Park, CA: Sage.

Williams, R. (1963). *Culture and Society 1780–1950*. London: Penguin.

Yankelovich, D. (1982). *New Rules*. New York: Bantam.

Index